3-48

Declining Grammar

Declining Grammar

and Other Essays
on the English Vocabulary

Dennis Baron
University of Illinois
at Urbana-Champaign

National Council of Teachers of English
1111 Kenyon Road, Urbana, Illinois 61801

NCTE Editorial Board: Donald R. Gallo, Richard Lloyd-Jones, Raymond J. Rodrigues, Dorothy S. Strickland, Brooke Workman, Charles Suhor, ex officio, Michael Spooner, ex officio

Staff Editor: Robert A. Heister

Cover Design: Doug Burnett

Interior Design: Tom Kovacs for TGK Design

NCTE Stock Number 10738-3020

Library of Congress Cataloging-in-Publication Data

Baron, Dennis E.
    Declining grammar and other essays on the English vocabulary / Dennis Baron.
      p. cm.
    Bibliography: p.
    ISBN 0-8141-1073-8
    1. English language—Lexicology. 2. English language—Semantics.
3. English language—Usage. I. Title.
PE1571.B37 1989
420—dc20
                                   89-34420
                                     CIP

Contents

Preface

The essays in this book, written over the past two years, began as responses to particular problems arising during my earlier work on attempts to reform the English language, and on the question of language and sex (Baron 1982a, 1982b, 1986). Although they started as discrete entities, a pattern gradually developed interconnecting the essays and establishing a progression from start to finish. Consequently, while most of the chapters may be read independently of one another, or in small groups of two or three, they also cohere to form a book about where the English language—particularly its vocabulary—has been, where it is now, and where it is going.

Declining Grammar is about English words, how we define them, value them, and argue over them. And it is about the importance we attach to English as the language of our individual and our national expression. One of the things readers will discover in this book is the extent to which mistaken ideas about language influence language development. We will look at some of the attitudes toward English frequently expressed by language commentators, and some of the ways in which our language—particularly our vocabulary—is changing and developing to meet the new demands placed on it.

In the first section, we will examine some of the myths and misconceptions that affect our attitudes toward language—and toward English in particular. False or skewed ideas about language crop up in everyday conversation. They influence the criteria we set for proper writing style and contribute to our hazy notions of what constitutes standard English. Ultimately they affect how English teachers teach about our language, a subject which continues to vex students, teachers, and the American public at large.

The second section examines some specific questions of meaning and usage. "Declining Grammar," the book's title essay, traces the ups and particularly the downs in the meaning of the word *grammar,* which went from something originally very positive to something that is now rather negative, though this latter fact is generally ignored by our dictionaries. The other chapters in this section look at specific usage controversies of the past and present to demonstrate that while there is little agreement on what constitutes proper English, the endless debate over language standards shows that language concerns are never far from our consciousness.

Section three examines some controversial trends in English vocabulary, and some developments too new to have received comment before. The final section treats several aspects of linguistic politics, from specific attempts to deal with the ethnic, religious, or sex-specific elements of our vocabulary to the broader issues of language both as a reflection of our public consciousness and constitution and as a refuge for our most private forms of expression.

A great many people have listened patiently to the ideas explored in this book. My family, colleagues, and friends have contributed examples and counterexamples too numerous to mention. I want to thank the staff and audience of WILL-AM, the American Public Radio affiliate at the University of Illinois at Urbana-Champaign, for the opportunity to air my views on language in a continuing series of commentaries. And I want to thank the National Council of Teachers of English, and its Commission on the English Language, for their active encouragement and support of my work. Released time provided by the University of Illinois allowed me to complete my manuscript.

Earlier drafts of some of the essays in this book have appeared elsewhere, sometimes under different titles. Parts of "Academies of One" appeared in the *English Journal,* and William Safire has cited a number of my usage comments in his books and his columns in the *New York Times Magazine.* "Nothing Like a Good Pun" was first published as "Public Cutespeak" in *Verbatim, the Language Quarterly.* "Sexist Language" and "A Literal Paradox" originally appeared in *Righting Words.* "The English Language and the Constitution" was published in *The Brandeis Review.* "Declining Grammar" appeared as "The Ugly Grammarian" in *English Today,* and "The Passive Voice Can Be Your Friend" was published in the same journal. Parts of "The Myths of Teaching English" will be published under the title "Watching Our Grammar" in *Essays for English Teachers,* edited by Gail Hawisher and Anna Soter (Albany: SUNY Press, 1989). All are reprinted with permission. I also want to extend my gratitude to Houghton Mifflin Company for permission to reprint the first 100 words of the Brown Corpus from Nelson and Kučera's *Frequency Analysis of English Usage,* and to Longman Group Limited for permission to reprint the first 100 words of the LOB Corpus from Hofland and Johansson's *Word Frequencies in British and American English.*

Most of all, I want to thank the teachers who participated in the Writing Outreach Workshop sponsored by the English Department at the University of Illinois at Urbana-Champaign, during the summers of 1986 and 1987. It was your enthusiasm for the English language and your dedication to our profession that inspired this collection, and it is to all of you that I dedicate this book.

I Language Lore

1 Weather Report

Language, like the weather, is a popular topic: everybody's got something to say about it. And like the weather, where there is language, there is also change. One of the most common weather sayings goes something like this: "If you don't like the weather around here, just wait five minutes." You hear this in New England and the Midwest, in California and the South, and while it is sometimes attributed to Mark Twain or Thoreau or Emerson, it has achieved the status of proverbial folk wisdom.

Language changes like the weather, cyclically, seasonally, according to forces that seem mysterious if not sinister to the average person, and we could modify our weather proverb to apply to language: "If you don't like the way language is used now, just wait five minutes; you'll like it even less," since those who complain about the language are never happy for long.

The metaphors we use to describe this change for the worse reveal our inner feelings about English. We think of language in terms of organic imagery: it may live and grow, like a garden, if properly nourished and weeded, while in the hands of the common crowd— so goes the opinion of the linguistic elite—language will sicken and die. Some critics see bad usage as a virus causing physical illness, usually gastrointestinal, in those most sensitive to its nuances. Language has a moral life (corrupt language may be a force for ethical as well as physical corruption), a political one (it may be anarchic, democratic, or autocratic in its structure), and an economic one as well (languages mint, lend and borrow their words, like coins, and the debts that they incur must eventually be repaid). Since we are used to thinking of language in terms of metaphor, and we rely on language as a social barometer measuring the class, education, and overall worthiness of our fellow human beings, a weather-model of language should not be all that revolutionary.

In terms of its metaphoric treatment, language has a psychological and social life too. One currently popular view, an extension of the Sapir-Whorf hypothesis, considers language a cognitive prison whose walls and bars control our thoughts and prevent our direct knowledge of reality. This theory sharply contrasts with the competing notion that language is the transcendental representation of the real world and thus the source of all inner and outer knowledge. In this view, words either are or bear an ineffable but nonetheless certain affinity to the things they represent. According to either model, we cannot know what we do not have words to express, a stricture which places depressing limitations on the human imagination.

Practically speaking, though, language is neither a mirror or a prison, but a prism, a lens which affects our perceptions to a certain degree, but which we can also control and focus. In a more down-to-earth social model, language is a set of laws, initiated individually but adopted by consensus, as with any social compact, changing in response to an ever-changing environment, and possessing in turn the power to alter that environment. Those who transgress the laws of language are open to censure. Frequently we view them as criminals in need of punishment. In the eyes of the language judges, for example, people should be imprisoned for using such supposed innovations as *gift* as a transitive verb—*They gifted us with a copy of the book* (a usage which goes back to the sixteenth century), or *aggravate* for *irritate* (a usage dating from the seventeenth century), while dangling *hopefully* at the start of a sentence (*Hopefully, this won't happen again*), which is indeed a new construction, dating back only to the 1960s, is considered by the authorities to be no less than a hanging crime.

If we are to believe most of what we hear about English at cocktail parties or in the popular press, we have been heading downhill in our speech since some unspecified point in the past. Something is always going wrong with the language; things are never as they used to be, or as they should be. Pessimists maintain that English is in a state of decay, and all our efforts to bring about or restore the "Golden Age," where people gave language its due and used it correctly, fall on deaf ears. The language forecast for these doomsayers continues to be dim: partly cloudy with a sixty percent chance of double negatives.

To complete the analogy between language and the weather, I have found that we trust commentators on language about as much as we trust meteorologists. Yet ironically, we can't seem to get along without either. No news broadcast is complete without the weather report, and while most of us don't open the newspaper simply to look for William Safire's language column, or Ann Landers's advice on good grammar, popular books and articles on the state of the language generate dependable, often devoted audiences. Just as many of us remember our schooltime exposure to English grammar with chagrin, if not outright pain, we also carry inside us a model of an English teacher whose perfection we never managed to emulate, whose disappointment in our performance did not make language study a dead issue but spurred us on toward new heights of correctness.

The Facts of English

Although we all may have something to say about language, a little knowledge often proves a dangerous thing. Much of what we do say is wrong, for few of us take the trouble to study the science of language, yet quite a few of us go about pretending that science simply does not exist. Consequently, our ideas about language are based on subjective preference rather than objective fact. There is nothing unnatural about this, since subjectivity is one of the main forces behind language use. But we seldom acknowledge that our language judgments, or the judgments of those whom we take for experts, are arbitrary, not graven in stone but inked on wood pulp.

Our attitudes toward language have a profound effect both on English itself and on those who use it, but it is never easy to characterize this effect with much precision because speakers of English display an astonishing ambivalence toward their language. On one hand we disparage our own abilities, constantly apologizing for our mistakes, real or imagined. More often than not we labor under the delusion that our English is riddled with error, that it is inadequate to the demands placed on us. In our unending desire to say or write it right, we seek out and defer to the opinions of teachers, editors, and usage experts. But on the other hand, although we bemoan our linguistic incompetence and fret over our insecurity, we are also loath to accept the advice we so desperately seek. How dare anyone tell us what to say or write, or how to go about it? It's undemocratic. There ought to be a law.

It is an unfortunate fact that many otherwise well-educated native speakers of English either reject or shy away from the formal study of their own language. Since it became a fundamental part of the American educational curriculum well over a century ago, students—and even some teachers—have resisted initiation into the mysteries of grammar, and the term *grammarian* has taken on a negative connotation that is difficult to counteract. It is a further measure of our linguistic waffling that we alternate complaints about too much grammar in our schools with cries of not enough.

Despite our endemic unhappiness with grammar instruction, informal interest in English remains keen. Language may not be a big-time issue in this country, like politics, religion, or the economy, but it is an issue that concerns everybody, and it surfaces all the time. The press regularly prints commentaries and editorials on the state of English. There are as well frequent stories about attempts to reform our pronunciation, spelling, and grammar. The bureaucratic style of governmental prose is continually held up for ridicule by all manner of essayists and media commentators. Watchdog groups seek out the deceptions embedded in public doublespeak. Individuals crusade against the misused apostrophe or the encroachment of quotation marks. And the introduction of new words is noted now with amusement, now alarm. More important, though it still receives nowhere near the attention it deserves, is the fact that many of our citizens pass through our schools without learning to read or write effectively.

There is no doubt, then, that interest in language is high. And we are not always defensive about our linguistic prowess. Sometimes we plead ignorance, but just as often we are language bullies, correcting our relatives and friends (they may not stay friends for long), and even our teachers. True, the public dutifully seeks out the advice of the numerous guides to good English, but should a usage authority make a mistake, scores of amateur guardians of our tongue are quick to respond with unkind censure.

I myself have been guilty of language hubris. Once in high school I dared to challenge a pronunciation by the severest of my teachers. The word in question was written *gaol,* the British spelling of our American *jail.* It is pronounced to rhyme with *rail* on both sides of the Atlantic, a fact which I knew in my precocity, but which my teacher had missed. Instead she said something with a hard *g* that rhymed with a drawn-out *cowl.* I knew nothing then of spelling pronunciation, the reading of words not with their traditional sounds, but as they appear on the page, and I knew even less of classroom decorum and respect for authority, but once the correction was out of my mouth I knew I had done wrong. The class was silent. The teacher became dangerously calm. I was made to walk the length of the room, up to the desk, and told to find *gaol* in the dictionary. This I did, though with difficulty, for I suddenly lost all sense of alphabetical order.

Of course I was proved right, but at what cost! My teacher took the correction gracefully, more gracefully than I had offered it, but things were never the same between us. Nor did I become an instant folk hero among the students—I was just the fool who corrected Mrs. N. on some amazingly trivial point. With language, as with everything else, we all must learn that there are times to be correct, and times to be still.

Grammar and grammar

When we speak of grammar we frequently confuse two of its basic senses. Sometimes we divide these into grammar as science and grammar as art. I prefer to call these *Grammar* with a capital *g*, and *grammar* with a small one. In any case, *Grammar* writ large refers to the structure, or the formal features of a language, its sounds and syllables, its morphemes, words, and sentences. It is a descriptive study, one which catalogues and inventories a language, accounting for its elements according to the general principles of linguistic science. *grammar* with the little *g* refers to the rules of preferred or prescribed usage associated with standard language. It is the etiquette of knowing which pronunciations or words or idioms are privileged, and which are stigmatized. It is the art of being correct.

These different grammars can get us into trouble, and the ordinary English speaker is often caught in the cross fire between (or is it *among?*) the experts. When descriptive linguists go after the facts of English, which they must do for us to have a record of our tongue in all the stages of its development, they are sometimes accused of abandoning all standards and approving language forms some people label as inferior. When prescriptivists attempt to lay out codes of behavior for all of us to follow, which they must do as well, for they too are part of the self-regulating system of our language, they seldom agree on general or specific principles. No matter how much we laud their efforts, we find the procrustean bed of the language commentators too much for our unsupple limbs. The language commentator Logan Pearsall Smith (1948) has called grammar in this prescriptive sense "the natural enemy of idiom." As hard as we may try to follow their advice, we become lost in the contradictory opinions of the prescribers. Aiming for an impossible standard of language perfection, we make new mistakes, pushing English in new and unforeseen directions, provoking the language critics further still.

In 1921 the Oxford philologist H. C. Wyld lamented that despite our persistent interest in things linguistic, too many of us resist the notion that a considerable body of well-ascertained facts about language exists, and that a knowledge of linguistics can illuminate the language questions which concern teachers, writers, editors, and the general public. I hope with this book to counteract in a small way this tendency to reject the facts of English, and to encourage my readers to pursue the subject in all its fact and fancy well beyond the confines of these pages.

2 The Myths of Language

Language commentators and weather forecasters depend to some extent on signs of the times for their predictions. Just as we look at clouds and test the wind to estimate the weather, we listen to words or read magazines and make claims about the direction of English. But we also depend on folklore for our guesses. Red skies tell sailors all sorts of things about storm and calm, and we deduce the severity and duration of winter from the likes of woolly worms and groundhogs. General forecasts about language and literacy are similarly grounded in misinformation and myth.

Some misinformation about language takes the form of advice: complete your sentences (many sentences are physically incomplete, yet completely understandable); never begin one with *and*; don't contract; avoid *I* and *you*. And, of course, avoid the passive voice. There is also myth: French is a rational language; Greek is democratic; Chinese is transcendental; English is in a state of decline.

The Myth of Elizabethan English

One common American language myth asserts the existence of a settlement in a remote corner of the Ozarks, or possibly the Appalachians, where time stands still, where English is spoken today exactly as it was in Shakespeare's time. Underlying this myth is another: that the original European settlers of this area were a racially homogeneous group of Scotch-Irish and English, an assertion that has been challenged and has never been proved. A recent public television series on the English language went so far as to locate this untouched-by-time settlement not in the mountains but in the Sea Islands off the Carolina coast. Viewers saw the resident fisherfolk speaking in their quaint, old-fashioned ways. Of course this linguistic fountain of youth cannot exist, for no speech community, whether ethnically homogeneous or not, can ever become frozen in time. Language never stops changing, no matter how isolated its speakers are from the world around them, or how old-fashioned they sound to others. As the sociolinguists Walt

Wolfram and Donna Christian remind us in their study of Appalachian English (1976), the language of any group may be conservative in some aspects but progressive in others. Although Appalachian, Ozark, or Sea Island speech may preserve a few features of older English that have been lost by other dialects, they also produce advanced forms that have not yet spread to other areas.

As the Elizabethan English story suggests, a major function of language myth is to mark one form of speech as purer than or otherwise superior to another. Some myths assert that language reflects the speaker's inner self. For example, it is a common but mistaken notion that the speech of city folk (or northerners), is too fast and too nasal and reflects an unfriendly disposition, while their southern (or rural) counterparts are wrongly characterized as slow of speech, with drawling vowel habits that are supposed to evidence a combination of sociability and decreased mental activity. Such commonly used terms as *nasality* and *drawl* are frequently subjective and invariably negative. To cite two personal examples, when I was in college a friend of mine from central Illinois, whose accent seemed to my then-unpracticed New York ears to evoke the deadly-drawling pace of antebellum Tara, likened the words of a Florida student we both knew to "bubbles slowly oozing up through the swamps." And more recently a colleague of mine at the University of Illinois, a professor with urban, east coast origins and an ivy league education—someone, in short, who would be described by central Illinoisans as a snooty if not downright nasal Yankee—once complained that the one thing he hated most about living in the Midwest was having his children grow up with what he called "that horrible midwestern nasal accent."

The myths sometimes deal with ways that language both channels and limits how we think. According to this view of language, we can only conceive what our language has words to express. By extension, the more words a language has, the more its speakers can do with them. In one bit of folklore we are asked to envy the semantic richness of the Eskimo, whose language offers countless words (the number varies with the teller) for different kinds of snow: according to the *Encyclopaedia Britannica* there is "falling snow," "snow on the ground," "drifting snow," "encrusted snow," and so on. On the other hand, we might pity speakers of those impoverished languages like English with only *snow* and *slush*.

We are also asked to sympathize with speakers whose languages distort or limit their cognition: some would argue that the syntactic structure of German interferes with comprehension, since its periodicity makes us wade through parts and parts of speech before coming to the verb. They also point to an unnamed, mythical, primitive language which, lacking a future tense, is supposed to prevent its users from developing any concept of time.

Cultural bias enters clearly into these myths about the relationship between language and cognition. English speakers seldom question their assumption that the only natural way to think is to put the verb between subject and object, not before or after, though in Old English the verb appeared in various parts of the sentence without any measurable interference with comprehension. And we never suppose that those earliest forms of our own language, which had no separate future tense, gave the first English folk any trouble conceiving yesterday, today, and tomorrow. Today's English offers several ways of naming what is yet to come, all of them dependent on the present tense: "I close (am closing, am going to close) the deal next Thursday." Even our so-called future tense requires the present inflection of the auxiliary *shall* or *will*.

Similarly, those who treasure lexical diversity often forget that despite its many words for arctic precipitation, the Eskimo language lacks a term for the general concept 'snow.' (Arabic similarly has words for different kinds of camels, though it lacks a generic term for *camel* itself.) This deficiency does not mean that Eskimo inhibits abstraction in its speakers, but rather that, in the case of snow, species outweighs genus. There is a similar situation in American English, though it is not quite analogous and hardly so picturesque: we readily distinguish at least two score types of *burgers* by brand (*Big Mac, Whopper*) or type (*pizzaburger, tunaburger*), having less and less recourse nowadays to the basic *hamburg*. Surprisingly, no one takes this as evidence of modern overspecializing, or concludes that the American preoccupation with chopped meat rivals what we naively suppose to be the Eskimo romance with weather.

The Myth of Greek

Language myths are subject to change, even to eventual debunking. We once thought that the form of government in a given society determined the nature of its language: an autocratic society fostered a rigid, authoritarian language, while a democratically constituted society literally reflected the voice of the people. In the eighteenth century, speakers of English regarded classical Greek as the ideal language to imitate because it was developed by the first and foremost democracy of the ancient world. They also thought that Greek persisted unchanged over a millennium, a sure sign of a language that has reached perfection.

Now we know better. Participation in Greek, or rather Athenian, democracy was limited by class and sex, which did not disturb eighteenth-century philosophers but seems much less congenial to our attitudes today. Furthermore, scholarship has shown that no language goes unchanged for very long. Greek varied over time and distance as much as English, or any other language, for that matter. There were sharp distinctions among the dialects of ancient Greek, in addition to the striking differences that have been so long apparent between the Homeric, classical, and modern tongues.

French, the Rational Language

The French will tell you, if you do not already know it, that French is a superior language because it is rational. Some go so far as to claim that French reflects the very structure of the human mind, assuming that structure to be rational as well. And the French perceive of themselves as more concerned with language than just about anyone else: they are a nation of grammarians who thrive on purity and unity. After the French Revolution, in an effort to solidify the power of the central government, the educational system of the country was nationalized, Parisian French became the standard, and all regional languages and dialects were virtually outlawed. But as the language historian L. C. Harmer (1954) has pointed out, the Gallic view of themselves and their language conflicts with linguistic reality.

For one thing, French is not pure and it never was. French is a language which borrows words, difficult as that is for its citizens to admit. The name *France* suggests as much: the French were originally Franks, a Germanic tribe (so were the Normans, or Northmen) who "borrowed" Latin more or less unwillingly from the conquering Romans. Today the purists in France object so much to the many English words adopted by their less chauvinistic comrades that non-French words have been outlawed: not only the new words like *le footing*, 'jogging,' and *le pull* or *pullover*, 'sweater,' but the good old words that crossed the Channel over two centuries ago, such as *rosbif, redingote*, and *club*. Vigilante groups monitor radio, television, and the press, and offenders must pay fines to the government for any vernacular contraband uncovered.

Officially, at least, the French position is that the language must be kept pure. In fact *purism* itself is a term we have borrowed from the French, and it is always negative: "Scrupulous or exaggerated observance of, or insistence upon, purity or correctness, especially in language or style" (*OED*, s.v.). In addition to keeping out foreign words, the French pride themselves on maintaining a standard language with little or no variation. They have an Academy charged with deciding matters of correctness, and a national system of education to promulgate these decisions and suppress local innovation and change. Unfortunately neither the French Academy nor the teaching cadre has been able to exterminate regional and social dialects or to clamp down on variation.

This variation is found not only in rare or isolated cases, but in common, everyday French. For example, evidence from no less central an area than Paris suggests that the markers of grammatical gender which gave so many of us trouble when we learned French in school are breaking down in the spoken language (Durand 1936). Also, while French teachers in American high schools still take off points for incorrect accent marks, the French themselves have become sloppy about these things: when I taught English to English majors at a French university some years ago, I noticed that my students, who did their written work in French because their English was so poor, evaded the problem of acute and grave accents on their vowels by drawing horizontal lines instead. Even the standard literary language of France is so full of disputed usage that a thriving business exists in usage and style manuals to guide the perplexed through the maze of variation.

So much, then, for the myth of French.

The Myth of Chinese

Because it is so different from English and the European languages both in speech and in writing, Chinese was romanticized by westerners and a variety of myths have arisen about the language spoken by so great a percentage of the earth's inhabitants. In the seventeenth century, for example, the writer John Webb praised Chinese as "plain, easy, and simple, as a *natural* speech ought to be," and he sought to prove that it was the first language spoken on earth. Webb (1669) found Chinese to be chaste as well as natural, for he was under the mistaken impression that the language had no way of referring to what he chastely calls "the privy parts." He also mistakenly finds that there is a basic human predisposition to speak Chinese: "The very first expression we make of life, at the very instant of our births, is . . . by uttering the Chinese word *Ya.*"

The Chinese language has both fascinated and repelled western observers from the start. Some commentators described it as "pure applied logic," but John Wilkins, the seventeenth-century philosopher of language who tried to create an ideal artificial language, complained that Chinese, like Latin and Greek, is imperfect: it has too many characters and words; it is ambiguous; and it is too difficult to pronounce. The Chinese writing system, certainly one of the world's oldest, is held up to ridicule by proponents of the alphabet. But as spelling reformers argue, the alphabet isn't perfect either.

The Myth of the Alphabet

Writing has always been associated with magic and the unknown, and it is not surprising to find myths about writing systems permeating our thoughts on language. Western intellectuals once supposed that both the Chinese and Egyptian writing systems offered transcendent representations of ideas and things, providing closer ties between the mind and the external world than the halting phonetic symbolism of the alphabet-dependent European languages, and in the seventeenth century some attempts were made to create universal, philosophical writing systems using ideographs. The decipherment of Egyptian hieroglyphics showed, however, that phonetic symbols—keys to pronunciation—were interspersed among the pictures. Similarly, although western myths about the Chinese charactery persist, linguists now know that not every character forms an independent word, as we think of words in English, and that some ninety percent of Chinese characters contain phonetic as well as semantic information.

The myth of the philosophical superiority of picture writing is counterbalanced by the myth of the developmental superiority of the alphabet. According to this story, the three major types of writing systems reveal an evolutionary pattern. The first stage in the development of writing is ideographic, each symbol standing for an individual word or concept. The second stage gives us the syllabary (used, for example, in early Semitic writing and in Japanese), where each written symbol represents a syllable, generally a combination of sounds. Finally comes the most advanced stage, the culmination of the graphic process: the alphabet, in which each letter represents a single, discrete sound.

Implicit in this myth is the notion that the alphabet is the inevitable outcome of the rise of writing or, put more simply, that last is best. Alphabetists fault ideographic systems for their complexity. It is a commonplace that illiteracy is rampant in China because the Chinese must memorize thousands of individual symbols before they can read their literature. Syllabaries are somewhat more efficient, but they still contain at least twice as many graphic elements to learn as alphabets, and they are often perceived as an intermediate and therefore imperfect stage in the development of writing.

The alphabet is last and the roman alphabet is not the least, claims the myth. Whether it is the most efficient is something else again. Unfortunately, most of the letters of the English writing system have more than one sound associated with them; sometimes letters are not pronounced at all; and in certain instances, such as *BarBQ*, we could even claim that English verges on the logographic. English writing may not present as much difficulty as Chinese, but it is clear that our vowels and consonants offer the learner of English—native speaker as well as second language learner—a phonetic maze from which few emerge without considerable difficulty.

Spelling Reform

Actually the alphabet may be the biggest problem we have with English. When I ask students what aspect of English they would change if they could, they invariably point to our illogical spelling system. Language experts too would like to reform orthography. Quite a few have tried and failed to do so. Thomas Spence, an eighteenth-century spelling reformer, likened English orthography to "the darkest hieroglyphics, or most difficult cyphers." George Bernard Shaw demonstrated that *ghoti* could be pronounced "fish" (*gh* as in "rough," *o* as in "women," *ti* as in "ammunition") and complained that although his own last name had only two sounds in it, he had to use four letters to spell it. Shaw called for a new, truly phonetic writing system, and his will (1950) established an "alphabet trust" to promote a new, rational English spelling.

Since the sixteenth century, spelling simplification or rationalization has been the goal of most English language planners and commentators, though their success has been minimal. The case of Chinese illegibility notwithstanding, readers of English, like their Chinese counterparts, must memorize countless patterns and irregularities—nonphonetic place names like *Cholmondeley* or *Cirencester* (pronounced Chumley and Sizister) not to mention such common difficulties as the *b* in "subtle" and "bomb," the *ough* in "rough, though, through, slough," and "ought," or the *p* in "pop, psychology," and "phonetic" itself—before they can tackle even the simplest of literary texts.

Reformers argued that phonetic spelling would save money as well as time: words would be shorter, resulting in lower printing costs, and children would learn to read more quickly. Spelling as a school subject could be mastered in a matter of months, instead of years, and foreigners would acquire English much more readily. But it is also clear that phonetic spelling would cost us something. Opponents of reform argued that books would have to be reprinted and everyone would have to be retrained in the new spelling. In addition, respelling would render the etymology and history of our words obscure. Replying to this, the reformers claimed that everyone would be temporarily bilingual so far as spelling went, with new generations learning only the newer forms of words. As for etymology, the spelling reformers pointed out that only a few classicists and linguists ever had any use for etymology, the bulk of English speakers being thoroughly ignorant of the sources and structures of our words anyway.

But there are deeper problems with orthographic revision. Despite their high-minded aims, the new spellings were inconsistent. The American Philological Association advocated simplifying double letters: *kettle* becomes *ketl*. But in *sapphire*, where *ph* is respelled as *ff*, the double consonant remains. Silent *e* was also dropped, but *decked* is spelled as *deckd*, while *thanked* becomes *thankt*, despite the fact that both final consonants have the sound of *t*. Greater still, however, is the problem that because the sounds of speech are in continual, albeit gradual, flux, and because pronunciation varies not only with time, but also with geography, education, age, class, and situation, among others, a phonetic writing system can only succeed at the expense of standardized spelling. Noah Webster, in his *Compendious Dictionary* of 1806, argued that our reluctance to allow spelling to change along with pronunciation "is destroying the benefits of an alphabet, and reducing our language to the barbarism of Chinese characters instead of letters." But standardized spelling is a goal that not only Webster, but most of our schools and dictionaries, as well as the general public, have fought long and hard to achieve, a goal they are unlikely to give up in the near future.

3 The Passive Voice Can Be Your Friend

> Righteously, mercilessly, he weeded out the passive voice.
> —Anne Tyler, *The Accidental Tourist*

The myth of alphabetic superiority is one that is held by many linguists and sinologists. Language professionals, particularly editors and English teachers, may also subscribe to an even more popular modern myth which claims that the active voice is preferable to the passive. The passive voice is frequently cited as a stumbling block for student writers, who run into trouble with the inversion and syntactic complexity which the passive requires. It is also clear, however, that professional writers, whose syntax is generally under control, do not sufficiently refrain from the passive to satisfy the usage critics.

Modern style seems founded on the premise that shorter is better, when it comes to language, and when the agent or doer of the action is not deleted, the passive form of an expression—see sentence (2) below—is just a bit longer than the active sentence (1). When the agent is deleted, of course, as in sentence (3), the passive is shorter than the active. But critics of the passive do not find this information comforting.

(1) *active (5 words)*: The grammarian parsed the sentence.
(2) *passive (7 words)*: The sentence was parsed by the grammarian.
(3) *passive with deleted agent (4 words)*: The sentence was parsed.

Embedded in our official distaste for the passive is an idea that the passive is a recent development in English, and that the only really good writing is essay writing and fiction, where use of the passive is said to detract from stylistic strength and directness of expression. However there is a clear prejudice among today's commentators on voice—particularly those who express themselves in writing textbooks—against one of the commonest types of prose, report writing, where the passive voice is not only common, it is generally less wordy than the active, more direct, and more efficient in conveying information.

The passive is not a form that is new to English, nor is its spread a recent phenomenon. Instead, it is the attack on the passive voice

that is a recent development in the history of English usage. Eighteenth-
and nineteenth-century commentators did not proscribe the passive,
though they did not hesitate to correct improperly formed passives
when they found them. A few language experts even argued that
English had no true passive voice, but most accepted it as an essential
element of our grammar and style. While today's language critics fault
it, our twentieth-century grammarians seem happy with the passive
as a fact of life. For example, in his grammar, George O. Curme (1935)
remarks without regret that the passive "has become a favorite form
of expression in English." The historical linguist F. Th. Visser (1973)
documents the popularity of a variety of passive constructions not
only in modern times but throughout the history of English. And
Michael Halliday (1970) is one of several linguists to observe that the
number of intransitive verbs with passive signification is expanding:
*The recruits trained; The house sold quickly; The book reads easily; The
soup that eats like a meal.* Quirk *et al.* (1985) find the active voice
"generally by far the more common," though the passive occurs more
commonly in informative than imaginative prose. They note that in
certain types of texts the passive may actually outnumber the active
by as much as ten to one.

Nineteenth-century usage guides do not advise against the passive,
though some do warn writers not to change voice in mid-sentence. In
fact, William Swinton, in his *School Manual for English Composition*
(1877, 41), tells student writers to use the passive for variety. Nor is
the passive the major concern in the early part of this century that it
was later to become. The usage critic Alfred Ayres (1901) goes to great
lengths to argue that brief sentences are preferable, and that excess
verbiage makes sentences weak. Objecting to nominalizations—the
turning of verbs into nouns— Ayres complains, "Why use six syllables
when three will suffice?" But, though he worries at great length
whether it is appropriate for the indirect object of the active to serve
as the subject of the passive (for example, *Alice was given the book by
Martha*), he doesn't find the passive wordy at all.

The Fowlers do not favor one voice over the other in either of their
extraordinarily popular works on usage (1906; 1926), though by 1907
American school texts were recommending the active voice, labeling
the passive as less direct or effective (Sampson and Holland 1907),
clumsy and wordy (Wooley 1907), sluggish (Hanson 1908), and less
emphatic (Hanson 1912). Greenough and Hersey (1918) say, "Use the
passive voice sparingly" because the active is more interesting. The
grammarians MacCracken and Sanderson (1919) advise that "inaccurate substitution of passive for active produces sentences that are

vague, wordy, or faulty in emphasis," and Maurice Weseen, in his *Dictionary of English Grammar* (1928), maintains that "the active form is nearly always preferable to the passive because it is more direct and forceful." While Johnson, McGregor, and Lyman (1939) find that the passive "is frequently a desirable construction," they prefer the active, which "adds a feeling of liveliness and vigor to the sentence." Even the linguist Albert Marckwardt (1940) finds the active voice more "effective," recommending its use "wherever possible." Among these textbook writers, only Cook and Chapman (1936) defend the passive as often more "convenient [than] . . . the crude and indefinite *they*."

It is not clear just when or why this negative assessment of the passive first arose, though for want of a better explanation we may attribute the spread of such comments to a general shift in English toward a concise, plain literary style. In addition, by the 1940s the passive, with its deletable agent ("The chemicals were added and the resulting change in temperature recorded; The requested item will be sent as soon as it becomes available") became associated not simply with the mildly distasteful traits of wordiness and confusion, but with the even more negative practice of conscious deception by deliberately hiding the doer of the action ("Funds have not been allocated; The bombs were dropped on innocent civilians").

Eric Blair, writing under the pen name George Orwell, reinforces this moral evaluation of the passive voice in his influential essay "Politics and the English Language" (1946), where he includes the passive in the catalogue of what he calls the "swindles and perversions" of modern writing. Of course pseudonyms are a most deliberate way of hiding the agent of an action, and Orwell does use agentless passives both in his condemnation of the construction—*the passive voice is wherever possible used in preference to the active*—and throughout his essay.

A survey of writer's guides shows that current advice about voice ranges from the practical to the rabid. For example, in their influential commentary Cleanth Brooks and Robert Penn Warren (1970) recommend choosing voice carefully to achieve appropriate emphasis, though they warn writers against using the passive simply because they are "too lazy or vague to think who or what the true subject is." The *McGraw-College Handbook*, by Marius and Wiener (1985), is typical in counseling its readers, "Use verbs in the active voice in most instances; use verbs in the passive voice sparingly and only for good reason." The authors further label the passive a means of evading responsibility, permitting its use "only when the recipient of the action in the sentence is much more important to your statement than the doer of the action."

Though Marius and Wiener acknowledge that the passive is a general feature of scientific and technical writing, their stress upon the active as essential for a clear and direct writing style demotes scientific prose to writing of a lower order.

Another textbook author, James Raymond (1980), maintains that writers use the passive "when they want to evade or conceal the responsibility for someone's behavior." The poet and essayist Donald Hall (*Writing Well*, 1976), after labeling the passive as hazy, distant, watery, and evasive, remembers its conventional use in science and concedes, "occasionally the passive is right, or unavoidable," or is at best a lesser evil. And Sheridan Baker, in his classic text *The Practical Stylist* (1981), does not even consider the needs of scientific, technical, or business report writers and their readers in his strong, yet wordy condemnation of the mushrooming passive:

> I reluctantly admit that the passive voice has certain uses. In fact, your meaning sometimes demands the passive voice; the agent may be better under cover—insignificant, or unknown, or mysterious.. . . But it is *wordy*. It puts *useless words* in a sentence. Its dullness derives as much from its *extra wordage* as from its impersonality. The best way to prune is with the active voice, cutting the passive and its fungus as you go. [Emphasis added]

For the writer William Zinsser (*On Writing Well*, 1980), the passive fungus may actually prove fatal: "The difference between an active-verb style and a passive-verb style—in pace, clarity and vigor—is the difference between life and death for a writer."

With apologies to *The Practical Stylist*, some texts geared to more practical sorts of writing do not reject the passive with such ferocity, though most subscribe to the myth of the evasive passive. A number of business and technical writing books do not even mention voice as a stylistic or moral concern. Those writers who clearly prefer the active argue that the passive is also necessary. John M. Lannon (*Technical Writing*, 1985) warns of passive danger, yet advises his readers to use both voices selectively. Nancy Roundy (1985), who also favors the active, recommends the passive for its impersonal and objective function, while the handbook of the Delaware Technical and Community College (1982) reminds us of the diplomatic power of the passive construction.

One standard composition book, *Writing with a Purpose* (James McCrimmon 1980), actually challenges the common belief that the passive is weak: "There are situations in which the passive voice is more emphatic." Unfortunately McCrimmon does not trust his readers' judgment or ability: "Because misuse of the passive voice often results in an awkward or ungrammatical sentence, it is wise to choose the active voice unless there is a clear gain from using the passive." Other writers defend the passive more strongly. Mills and Walter (1970) call the active-passive debate subjective, crediting the passive with the ability to produce "crisp and effective sentences." Waldo H. Willis (1965) argues that in technical writing, which is largely impersonal, the active voice has no particular advantage, adding that "a blanket ban on the passive robs the author of more freedom of expression."

Doris Whalen (1978) finds the passive important in reports and in the writing of minutes, while Harry M. Brown (1980) recommends it to soften bad news. Fielden, Dalek, and Fielden (1984), who generously claim "the passive voice can be your friend," observe that most writers who object to its use have no experience in the business world, where the passive is often called for. The authors stress that the deceptive powers of the passive may be used to advantage, for example when conveying negative information to a supervisor or an important customer. However, they also warn managers that the passive voice in the writing of subordinates signals deception or evasion, and should be looked into.

Today's bias, however, even in business and technical writing guides, is toward the active voice. Writing theorist Elaine Maimon and her colleagues (1981) favor the active in all sorts of prose and, noting that it is becoming increasingly popular in scientific writing too, advise technical students to pepper their work with active sentences. But Carolyn J. Mullins (1983) goes further, urging the replacement of passives by actives in scientific and social science writing because the passive does not mark objectivity, as is generally assumed, but masks uncertainty instead, permitting both bias and imprecision in a text. Conversely, the active form is often used when science writers want to emphasize their fallibility. According to the rhetorician Charles Bazerman (1986, personal communication), the active appears as a sign not of hubris but humility, a call for other researchers to validate the writer's experiment or theory.

Of the modern usage critics, Bergen and Cornelia Evans (1957) are virtually alone in supporting the passive construction. Though educators seem bent on eradicating the passive, Evans and Evans describe it as a sophisticated device popular among educated speakers and writers. They dismiss claims that the passive is weak or clumsy, finding it often just the opposite: "When the agent is mentioned in a passive construction it has more emphasis than it would have with an active verb." While they do not recommend the passive for description or narration, Evans and Evans find it "almost indispensable in presenting ideas and generalizations." And while they concede that the passive may be used to disguise responsibility for a given act, they sensibly urge us to "blame the person who is not being candid, and not the grammatical form that makes this possible."

Unfortunately, accurate information on syntactic frequency is not readily available, and it is difficult to judge whether the passive is spreading or declining in specialized types of writing, or in writing in general. Even if we did count the syntactic structures of published prose our results would mislead us, for many an active voice owes its appearance to the vigilance of an editor with an antipassive outlook.

One textbook laments that writers do not follow advice against the passive because they do not understand the concept of voice. It is true that naive writers, in their efforts to clean up their prose, tend to suspect any form of the verb *to be* of passive affiliation. But this hardly explains why the passive is so common. Indeed we may even argue that the multitude of passives in the writing of nonprofessionals indicates the naturalness of the construction. We freely and effectively use all sorts of syntactic constructions whose nature and function we cannot explicitly analyze. Nor is it wise to ban a syntactic form just because it is difficult to master. Considerations of style notwithstanding, to view the passive as unnatural or inappropriate is to accept uncritically the myth that twentieth-century commentators have spread about the voice. Apparently the passive is alive and in some cases it may even be well, despite the poor press it has been given. It is more than likely that the passive cannot be restrained because it is so much a part of English, always has been, and still needs to be. Why else would Orwell begin "Politics and the English Language" with an agentless passive,

> Most people who bother with the matter at all would admit that the English language is in a bad way, but *it is* generally *assumed* that we cannot by conscious action do anything about it,

and strategically place one in his closing paragraph as well?

> Political language—and with variations this is true of all political parties, from Conservatives to Anarchists—*is designed* to make lies sound truthful and murder respectable, and to give an appearance of solidity to pure wind. [Italics added]

4 Brevity and Style

I cannot speak well enough to be unintelligible.
—Jane Austen, *Northanger Abbey*

One problem with passives for the modern critic is their length. Commentators on style have always linked sentence length with comprehension, but only recently, with our twentieth-century insistence on brevity as the soul of a natural style, do we hear the universal cry that long sentences, whether active or passive, tend toward affectation, and that while good style demands a mix of sentence lengths, most of our sentences could stand some cutting.

Natural Style

We often praise a writer for a natural style, yet like other critical terms of language, such as *standard* and *grammatical,* there is an uncertainty built into the notion of natural writing that merits exploration. *Natural* itself is a word that conjures vagueness. It is a popular label for foods as well as styles, though the Food and Drug Administration, which strictly prescribes our food terminology, does not define *natural* at all, and permits manufacturers to call products high in salt, sugar, fat, and all manner of preservative chemicals *natural* foods.

Natural is also one of many stylistic labels we attach to English prose and poetry. There are the high, middle, and low styles, echoing Aristotelian categories. In the nineteenth century we spoke of the nervous (or strong) style and the feeble; and there are the dry, plain, neat, elegant, and florid styles. Some of these stylistic categories overlap, and commentators frequently mix terms from several categories. So the middle style may also be the plain style for some, while others will insist the middle style has more ornament than the plain style, which in turn is fancier than that style they call dry. To the ordinary reader this confusion of terms underscores the subjectivity of stylistic assessment. But one point critics have agreed on throughout the centuries: they call the best style, whatever its features, natural, while the epithets *rude* and *affected* apply to any style they find displeasing.

Although we should know better, we are many of us disposed to believe the pretense of modern literature that it invented the plain, natural style as a reaction to the linguistic excesses of some twelve hundred years of prose and poetry in English. In fact, the natural style, whatever its definition, has always predominated among our writers, and it has been set forth by many commentators since the Renaissance as the preferred mode for formal discourse.

While Aristotle defines the terms somewhat more specifically, English writers generally think of the high style as formal, elevated, ornate diction. In contrast, the low style is not only informal, it is blunt and crude as well. It has always been the case that the high and low styles are extremes reserved for special functions in English prose. They are available to create localized emphasis, usually humor or a temporary shift in the degree of formality, but when they predominate in a work or with a group of authors, they are generally marked as faddish and are considered outside the mainstream of a given age.

In contrast, the natural style represents a mean, an average, comfortable, ordinary kind of language suitable for a broad range of occasions. The basic problem in defining the natural style is the slipperiness of the term: what is natural for one critic or literary period is unnatural for another. Although we are quick to characterize modern writing as plainer and for that reason more natural than what has gone before, we are apt to forget that what is plain to one age may appear hopelessly ornate, confused or self-conscious to its successors.

That natural diction is plain, concise, and exact is seldom questioned today, for modern notions of style associate ornament, whether in diction or syntax, with a past whose modes of expression are no longer appropriate. No one will deny that a plain style is still preferred for what we loosely denominate "expository prose." Moreover, the high or elevated style has little place any longer in our own discourse, even on the most severely formal occasions. Our scholars and wits do not use it, except perhaps in parody, and the closest we come to it may be the inflated language we associate with bureaucracy and occasionally with the writing of students, or the technically dense jargon of specialists in the arts, sciences, and professions, whose use of language tends to challenge the common notion that the purpose of language is to facilitate communication. The low style remains in a variety of dramatic representations of speech: in plays and the novel, film, radio, and television. It has never been a significant part of expository writing, except as the subject of analysis.

At any given time, the term *natural* may be applied to the style of writing currently in vogue, or to the style which is proposed as superior to the current favorite. Even more troublesome is the fact that some critics use *natural* to mean writing that is like informal speech, while for others it is writing that does not draw attention to its own artifice. But there seems to be one distinction between the modern notion of natural style and its precursors that all critics share: until the twentieth century, the mainstream natural style of every age aimed at simplicity in diction and, perhaps to a lesser extent, the avoidance of elaborate and intricate sentences. To this, modern English critics, teachers, and editors have now added the goal of shortening all sentences.

Style and Sentence Length

As part of his definition of the sentence, Aristotle notes that it must be "of such a length as to be easily comprehended at once." In his *Philosophy of Rhetoric*, George Campbell (1776) advises against sentences that are too complex, either ones with many layers of embedding, or with lengthy parenthetical inclusions. He also faults sentences that are too long: his illustrations are from Bolingbroke and Swift, one sixteen lines in length, the other fourteen. The rhetorician Hugh Blair, in his *Lectures on Rhetoric and Belles Lettres* (1783), agrees that "using long periods . . . overloads the reader's ear," but he warns as well against excessive brevity, "by which the sense is split and broken, the connexion of thought weakened, and the memory burdened by presenting to it a long succession of minute objects."

Blair prefers a style that intermixes long and short sentences. He also argues for simplicity in writing, which includes both unity of construction and clarity of thought. The simple style is neither dry— that is, totally lacking in ornamentation—nor is it excessively figured. It contains, furthermore, a naturalness of expression that is opposed not to ornamentation but to the affected use of ornament. Natural writing for Blair is artless—it does not draw attention to itself—because natural writers, the classical authors, for example, are more in tune with nature than the moderns. Blair cites Addison as one modern who shows some of this natural style: "There is not the least affectation in his manner; we see no marks of labour; nothing forced or constrained; but great elegance, joined with great ease and simplicity."

In *English Prose*, John Earle (1890) finds sentence length varying from language to language, with the English sentence both simpler and shorter in nature than its Latin equivalent, though English is more likely to string together coordinated clauses. Earle argues that the earliest English writers mix concentrated, latinate sentences with the more expansive, serially organized English types, "the one being the fruit of their scholastic discipline, the other the gift of boon Nature." He maintains, however, that the "alien structures" of Latin are inappropriate for modern prose. Earle cites a twenty-line sentence of Ruskin's to prove that the short, varied sentences of modern English are preferable.

Like his predecessors, Earle favors a plain, natural style rather than an affected one. He also stresses the individuality of style, and he takes the notion of idiosyncratic style a step further by drawing an analogy with gardening. As a good gardener does not simply repot flowers already in bloom, so whoever "would write with anything worthy to be called style must first grow thoughts that are worth communicating, and then he must deliver them in his own natural language."

Simple and Direct

The nineteenth-century rhetorician Alexander Bain (*English Composition and Rhetoric*, 1887) is in basic agreement with the tradition that prefers a mix of short and long sentences, though he is one of the first commentators to emphasize that "short sentences are simple and direct." Although virtually all of today's critics consider varying sentence length essential to good style, many of them also advise writers to slim down every sentence as much as possible. Modern writers, particularly student writers, are faulted for wordiness, though critics sometimes substitute more colorful pet words for this phenomenon. The editor Claire Kehrwald Cook (1985) speaks of "baggy" sentences. Richard Lanham (1979) gloomily predicts a "lard factor" of 33 to 50 percent in unrevised sentences. Language historian and stylist Joseph Williams (1981) encourages writers to control sentence "sprawl." And in *Simple and Direct,* the writer Jacques Barzun (1975), though he is no Saxonist, aims to reduce *surplusage* in syntax and in diction: "Communication is most complete when it proceeds from the smallest number of words—and indeed of syllables."

Some studies actually turn the notion that short in language is better than long into a law specifying readability factors for sentences. The critic L. A. Sherman (1893) observes a decline in sentence length in literary prose from the Elizabethan period to the late nineteenth century. Though much of this decrease in sentence length can be attributed to changes in punctuation practice that result in simple rather than compound sentences, Rudolf Flesch (1949) seizes on

Sherman's tentative statistics and charts a more drastic decline from an Elizabethan average of 45 words per sentence to a Victorian average of 29, a turn-of-the-century figure of 20, and a more recent tally of between 13 and 17 words per sentence. Flesch also considers word length in computing readability, with an implicit preference for the native word. For a 20-word sentence—a long one by his standards— to qualify today as standard on Flesch's readability scale, it must have an average of 1.4 syllables per word. Flesch excludes any consideration of genre from his calculations, recommending that all writers aim at the sentence and word limits of newspaper stories.

In *Style: Ten Lessons in Clarity and Grace,* Joseph Williams (1981), of the University of Chicago, is more sensitive to the contextual require- ments of writing: newspapers have short sentences, magazine writing has 20–22 word averages, and technical and academic prose runs longer still. Williams does not hold writers to a predetermined length, though he does suggest that writers reconsider sentences more than 2.5 lines long. John Lannon's *Technical Writing* (1985) imposes a twenty- five word average limit on sentences in technical documents. The Bell Laboratories style programs in *Writer's Workbench* (1983), using four different readability formulas, set an acceptable range of 16.7 to 25.3 words per sentence, flagging for possible revision sentences that are too short as well as those that are too long. *WWB* further recommends that the total number of short sentences in a text range between 29.2 percent and 38.0 percent, while the mix of long sentences should be from 11.7 percent to 18.9 percent. According to *WWB*, the present chapter has an average sentence length of 29 words, somewhat longer than that recommended by the program for technical memoranda.

Whose Default?

Whether or not we have the statistics for documentation, it certainly *seems* true that writers today create shorter sentences than their counterparts in times past. It is not clear however that this change is the result of any cognitive shift that has taken place among readers and writers. Shorter sentences may be easier in general for readers to process, and some less-accomplished readers may not be able to decode sentences whose length and structure go beyond certain testable limits. But we cannot claim that shorter sentences are either more or less natural than longer ones. Nor are they demonstrably better, even though we may sometimes prefer them.

In *Writing Well,* Donald Hall (1985) suggests that short sentences are easier for everyone to write, while only practiced writers are likely to succeed at longer ones. This may indeed account for the emphasis in textbooks and writing guides on cutting long sentences, and it may explain the problems novice writers have with passive constructions. But if novices do not grapple with hard forms, they will never master them. While newspaper sentences may be quite short, it is not clear that sentences in other types of writing should adhere to the same standard. True, the notion of readability has directed textbook prose for twenty years or more. And the recent strength of the Plain English Movement has led to the simplification of many legal documents so that the average person may better comprehend them. But this is only part of the story, for despite Flesch's claim to the universality of his formulas, both the degree of readability and the plainness of language depend to a great extent on the content and presumed audience of a text.

The need to pitch college textbooks at a ninth grade reading level, apparently the limit of the average college student, has caused concern among writers and educators, who would prefer to raise reading levels, not simplify materials. And the translation into plain English of the technical language of contracts, leases, guarantees, and other official documents, which is part of a larger move toward consumer protection, represents a limited attempt to make these important aspects of modern life accessible to all the citizenry. No one seriously proposes to reduce every text to the least level of difficulty. Despite the passion to cut fat from sentences, the more sensible writing guides stress comprehensive revision rather than cutting alone, for good editing involves amplification as well as reduction. Even the computer style checkers, whose major concern is with the readability of technical documents, recognize the need to vary sentence length, and both *Writer's Workbench* and IBM's style program, *Critique,* allow users to define their own criteria for sentence length rather than accepting the default.

The movement of natural style in the direction of shorter words and phrases thus proves to some extent illusory. For one thing, we cannot with any confidence assert that modern writing is in fact shorter, more concise, or more natural in every context than writing in any other age. For another, we recognize that a natural style does not come naturally. As Sir Philip Sidney knew four centuries ago, natural style is the art of making the difficult look easy. Claire Cook, in *The MLA's Line by Line: How to Edit Your Own Writing,* illustrates this by connecting today's passions for physical and syntactic fitness: "Trim sentences, like trim bodies, usually require far more effort than flabby ones."

It is what readers perceive as effortless, not the effortlessness of production, that brands a style as natural. Because readers bring to a text varying degrees of ability and experience, what is comfortable prose for one may prove difficult for another. Readability formulas that aim at the least common denominator will not solve this problem, for prose that is too easy can be as unnatural as prose that is too hard. One difficulty in constructing reading texts for use in schools is the fact that the simpler the words and sentences, the less interest the material has for students. A similar problem for writing instruction is the fact that naturalness is also a function of the appropriateness of language to the context of writing, and here no one can safely claim that less is always better than more, or vice versa.

5 Going Native

Good authors too who once knew better words,
Now only use four letter words, writing prose.

—Cole Porter, "Anything Goes"

The push for simpler sentences and shorter words has been aided and abetted through the centuries by a fringe element among language commentators who claimed that native words are better—shorter, purer, and more natural—than words that come from other languages. These "Saxonists" called for the expulsion of all foreign words from English and their replacement with words of native, Anglo-Saxon origin.

In *The King's English* (1906), the brothers Fowler urge us to prefer the concrete word to the abstract, and the Saxon to the Romance. Their recommendation—hardly a new one in the history of English style—is echoed almost verbatim, though without attribution, in George Orwell's frequently reprinted essay, "Politics and the English Language" (1946), and is now repeated by almost everyone in the business of giving advice to writers. Like warnings against the passive, the Saxon rule assumes that ideal prose is invariably simple and direct, and it presents a misleading picture both of the complexities of writing and the mixed nature of the English vocabulary. Carried to its extreme, Saxonism produces a style that is anything but natural.

From the sixteenth century down to the present day, the Saxonists have celebrated both the antique English of *Beowulf*, untainted by Latin or French, and the "pure" speech of the uneducated rural folk. The Saxonists urged the revival of archaic, disused words like *boon* and *doughty*, freely coining new words on native models when the old words could not be adapted to modern circumstances. For *perambulator* or *baby carriage*, both newer words of foreign origin, the Saxonists recommend the domestically manufactured *push wainling* (*wainling* is an old word for 'small wagon'). *Butler*, from the French *bouteilleur*, 'bottler,' bows before the made-up, but native-sounding compound *cellar thane*, while *escalator* gives way in modern Saxonist vocabulary to the Germanic monstrosity, *upgangflow* (in contrast, the German word for this contraption is *die Rolltreppe*).

Traditionally, the Saxonists claim they are restoring the purity of English and celebrating the unspoiled language of the common people. Like the sentence shorteners, whose goal is *natural* syntax, the Saxonists aim for a *natural* vocabulary. But once again the definition of *natural* proves slippery. In the *Rhetoric*, Aristotle recommends using words that are clear, current, and appropriate, "so that we may seem to be speaking not with artifice, but naturally." This sentiment is almost universally affirmed among English writers, though there is some disagreement over whose words are natural and whose are not.

In *The Art of English Poesie*, George Puttenham (1589) defines natural diction as that which is pure and national, specifically the language of the royal Court, the good towns, and the great cities. It is definitely not the speech of rustics, nor is it the language of foreigners, or professors, whose words are characterized as local, mongrelized, and affected. Sir Philip Sidney also faults the deliberate, pretentious, scholarly style, preferring instead the language of the "smally learned Courtiers," whose style naturally hides the art that produces it.

A few critics locate natural vocabulary not among intellectuals, artists, and the court, but exclusively among the common folk. For example, E. K., in his Epistle Dedicatory to Spenser's *Shepherds' Calendar* (1579), applauds the poet's attempt to restore the archaic language of rustics, those "good and natural English words as have been long time out of use." The natural words of the commoner are more officially endorsed in Thomas Sprat's *History of the Royal Society* (1667). In a view of language that reflects a Renaissance preference for the imagined speech of shepherds, and prefigures a similar Romantic taste for the bucolic, or rural, Sprat links philosophical or mathematical discourse not with writers and philosophers but with those who are unspoiled by too much knowledge, a class of people, interestingly enough, who do not typically engage in writing:

> [The Royal Society] have exacted from all their members, a close, naked, natural way of speaking; positive expressions; clear senses; a native easiness; bringing all things as near the Mathematical plainness, as they can: and preferring the language of Artisans, Countrymen, and Merchants, before that, of Wits, or Scholars.

Natural words are not only unaffected, according to Sprat, they are also concise (113). Instead of "extravagant" speech and "swellings of style," the negative features of a high style gone wrong, English scientists are advised, in what may constitute the first official recommendations on the language of scientific and technical writing, "to return back to the primitive purity, and shortness, when men deliver'd

so many *things*, almost in an equal number of *words*." Just as in a less
scientific context, Adam is credited with naming the animals, in the
seventeenth-century view language was tightly bound with the natural
world. An ideal or philosophical language, such as that created by
John Wilkins (1688), himself a member of the Royal Society, seeks to
return human communication to the state of nature from which it has
strayed, if not to Eden itself at least to a time before the incident at
Babel, when each word unambiguously signified one thing or concept,
and economical language was the rule rather than the exception.

Regenerating Saxon English

In the mid-fifteenth century, Reginald Pecock, Bishop of Chichester,
used foreign words whenever they were handy, but created native-
looking English words to render Latin terms for which there was no
ready equivalent. Pecock produced such uncomfortable English compounds as *un-to-be-thought-upon*, 'unimaginable,' and *unagainsayably*,
'undeniably,' as well as the folksy *netherer*, 'inferior,' and *outdraught*,
'extract.' One of the earliest practicing Saxonists was Ralph Lever, who
in 1573 wrote a treatise on logic with a technical vocabulary largely
of native origin, or more precisely, native-like origin, for Lever forms
his terms of *witcraft* (logic) from familiar building blocks, creating
strange words the average reader cannot decipher without a glossary:
backset for predicate, *likemeaning word* for synonym, *foresay* for premise,
and *saying* for sentence, to cite but a few. The Baconian scientist
Nathaniel Fairfax (1674) also replaced words of foreign, or as he
preferred to call them, *outlandish*, origin with homespun neologisms:
forespeech, 'preface,' *brack*, 'atom,' *everbeing*, 'eternal,' *flowsom*, 'liquid,'
sturt, 'a sudden impulse,' and *whereness*, 'position, location.' Fairfax's
prose is dense with such Saxonisms, whose idiosyncrasy makes for
rough going. For instance, instead of simply recommending that his
readers choose native words in preference to foreign imports, he
attempts to illustrate his notion that native English words are closer
to the things they represent than borrowed ones:

> Call in from the fields and waters, shops and work-housen, from
> the inbred stock of more homely women and less filching Thorps-
> men, that well-fraught world of words that answers works, by
> which all Learners are taught to do, and not to make a clatter;
> and perhaps, if we slip this tide, we shall never come again at
> such a nicking one. (B7ʳ–B7ᵛ)

Although he is certainly alone in his assumption, it is clear that Fairfax considers his writing natural in contrast to the ornate style of his contemporaries:

> As for the way of wording it, I know aforehand, 'tis not trim enough for these Gay days of ours; but dressing is none of my business. . . . I had rather speak home than fair, nor do I care how blunt it be, so it be strong. (B5ᵛ)

Unlike Lever, whose neologisms were ignored by lexicographers, many of Fairfax's words made their way into the *OED*, though we have no trouble understanding why only a few of his "natural" terms managed to live on outside the dictionary.

In the nineteenth century the Saxonists, encouraged by a renewed interest in medieval chivalry, took the field again. The philologist William Barnes campaigned for native words by writing poems that incorporated his local Dorset dialect. A cleric, Barnes treated his parishioners to Saxon-tinged sermons, and filled his studies of grammar, or *speech-craft* (1878), and logic, or *rede-craft* (1880), with Saxon terms as well. Like Lever, he substituted nativized technical terms for traditional ones: *thought-wording,* 'proposition,' *speech-thing,* 'subject,' *free-breathing,* 'vowel,' and *three-step thought-putting,* 'syllogism.' Among his many nontechnical neologisms or revivals, Barnes proposed *book-lore,* 'literature,' *folkdom,* 'democracy,' *gin,* 'machine,' and *teachsome,* 'didactic.'

The American language reformer Elias Molee's thoughts on nativization were even more comprehensive. An enemy of grammatical gender, arabic numerals, and uppercase letters, as well as an advocate of phonetic spelling, masculine and feminine nominal suffixes, and the use of abbreviations to replace the commonest English words, Molee argued in several works published between 1888 and 1919 for the creation of an international "union" language to serve not just the United States but all the "Germanic" nations. Its vocabulary consisted of an anglicized, but thinly veiled German: *dir,* 'animal,' *deerlore,* 'zoology,' *spraki,* 'language,' and *wishfeineri,* 'luxury.' Finally, Charles Louis Dessoulavy (1917), a translator by trade, published a list of hundreds of native synonyms for borrowed words, including *beword,* 'report,' *bow-wow* 'onomatopoetic,' *cranky,* 'abnormal,' *holed,* 'porous,' *reckoning,* 'arithmetic,' *sawbones,* 'surgeon,' and *self-working,* 'automatic.'

Such outbursts of radical Saxonism occurred during periods of intense antiquarian interest, both in the Renaissance and again in the nineteenth century. They also coincided with reactions against an ornate, latinate style in diction. The Renaissance ultimately rejects the coining of the inkhorn terms that make the language of some of its writers both difficult and distinct. The Romantics, dismissing the literary pretensions of the immediate past, show a predilection for the doughty ways of Arthurian England, and pretend to imitate the unspoiled language of the common folk.

Most of the Saxonists' suggestions appear bizarre and distinctly unnatural to the native English speaker. Though the various nativist movements never achieved their aim of ousting the Romance and Hellenic elements that permeate English, they did have some effect on the English vocabulary, and on our general thinking about language. The Saxonists are directly responsible for the revival of the word *handbook*, the exact equivalent of the latinate *manual*. The rhetorician John Earle (1890) credits the Saxon movement with popularizing such new or revived words as *ashamedness, featureliness, knowingness, livingness, open-mindedness, seamy, settledness, shaky, unknowable, unyieldingness,* and *uphillward,* several of which are still common today, and he himself tries to introduce *formlore* in his discussion of English verbs.

More important, though, Saxonism ultimately confirms a number of our modern stylistic assumptions. Many eighteenth-century writers on language viewed Chinese as an ideal language—indeed as we noted above, one commentator even argued that it was the first language—because its supposed monosyllabic vocabulary was thought to reflect most directly the world of nature. While Anglo-Saxon was not so terse as Chinese, it was certainly more available to English writers. Disregarding the many compounds and near-compounds in our language (*bookcase, firehouse, personal computer*) or viewing them as composites of unaltered monosyllables, commentators found Saxon words shorter and therefore more natural than their Romance counterparts. Short words are characterized as purer, stronger, or more active than polysyllables. Short words are also thought to be concrete rather than abstract, and it is sometimes even maintained that although they are supposed to be *natural*, Saxon words come less easily to us than latinate terminology, which is consequently characterized as lazy. Ultimately, native words are portrayed as more democratic because their etymology is transparent to the unlearned, while the derivations of borrowed words, and therefore their meanings, are clear only to those with a knowledge of the classical tongues.

Of course these assumptions are not entirely correct. While it is true that the most frequent words in English are also native ones (see the next chapter), many of these are abstractions (*love, hate, thought, god*), and many borrowed words are concrete (*people, bagel, ventricle, squash, telegram*). A computerized analysis of the vocabulary in this chapter (excluding the Saxon examples) indicates that some 45 percent of the

abstractions are of native, or Saxon origin. Nor is the native word always more concise: *foreword* is a bit longer than *preface,* if we measure size either by number of letters or length of vowels, and *afterword* similarly outruns *appendix.* We must also acknowledge that abstractions are as indispensable to human communication as concrete terms, and that the etymologies of most words, native or borrowed, are obscure to the average language user, who will not recognize Old English *aeng,* 'pain,' in *hangnail,* and who will tend to "correct" the *wend* in *wend one's way* to *wind,* or the *wright* in *playwright* to *write* (chapter 13).

The nativist movement has affected other languages besides English. In the nineteenth century, and again during Nazi rule, Germans sought to purify their language from romance influence. During World War II, the Japanese outlawed the use of English in the territories they controlled, and the French, always on the *qui vive,* continue to fight English encroachments. Graham Pascoe (1988) reports in *English Today* that a recent deanglification competition held in French schools produced such nativizations as *automaison* for *camper, saucipain,* literally a clipped and blended 'sausage bread,' for *hotdog,* and *flanophone* for *Walkman,* a trademark name used by Sony, a Japanese corporation, which has become one of the newest international generic terms. Although he is certain these new coinages will have as little effect as the efforts of the Saxonists, Pascoe reflects his own Saxon bias, noting that the French neologisms are roughly one third longer than their English counterparts.

Like the Saxonists, spelling reformers, who were most active in England and America during the later nineteenth and early twentieth centuries, also argued that their reforms would result in shorter words. And like the Saxonist movement, simplified spelling has affected our usage to a small degree: *catalog* is common, *analog* is preferred to *analogue,* and such forms as *thru, tho, nite,* and most recently *lite,* regularly appear in advertising and in some informal writing. While most of these forms are not considered standard, the Saxonists' emphasis on monosyllables, combined with the abridgement tactics of the spelling reformers, no doubt influenced the modern English preference for short words and possibly short sentences as well.

6 Basic Words

I find vocabulary a great drawback.

—Elizabeth Taylor, *A Game of Hide and Seek* (1951)

The Saxonists took an extreme position on our vocabulary, but they were right about one thing. Of the 100 commonest words in English, only a handful are of non-native origin.

Two new frequency lists of Modern British and American English were recently published, allowing us to judge quite accurately the popularity of today's words, to see just what is on everybody's lips, or more precisely, to count the words everyone is writing. One of the lists is based on the Brown Corpus, a collection of one million words of published American prose drawn from a wide variety of sources by researchers at Brown University (Francis and Kučera 1982). The other comes from the Lancaster-Oslo/Bergen, or LOB, Corpus, a similar collection of one million words of British prose made at Lancaster and Oslo Universities, and at the Norwegian Computing Centre for the Humanities in Bergen (Hofland and Johansson 1982). These two lists (see chapter end) differ somewhat partly because of differences between British and American English, and partly because Brown lumps together all variants of the base form of a word. For example, in making its frequency tally, Brown considers *me, my,* and *mine* the same as *I,* while the LOB Corpus treats each form separately. Thus *I* and its variants rank 13th in the Brown frequency list, but the LOB list places *I* in 17th place, with *my* in 59th and *me* in 66th, while *mine* does not appear at all in the LOB top 100.

In either case, the top 100 are clearly words we cannot do without, lean words of one syllable, by and large, and mostly words of native origin as well. There are a few two-syllable words among the 100, and no trisyllables. Only a few borrowed words—about 5 percent—appear in the lists: *they* comes from Old Norse but enters English very early, and even the stoutest Saxonist would claim it as a native word. Also from other languages are *Mr.* and *just,* from Latin, and *very* and *people,* ultimately from Latin as well, though we actually borrowed them from French. These 100 words, the first century of the English

37

language, if you will, may be short and common, but they tell us a lot about the way we use (and abuse) our language.

Frequency and Sex

Comparing the lists at the end of this chapter can reveal some differences between British and American English. In the LOB Corpus, the noun *Mr.* occurs 1,535 times in a corpus of 1,000,000 words, while in the Brown Corpus it is used only 857 times. This may indicate that British usage is almost twice as formal as American when it comes to naming adult males in print. Furthermore, the fact that the titles *Miss, Mrs.,* and *Ms.* do not appear in either of our lists of top 100 words confirms what many feminists—both men and women—have alleged all along, that males are more likely to be the subjects of reference in written discourse than females.

Consistent with our sexist grammatical tradition of placing women and children last, the word *man* is the most common noun in written American English. Even so, it just barely makes it into the first half of the Brown frequency list, where it ranks 44th, and it is an even less popular 88th in the LOB list. Although some commentators still argue that *man* includes *woman* in most of its incarnations, many language authorities and a good number of researchers in psychology maintain that the word has primarily masculine connotations. Further documenting this imbalance in gender reference, the word *woman* is clearly nowhere near as popular as *man*. Brown ranks *woman* 199. While *boy* is 227 in Brown, its feminine counterpart, *girl*, is a less common 254. *John* is the most popular masculine name, ranked at 244 in the Brown Corpus, but *Mary*, the most common female name, is ranked a distant 1167 in frequency. Even *God* is less common than *man*, weighing in at a relatively infrequent 292, occurring less often than such nouns as *woman, John, doctor, student, president,* and *life.*

Our sex-stereotyping culture demotes *woman* to the bottom of the list. The gender-neutral word *child* is only 138, beating out *woman* in popularity. Even *Mrs.,* at number 165, is more common than *woman.* Ranked 445, *Miss* is clearly out of favor as a title. But both *man* and *woman* are more frequent than their gender-neutral alternatives, *person* (341), *human* (396), and *individual* (641). *Lady,* frequently considered euphemistic and frowned on by usage critics and by feminists, is not a popular word in print. Brown ranks it 924. Although women make up slightly more than half the population in the United States, *son* is mentioned in texts twice as frequently as *daughter,* corroborating the suspicion that many speakers and writers prefer male children.

The evidence of these gender-specific words suggests that women are less visible in public discourse than are men, and while this fact reflects a sexist bias in our culture, it also represents a linguistic bias that makes the status quo more difficult to change. Even the two exceptions to this pattern of masculine domination tend to reinforce the pattern of discrimination by allowing women to become more visible than men only in words describing their familial function. The two feminine words that occur more frequently than their masculine counterparts are *mother,* which is 368 in the Brown Corpus, while *father* is 434; and *wife,* which is 391, while *husband* is out of the running at 653.

The personal pronouns also offer some information about sex differentiation in our vocabulary. In both the Brown and LOB lists, the masculine forms of the third person pronoun are more common than the feminine forms. The masculine third person pronoun *he* is even more common than the gender-neutral first person *I,* an indication that on both sides of the Atlantic we refer to males more than we refer to ourselves, and to females less. Complicating this conclusion further is the fact that we do not know the extent to which the author's sex skews the numbers. In addition, the two lists are compiled from texts published in the early 1960s. It is clear that the women's movement has had a significant effect on the formal vocabulary of American English in the past twenty-five years, and the relative frequencies of words like *he, she, man* and *Ms.* might be quite different if measured in texts published today.

Speaking of *she,* we can safely say that the most popular feminine pronoun is a mystery word of sorts. In Old English, the feminine personal pronouns all began with *h: hio, heo, hie.* By the twelfth and thirteenth centuries, however, the feminine pronouns were almost wholly indistinguishable in pronunciation from the masculine ones, and it is during this time that *she* begins to appear in written texts. But the origin of our feminine pronoun is still a subject of contention for etymologists.

She may derive from the feminine form of the Old English demonstrative pronoun *seo,* meaning 'that.' The masculine demonstrative, *se,* developed into the definite article, *the.* It is not entirely clear why English would preserve a feminine word beginning in *s,* while transmuting its corresponding masculine into *th,* though separate use of *seo* as a feminine pronoun might account for the different development patterns of the two words. In Old Norse, demonstratives could function as personal pronouns as well, and there is some evidence that *she* arises in areas of England settled by Norse invaders in the Middle

Ages. Furthermore, a feminine pronoun in *s* has some precedent in the Germanic languages. Both Gothic and Old High German had feminine personal pronouns analogous to *she* (compare the Modern German feminine pronoun *sie*).

Perhaps the most bizarre account of the origin of *she* derives the feminine pronoun from the masculine, as Eve is supposed to derive from Adam. According to this thoroughly erroneous explanation put forth by a nineteenth-century writer known only as S. S. S., *she* consists of *he* plus the prefix *s*, a letter whose sound and shape remind the author explicitly of the serpent in the Garden of Eden. The same author saw *her* as the masculine *he* with the addition of the letter *r* symbolizing Adam's rib.

While English pronouns changed in the Middle English period to preserve the threatened masculine/feminine distinctions in the third person singular, the counter tradition in which gender distinctions are blended also lived on. For example, in British and American informal folk speech the masculine, feminine, and neuter pronouns can refer indiscriminately to masculines, feminines, and neuters. Furthermore, there arose in Middle English a precursor to the sexless pronouns that have been proposed over and over for Modern English (see below, chapter 23), a gender-neutral form of the pronoun, represented as *a* or *un*, which still occurs today in British folk speech.

The Most Common Word

Most of us know that *e* is the most common letter of the English alphabet. *The*, the definite article, is the most common *word* in English, occurring almost three times as often as the indefinites *a* and *an*, and forming about 7 percent of our written speech. And *the* has nothing to do with sex. Incidentally, the least common words in Brown are *shopping* (noun) and *chip* (verb); in LOB the last word is *psalm*.

Despite the frequency of *the*, it is a newcomer compared to some of our words. Old English did not even have a definite article. Instead, it used a set of demonstrative pronouns with the separate forms *se*, *seo*, and *that* for masculine, feminine, and neuter. These demonstratives also functioned as articles and eventually, under the influence of the other forms of the paradigm, which began with *th-*, they coalesced into the modern word *the*. The neuter gives us Modern English *that*, now a pronoun, adjective, adverb, and conjunction. And as we have seen, the feminine *seo* is the likely source of *she*. According to the *OED*, *the* was firmly established by the year 950 in the north of

England, and had become the most popular form of the definite article by 1150 in the small but growing English-speaking world. The *s*-forms of the definite article had completely disappeared by the fourteenth century.

Like many little function words, the definite article has a great variety of uses. Mostly *the* alludes to knowledge shared between speaker and hearer, or writer and reader. *The* is used to specify something already known or mentioned, or somehow defined by the context in which it is found. *The* may be a directional word. It can refer back to something already mentioned: *She found fifty cents. The money was lying on the sidewalk.* It can also refer forward: *She found it on the afternoon of February 3;* here the specific date justifies the use of the definite article. In some cases, the article simply points to the attached noun as generally known: *The sun is very hot.*

The use of *the* may also be a pure convention. For example, rivers and mountain ranges commonly take the definite article: *The Thames, The Hudson, The Alps, The Smokies.* So do certain other place names: *The Bronx* (but not *Manhattan, Queens, Brooklyn,* or *Staten Island*). Universities vary on the use of the article: *The Sorbonne, The University of Illinois, The Johns Hopkins University,* but not *Harvard* or *Brandeis.* College sweatshirts tend to drop the article, however, and even the preposition: *University Illinois, University Hawaii.* It was once customary to refer to professional or recreational activities using the definite article: *the chess, the dressmaking.* We have remnants of this pattern in *the law, the ministry, the hunt,* and *the arts. The* is also found in titles: *The Aeneid, The Mona Lisa, The New York Times.* And it is common in expressions of time: *the hour, the roaring '20s.*

The is used as an emphatic device (and as such is stressed in pronunciation so that it rhymes with *thee*): *Urbana is the place to be this season.* In other cases, *the* may be a stylistic or geographical option. A work may be translated *from German,* or *from the German.* Americans speak of *Lebanon,* while the British use *The Lebanon.* Similarly Americans say *The doctor is in,* and *Harry was in the hospital,* while British English shows *Doctor will see you now,* and *She spent two days in hospital.* We may suffer from *the Plague, the shakes,* and *the blues,* but we also get *(the) toothache* and *(the) flu.* Formerly, *the* could introduce abstracts: *the posterity.* In weights and measures *the* can alternate with the indefinite: *Fifty cents a/the pound.* It is also used as an alternative for the possessive pronoun in reference to the body parts of a person already mentioned: *They led Charlie around by the/his nose.*

Colloquially, *the* occurs in such expressions as *How's the boy?* (referring to the person addressed, rather than a third party), as well as in reference to relatives: *How's the wife/the mater and pater?* And it occurs in imitation of European usage in the names of prominent women actresses or singers, as in *The Duse*. *The* is used in proverbial reference or generically: *The good die young; The police officer is your friend.* It also occurs in comparatives and superlatives: *The better part of valor is discretion; The best is yet to be.*

One interesting use of *the* is found in expressions like *The worse for wear; She is the better for it;* and *The more fools they.* Here we have not a definite article but a remnant of an Old English instrumental *þy* functioning adverbially. A similar formula pairs the instrumentals, *the . . . the,* the first being relative, the second, demonstrative, as in *the sooner the better; the more the merrier; the bigger they are, the harder they fall.*

The may seem like a versatile word, but in fact it is less various than another function word, *of* (number 3 in the Brown list). *The* takes up eleven columns in the *OED*, while the little word *of* occupies some nineteen columns, not counting its variants *o'* and *off*, which are treated separately. In contrast, two other words in the Brown top 5 pose less complex tasks to lexicographers. The conjunction *and* occupies four columns of print in the *OED*, and the dictionary deals with the indefinite article *a* in only three. One reason for the complexity of *of* is the fact that it has been influenced in the course of its history by both the Old English and Latin genitive (or possessive) case, as well as Latin and French *de*. Also, *of* serves as a particle attached to a great number of English verbs (for example, *cure of, rid of, think of*). In the process of its development, *of* has completely lost its original sense, 'away, away from,' now retained only in the spinoff word, *off*.

Basic English

While the words in the top 100 are necessary words, they are clearly not sufficient, for if we relied on them and them alone we would be unable to express most of the things we need to express in formal and informal speech and writing. How many words do we really need? The *OED* and its recently completed supplements contain about 500,000 separate word entries. *Webster's Second* boasts more than 600,000 entries, and *Webster's Third* lists over 450,000 (many archaic words were omitted in the new edition to allow room for more recent terms). The newest unabridged, the second edition of the *Random House Dictionary* (1987), treats 315,000 words. The more selective desk dictionaries record about 170,000 words in current use. And lexicographers estimate that several thousand new words are added to the language every year. There are some writers who maintain that we could make do with much less with just a little effort. After all, Shakespeare got by with a writing vocabulary of about 17,000 words (presumably his reading vocabulary was somewhat greater), and it is hard for us to imagine him ever being at a loss for words.

In the 1930s, the philosopher and literary critic C. K. Ogden devised a means of communication that he called Basic English, consisting of some 850 words and a set of simple grammatical rules for combining them to express anything a language needs to express. Basic English was designed as an international language like Esperanto, but unlike Esperanto, it was meant as an introduction to and not a replacement for, English. The supporters of Basic English claim that as a language it can stand alone, dealing efficiently with the matters of business, industry, science, medicine, and with the addition of specialized technical vocabulary, fulfilling the specialized needs of the arts, sciences, and trades. Through the process of combining and recombining the 850 words of Basic, the *General Basic English Dictionary* renders the senses of 20,000 other English words (Richards 1943).

The 850 words of Basic are not ranked, but they are divided into categories. One hundred words dealing with "operations" include the pronouns and prepositions, some adverbs expressing time and direction, conjunctions, articles, and the verbs *come, get, give, go, keep, let, make, put, seem, take, be, do, have, say, see, send, may,* and *will.* One verb from the Brown 100 does not appear in Basic: *know,* though it could be expressed by a combination of three Basic English words, *have knowledge of.* There are 600 "things" (we would call them nouns) in Basic English, 400 general and 200 "picturable" things, including some nouns on the Brown list at the end of this chapter, but not *Mister, people, state,* or *world.* Basic English also contains a category of "verse" or poetic words, mostly nouns, designed to be suitable for literary expression. These words include such relics of romantic British and American poetry as *angel, dawn, dream, fountain, joy, lamb, lark, meadow, raven, rapture, robe, sorrow, spear, veil,* and *weeping.* Understandably, not much poetry has been written using Basic English.

Basic English did not catch on as an auxiliary language like Esperanto. Nor has its use to introduce English to non-anglophones been accepted with universal enthusiasm, although it retains enough supporters among teachers of English as a second language to warrant its own computer program, called "Basic English" for the IBM PC and compatibles (1988), which will flag words in a text that are not among the sanctioned 850. Lancelot Hogben (1963) argued that Basic English was too limited in its vocabulary, forcing the small number of Basic words to carry too many different and confusing meanings. He proposed instead what he called "Essential World English," expanded to some 1,300 words, or semantic units. However, Hogben's suggestions did not draw much response. Since the average child masters several thousand words by the age of six, 850 words, or 1,300 "semantic units," even when they are combined indefinitely like the squares of a Rubik's Cube, just don't fill the bill when it comes to expression. On the other hand, we don't need to have all of the 170,000 words of the *Random House College Dictionary* at our fingertips, either.

The rank list of the Brown Corpus contains just under 6,000 words which occurred eight or more times in the materials sampled, and the LOB rank list has about 7,500 words occurring at least twice. These studies of the natural frequency of our written words suggest that we might get by with a vocabulary of about 10,000 words, including technical or specialized terms not necessarily shared by many other users of English. But even that number is insufficient. According to reading specialists William Nagy and Richard Anderson (1984) of the Center for the Study of Reading at the University of Illinois at Urbana-Champaign, many important words have a frequency of less than one in one hundred million, for example *amnesty, elevate, furor, jellybean, raccoon,* and *stenographer.* Furthermore, half the words in printed school English occur with a frequency of only one in a billion. Such ultra-low-frequency words include *billfold, cyanide, emanate, extinguish, inflate, nettle, saturate,* and *ventilate.* Clearly our word hoards must contain the rarest as well as the most common words for us to communicate effectively.

Words for Success

Experts differ on their estimates of actual vocabulary size—sometimes by as much as a factor of 12. I myself have seen guesses placing the average vocabulary as high as 100,000, and even an incredible 250,000. Much of this variation results from different definitions of what constitutes a word, but one reliable estimate made by William Nagy and Patricia Herman (1987) puts the average twelfth-grade vocabulary at about 40,000 words.

Despite this healthy figure, many Americans feel a yearning to increase the size of their vocabulary. We are constantly reminded in and out of school of the need to acquire new and bigger words. When I was in school, and later on, when I taught in high schools, students got weekly lists of ten or twenty words to learn by looking them up in a dictionary and using them in sentences. These words were always stripped of context, just lists of free-floating words arranged alphabetically and according to level of difficulty by some state educational authority, and the resulting sentences frequently demonstrated the dangers of such an educational approach.

This kind of list learning, based on an incomplete understanding of meaning, all but guarantees that words will be misused. For example, *adulterate* means 'cheapen,' according to a pocket-sized lexicon popular among my former high school students. This is hardly an adequate definition, and I still recall one well-intentioned sentence that missed the mark but told me something about adolescent attitudes toward school: The teacher adulterated the student in front of the class.

The learning of words out of context is an inefficient way to increase vocabulary. Rote memorization of word lists may provide a short-term gain, but such words, deprived of context, are also quickly forgotten. I can cite a personal example of an uncontrolled but instructive case of vocabulary development. When I was in high school, I prepared for the College Board achievement test in French by reading several books of French short stories in the month before the test. My French was good, but there were many unfamiliar words in the text, so many, in fact, that I frequently had little idea of what was happening in the stories. But I resolutely plowed through, soaking up what I could, looking nothing up as I went along. A friend of mine, whose French was equally good—we had been in the same honors French classes for three years and received identical grades—studied for the exam not by reading but by poring over word lists and testing herself with flashcards. I received a nearly perfect score, while my friend got over 100 points less on the 800 scale of the test. Two weeks later she had forgotten most of the words she memorized. I seldom read French now, but when I do, I find much of the vocabulary still with me.

We *learn* words, really making them our own, from hearing or reading them in context, not from looking them up and memorizing them. Nagy and Herman find that average readers encounter about 2,000,000 running words of text annually in their school reading, adding about 3,000 words per year to their vocabulary from reading alone, and not from the study of lists. College students may hear and read a million words a week in their studies, and their vocabularies will increase accordingly. Nonetheless, commercial and academic vocabulary improvement courses abound.

According to Rudolf Flesch (1974), the commercial word-building industry got its impetus from studies showing that successful executives had large vocabularies. The reason, to be sure, is that successful people need to have a lot of experience, and that experience does indeed broaden vocabulary. But the simple-minded response to this finding is that large word hoards make for quick personal success, and *how to* books and courses on word power proliferate almost as fast as fad diets and fitness programs. Enterprising word peddlers now sell a calendar with a new word to learn for every day of the year, and a cassette tape that you can listen to in your car while you're stuck in traffic, for those budding executives who don't even have time to look at the calendar.

According to Flesch, the push toward bigger vocabularies coincides with a push to use overly fancy words. Flesch is only one stylist to fight long and hard against verbosity in writing. From the good old days of Strunk and White's *Elements of Style* (still in print and very much in use) to the National Council of Teachers of English *Committee on Public Doublespeak*, with its annual awards condemning the use of words to mask reality, and the Plain English movement mentioned earlier, language critics have urged simplicity and directness in writing and speech. According to this school of thought, we should know more than we say. But like many aspects of language use, we are continually striking an equilibrium between pushes toward simplification and pushes toward complexity. That happy medium, the natural style in our words and in our sentences, while not always easy to maintain, is what we head toward, intentionally or not.

The 100 Commonest English Words

Brown Corpus

1 the	26 from	51 up	76 also
2 be	27 do	52 other	77 find
3 of	28 but	53 that	78 first
4 and	29 or	54 year	79 way
5 a	30 an	55 out	80 must
6 in	31 which	56 new	81 use
7 he	32 would	57 some	82 more
8 to	33 say	58 take	83 like
9 have	34 all	59 these	84 even
10 to	35 one	60 come	85 many
11 it	36 will	61 see	86 more
12 for	37 who	62 get	87 think
13 I	38 that	63 know	88 such
14 they	39 when	64 state	89 where
15 with	40 make	65 two	90 so
16 not	41 there	66 only	91 through
17 that	42 if	67 then	92 should
18 on	43 can	68 any	93 people
19 she	44 man	69 now	94 each
20 as	45 what	70 may	95 those
21 at	46 time	71 than	96 Mister
22 by	47 go	72 give	97 over
23 this	48 no	73 about	98 world
24 we	49 into	74 as	99 seem
25 you	50 could	75 day	100 just

Source: Francis and Kučera 1982, 465–66.

The 100 Commonest English Words

LOB Corpus

1	the	26	have	51	more	76	Mr.
2	of	27	are	52	said	77	made
3	and	28	which	53	out	78	first
4	to	29	her	54	about	79	should
5	a	30	she	55	what	80	over
6	in	31	or	56	up	81	very
7	that	32	you	57	some	82	our
8	is	33	they	58	only	83	like
9	was	34	an	59	my	84	new
10	it	35	were	60	them	85	must
11	for	36	there	61	can	86	such
12	he	37	been	62	into	87	after
13	as	38	one	63	time	88	man
14	with	39	all	64	than	89	much
15	be	40	we	65	could	90	years
16	on	41	their	66	me	91	before
17	I	42	has	67	two	92	most
18	his	43	would	68	then	93	where
19	at	44	when	69	other	94	many
20	by	45	if	70	its	95	well
21	had	46	so	71	these	96	even
22	this	47	no	72	now	97	also
23	not	48	will	73	do	98	being
24	but	49	him	74	may	99	those
25	from	50	who	75	any	100	people

Source: Hofland and Johansson 1982, 44.
Copyright © 1982 by Longman Group Limited.
Used with permission.

7 The Myths of Teaching English

> You taught me language, and my only benefit is
> that I learn'd how to curse.
>
> —William Shakespeare, *The Tempest*

The study of the English language is an essential and unquestioned part of every level of our educational system. We actually take it for granted that without formal instruction, the language we so carefully guard and cultivate would languish or worse yet, that it would deteriorate into unrecognizable grunts and scrawls. While most of the students we teach English to already know how to speak it quite well before they are of school age, we assume that their English is either not very good to begin with, or if in some few cases it is good, then we try to make it better. But we are wrong to view the situation of language so bleakly.

Despite its present position in the curriculum, the centrality of English is a recent phenomenon in the history of education. Although English grammar and spelling were frequently taught in the eighteenth century, English language and literature did not become a universal subject until well into the nineteenth century in the United States (and even later in England), and it is clear from the complaints lodged against our schools, and from the uninterrupted string of diatribes against the misuse of English that have appeared over the past two centuries, that the spread of English education has reinforced rather than stemmed our fear of linguistic barbarism.

One reason why language instruction is felt to be central, yet perceived to be inefficient, is an educational philosophy that characterizes the teacher as an expert imparting knowledge to the student-novice, combined with an educational practice that effectively limits how much teachers may learn about the language they must teach. This may not be the most appropriate model for English language instruction, and it puts teachers in an unfair position. In learning to speak their language before coming to school, students have already become experts, mastering a much more complex form of verbal behavior than that required by any reading or writing task we are likely to set before them. Moreover, though students are skilled in oral communication (their writing is something else again), English teachers do not generally qualify as experts in the English language for, although the curriculum emphasizes the importance of their literary training, it does not prepare teachers in language as a subject.

The focus of English language instruction, particularly at the upper levels, is on writing, but teachers are not encouraged to become writers themselves (few of them have the time to indulge the urge to write), nor are they provided with adequate training in writing instruction. As a result of this curricular inadequacy, there is a great deal of myth and misinformation associated with the teaching of the English language, and often no more than a smidgin of what might count as good linguistic or pedagogical theory. Specifically, we find confusion about the notion of Standard English, ambivalence over the linguistic expertise of English teachers, and a failure to understand the writing process and the cyclic nature of writing competence.

Standard English

While much of our grammatical terminology dates back to the earliest grammars of the classical languages, the now prevasive phrase *Standard English,* referring to the prestige literary dialect of spoken or written English, is fairly new. The word *standard* as a measurement of correctness or perfection first appears in the fifteenth century, but it is not connected with language until the eighteenth, when it is applied to Greek and French, languages whose reputed superiority was frequently held up for users of English to envy.

Standard is not joined to English until the late nineteenth century. Such expressions as *the King's English, the King's language,* and *received English* do occur before that, giving evidence for our early and ongoing concern with correct, good, or approved English. However, the association of the term *standard* with precisely defined and regulated weights and measures, as well as with monetary systems, creates the illusion that Standard English has scientific validity, that it can be defined and copied, like the standard meter or kilogram, and that it has the same currency for everyone.

We commonly suppose, for one thing, that a standard of usage exists which we all agree upon, a standard which may be described with some precision, reduced to a few simple rules, and imposed on the entire nation, if not the whole English-speaking world. As a concession to the varieties of English used in such diverse areas as

Australia, Britain, Canada, India, Ireland, New Zealand, Nigeria, and the United States, we commonly—though sometimes reluctantly—acknowledge the existence of regional or national spoken and written standards. But whether we are dealing with standards or Standard, we are invariably thwarted by the problem of definition.

Try as we do, we have yet to achieve anything even closely approximating an exhaustive description of the varieties of English, or to arrive at an understanding of the complex nature of language standards and the degree of variability permissible within what we broadly term acceptable English. Put simply, our grammars and dictionaries are all open-ended. No matter how many correct ways of saying things we manage to collect, there are many we have missed, and more still that have yet to be invented.

Nor can we agree on how such acceptable language use is to be enforced. What we mean by Standard English, beyond our identification of it with a vague prestige norm, is never entirely clear. Instead, it is generally easier for us to say what is *not* standard, for example, errors in subject agreement (*they was*) or in the concord of pronouns with their referents (*everyone . . . their*). We further assume that students of English, native speakers as well as second language learners, will make such errors given half a chance, and that these errors may be avoided by offering models of good usage to be imitated, or sentences containing errors for correction.

Such assumptions will not profit us: the listing of standard deviations, even in combination with a catalogue of the supposed rules of correctness, is not an efficient way of getting at good English, for as the linguist and usage critic Bergen Evans maintains in *Comfortable Words* (1961), "There is no simple rule about English that does not have so many exceptions that it would be folly to rely on it." It is impossible to deny the existence of acceptable variation in English even in so apparently standard an area as subject-verb agreement. In British English, collective nouns like *government* and *corporation* are treated as plurals, while Americans employ them in the singular. Even within America there is disagreement over the status of *data*, scrupulously construed as a plural by number-crunching researchers unwilling to seem ignorant of Latin, but more freely treated as a singular among the general population.

Variation in pronoun concord is permitted as well. To illustrate, Evans contrasts our unquestioning faith in the agreement of pronoun and referent with the unquestionably binding, if grammatically discordant, language of the federal Constitution: "Each House shall keep a journal of its proceedings, and from time to time publish the same, excepting such parts as may in *their* judgment require secrecy" (Article 1, sec. 5, subsec. 3; emphasis added). *Their* is no slip of the federalist quill. Rather it is clear evidence—one of countless examples cited by the chroniclers of English—of the perfectly standard process of meaning controlling form.

As we shall see in chapter 10, even so stigmatized a word as *ain't* has its defenders, and its place in informal, standard speech. In fact, complaints against variant pronunciation, morphology, syntax, or diction frequently signal that the offending form is either threatening to become standard, or has already become so.

The Standard English Teacher

While Standard English may not exist as a body of discrete linguistic facts, it certainly does exist as a widespread and powerful concept affecting our attitudes toward language variation and change. *Standard* may fail as a technical term because, despite its pretense at scientific exactness, it is as subjective and shifting as our notions of good or bad English have always been. Nonetheless, it has become a force for shaping the destiny of our language because of its exclusionary power. Despite our inability to pin it down, we all know what Standard English is, and what it isn't, though our lists of errors may not always agree.

We further assume that language errors are the result of ignorance, or even worse, of memory lapse, for we have a notion that the rules of English are something most of us learned in school but have since forgotten. Such an idea is unthinkable. As Bergen Evans points out, "If one forgets the significant facts about one's native language, one becomes unintelligible and will probably be locked up."

True, what we know about our language and what we learn about it in school are often at variance, and it may do us no harm to forget our formal schooling in English now and then. Before the English teachers who read this slam shut their books let me assure you that I am not slurring the knowledge of English teachers—I am one myself. Nor am I undervaluing our ability to do a most difficult and under-rewarding job. Rather, I wish to debunk a pernicious *myth* that stereotypes and handicaps those of us who profess English to students who may or may not want to learn about their language.

Our English teachers are well trained in literature and pedagogy, not in the history and structure of our tongue, standard or otherwise. They are not generally required to take more than one or two language courses out of the forty that make up a B.A. Yet the driving need of Americans to be correct in matters of language has forced English teachers to function as experts in the English language as well.

English teachers are generally set up as arbiters of linguistic correctness and taste by the usage-anxious public. We are expected to authorize pronunciation, a throwback to the days when prospective teachers were excluded from the profession if their speech revealed the barest trace of ethnic origin, and those who made it to the classroom were forced to speak in an accent natural to no one but the teaching cadre itself.

English teachers are asked time and again where to put commas, and what plurals are correct. We are expected by society to become language guardians, protecting English from external invasion or internal rot. Reluctance to judge such matters is seen by the public not as a concession to linguistic sophistication but as an admission of ignorance, and that in turn may have a disastrous effect on our employment status.

Ironically, teachers who accept the role of English monitors develop a reputation for unwarranted interference with other people's language and are shunned. Announcing to someone I have just met that I teach English draws one of two responses: fear or a collusive sort of camaraderie. I'm either told, "English was my worst subject, I'd better watch my grammar," which severely limits further conversation, or I'm asked to agree with my interlocutor that English is certainly in a bad way, a position which contradicts all that scholars know about language use and change.

Occasionally I am required to proscribe a phrase whose legitimacy has stood the test of time, but which my idiosyncratic new acquaintance finds objectionable. Once I was prodded to condemn what seemed to me to be the perfectly innocuous phrasing of "Keep off the grass." Another importunate individual asked me to confirm his suspicion that *surpluses* was an illegitimate form of a word that actually had no plural. In neither case did I oblige, and in neither case, I am almost sure, was I believed, for although people claim they wish to adhere to the standards of language, they are strangely unwilling to accept the facts of English that they seek to master.

The Writing Cycle

Society treats its English teachers paradoxically, blaming them for doing exactly what it expects them to do, as far as language goes, and blaming them as well for failure. We have heard in the past decades about the reading crisis that forces college textbooks to be written at junior high school reading levels. It is common now to read as well that the schools do not teach our children how to write. This writing crisis forms part of our general worrying over literacy, but its solution, make people write more, is both too simple and too hard.

We may value good writing, but we frequently take a dim view of writing instruction. Mention the debased state of the writing done by otherwise well-educated Americans, and heads will shake their sad assent. But try to get something done, for example more writing in more subjects in high school and college, and there is no general stampede of volunteers from either side of the desk, for the teaching of writing has become firmly associated with the drudgery both of composing and of grading papers on trivial subjects, and even more with painfully negative evaluation. As Jo McMurtry writes in her study, *English Language, English Literature* (1985), "Neither students nor teachers . . . are drawn to a pursuit in which the chief activity seems to be finding out how wrong one is, or . . . how much more effective one might become if only one did this or that."

While writing instruction often seems a no-win situation to teachers and students alike, instead of banding together to defend themselves, teachers frequently blame one another for what they perceive to be the failure of their common educational mission. As a result, at each stage of writing instruction from elementary through graduate school and beyond, we find ourselves bemoaning the inadequacy of the stage before. High school English teachers claim their students learned nothing about writing—in some cases not even penmanship—in the early grades. College rhetoric instructors commonly tell their freshmen to forget everything they were told about writing in high school. Upper-level college professors complain that the freshman writing teachers haven't done their job. Graduate faculties lament the inability of each new crop of graduate students to write coherently. And all editors know how difficult it is to rid newly graduated writers of the rhetorical baggage they picked up from generations of well-meaning but misdirected English teachers.

Complaints about the ineffectiveness of earlier stages of language education do not necessarily mean that our teachers or our students are failing. Rather, the cyclical nature of such complaints signals that each stage has its own criteria for success, and that each time we enter a new part of the education cycle we become beginners who need to learn the ropes and master the conventions before we make the grade.

The cognitive psychologist James Voss and his colleagues at the University of Pittsburgh (1983) have shown that beginners behave quite differently from experts when it comes to problem solving in the social sciences. And the linguist Joseph Williams of the University of Chicago (1985) adds that if we take out the notion of social science, these authors seem to be describing the difference between basic and accomplished writers.

For example, Voss and Williams show that novices attacking social science problems rely heavily on the phrasing of the problem and proceed directly to simplistic solutions, failing to consider related problems, alternative strategies, or complications that might arise. Most significantly, novices do not support their point of view with appropriate arguments. In contrast, experts are not confined by the way in which the problem is stated. They go beyond the words to the underlying conceptual relations, weigh a variety of answers, and examine the implications of solutions, preferring general approaches that will solve a number of subproblems. Unlike novices, experts spend much of their time in argumentation. They recognize that answers are not simple, and that others may disagree with their approach. Experts tend to be more aware of their audience than do novices, and consequently they recognize the need to defend their choice of solutions, heading off objections, explaining counterexamples, illustrating strengths and admitting weaknesses in their positions.

As with social science problem solving, we know that successful, or expert, writing depends upon mastery both of subject matter and of the conventional context of writing. The late Mina Shaughnessy of the City College of New York (1972) has shown that basic writers are stymied by their unfamiliarity with the process of putting words down on paper. Since writing is something that few people do voluntarily, even those who are comfortable with the notion of Standard or edited written English find writing an unusual and unnatural act.

Beginning writers are further hampered by their ignorance of factual and theoretical material, and by their unfamiliarity with the subject-specific conventions that exist for manipulating this material. Novice writers are tied to the surface structure of their writing problem, usually an essay question or assigned topic. All too often they begin an answer by rephrasing the question or restating the topic. Some of us, opting for a mechanistic approach to writing, actually teach writers to do this. The organization of their writing is similarly limited by their lack of knowledge. Novices forget to argue their positions, fail to make connections, take too much or too little for granted, and produce essays that are halting, uneven, and ineffective. Even their sentence structure suffers. They cannot foreground or deemphasize effectively, nor can they coordinate or subordinate their clauses well, if they do not understand the relationships that pertain among the ideas in a new field. And they cannot free themselves from dependence upon the style handbook, real or imagined, that accompanies each field, so their writing is forced rather than natural.

Expert writers approach their task differently from beginners. Their analysis of problems is more acute, their writing less choppy. They are able to identify their audience and address it at an appropriate level, to sort out significant details from insignificant ones, to focus and generalize appropriately, and to argue with conviction. They are comfortable breaking the handbook rules which so distract the novices; in fact they seldom think of the rules they break.

However, as Voss and his coauthors show, and as writing teachers have always known, we can only be expert in one area at a time. Expert chemists show no more skill in solving social science problems than do novice social scientists. Similarly, expert writers are only expert when they are at home with their subject. What makes things hard, however, is that fact that when it comes to writing, we are repeatedly cast in the role of novices.

Even if we know how to construct sentences and paragraphs and arguments, we are continually starting over. It's not just that we must discover and satisfy anew the expectations of high school or college or professional writing, we must also relearn how to write each time we face a new subject matter, and more narrowly still, each time we develop a new topic. The familiar image of the writer staring apprehensively at a blank page becomes a metaphor for the unending cycle of beginnings that writing forces on us.

Looking at writing this way has important consequences for teaching. Too often we treat composition as if it were a skill independent of content. We assume that if a student can get through five paragraphs using a variety of sentence types, conventional spelling, and recognizable punctuation, but without dangling modifiers or splitting infinitives, then he or she is ready for any writing challenge the world may offer. Unfortunately such an assumption may be overly optimistic. It identifies students who observe a few of the conventions of standard written English—like subject-verb agreement—most of the time. At best the writing facility we develop in these students will make other writing tasks if not easy at least less formidable. At worst, we falsely certify students in a skill in which they will quickly find themselves deficient when they arrive at their next writing task. In our writing courses we are training students merely to be novice writers; they must develop their own writing expertise for each new field they study.

Ultimately the problem of writing instruction is this: no matter how well we master the conventions of one writing situation, each time we write for a new field, or a new audience, we must begin again at the beginning. Until there is a body of knowledge that students can control, that they can become experts on, their writing will remain more or less concrete, unconvincing, and ineffective—which means that we cannot expect to do a good job in the writing classroom if there isn't something for us to be writing about.

This affirms two convictions writing teachers frequently express— that students who have something to say write better than those who don't; and that adults are easier to teach in writing classes because they have more experience, and therefore more to write about, than school children, or college students. But it also means that our college freshman writing instruction is frequently misdirected, if not impractical, for most such courses are conceived as general, and subject-independent, providing students with a skill that may be transferred to any situation.

Writing in the Curriculum

This brings us to the problem of locating writing in the curriculum. It seems only a little while ago that theorists were fighting to divorce writing instruction from literary study, on the grounds that traditional, literature-based writing courses were a disservice to anyone not majoring in English. The writing needs of students differ, went the argument, and no one should be forced to write in what is sometimes considered the unenviable style of English majors.

It was English majors themselves who argued thus, exhibiting ambivalence over the value of their own enterprise, if not outright self-hatred, and romanticizing the writing done in what they fondly characterized as the real world. As a headline in *The Chronicle of Higher Education* (December 4, 1985, p. 29) reports, the fight against writing the expository essay still goes on: "Writing Skills Taught in College Said to Muddy Clear Expression; Belle-lettres [sic] style called ill-suited for professional life." The accompanying article reports the opinions of English teachers presented at the 1985 conference of the National Council of Teachers of English, who call for training in professional writing, perceived as clean, concise, and straightforward, rather than the murkily literary essay of the "traditional" writing class.

While the Renaissance and the Romantic age celebrated the "natural" language of shepherds, the modern, bureaucratic era looks to business writing as the most natural form of communication. Professional writing, according to the English teachers cited in the article, is top-down writing: the reader is told right off what the subject is, and what to think about it, whereas the principle of organization of the belletristic essay is often obscure, requiring the reader to think about the subject, and perhaps about other things as well. Of course many essays are clear and to the point, and if I am not mistaken the fashion in literary criticism has been for some time to state right off what you are going to do, and then to do it. In contrast, I have read many a piece of "professional" or corporate prose that is awkward and inflated, muddied and bumbling, with no discernible subject, and that contains nothing worth thinking about.

The argument that English teachers are teaching the wrong kind of writing is not particularly telling. Good and bad professional writing exist alongside good and bad expository essays. However, it appears that many of us want to believe that English and writing do not belong together, or at least we question whether they do. A number of colleges and universities, taking up the chant that English instructors do not warrant the composition monopoly they have almost everywhere acquired, have gone so far as to separate writing from its traditional home in English departments. Some English departments, in turn, preferring to teach literature but only too aware that they teach writing because no one else wants to, consider such divestment a relief, despite its economic and political consequences. Even with this separation from literature studies, many of the new departments or divisions or programs in writing are still headed and staffed by English teachers, who now specialize in writing as a subject-independent subject and who can no longer rely on the clout that goes with membership in one of their school's larger departments to get funds for staff or equipment. Worse yet, locating composition in a discrete but subjectless university division brings with it the danger that the problem of writing will be considered solved, and that writing will receive less rather than more attention from the university as a whole.

More popular than writing divestment, at least in theory, is the movement that we call *writing across the curriculum.* Here at last is an attempt to recognize the writing cycle and to confirm writing as discipline-specific, to place the responsibility for making students write not just with English teachers, but with every subject area from accounting to chemical engineering to veterinary medicine. With such an approach we spread the responsibility around, sending students the message that writing is something we expect of them as a matter of course, not just in the humanities but in fine arts, science, and professional studies. And writing assignments coming out of courses with a recognizable subject matter will not be the kind of essays that we associate with the freshman writing class, exercises made up out of thin air and destined to return there once they have been scanned and graded.

The idea behind writing across the curriculum is further supported by research which shows that people read better when they are reading material about which they already know something than when they are reading in a new and unfamiliar subject. Ideally, writing across the curriculum allows English teachers to teach the kind of writing they have some competence in, writing about literature. In other departments as well, this approach should provide a subject matter for writers to become expert in. In practice, though, this does not always happen.

In many cases, writing across the curriculum simply means writing in two or three parts of the curriculum, a freshman level course, probably taught by English teachers who are constrained *not* to make it a literature course, and an upper level course or two in a student's major field, where some sort of paper is expected. However, according to Voss, undergraduate majors are probably not that much more expert than nonmajors. Writing may be a skill, but it is not a skill we learn only once, like riding a bicycle. Instead, it is something that must be practiced continually or it will atrophy. Research shows that if you don't use it, writing proficiency actually falls off. So the addition of a single advanced writing course, while better than nothing at all, may not make a great deal of difference to students if they are not expected to write much anywhere else, since whatever expertise they do develop in the additional course is likely to erode. Furthermore, not every faculty member wants to step into shoes left vacant by English department colleagues. True writing across the curriculum means a mandate to include writing in every course a student takes, not just in two or three. Although this would boost overall writing competence, it would be difficult if not impossible to impose on our faculties, who rightly insist on determining their own academic requirements.

Unfortunately there are no simple, universal answers to the instructional problems writing poses. But there is one more thing we should take into account: we must be prepared to admit that the writing crisis, like the other language-related crises in our history, is in part a fiction arising from our inability to reconcile the democratic spirit of free public education with the elitist judgment that some people are simply smarter than others.

We don't expect everyone to achieve equal facility in the complexities of algebra, but we would like to think that anyone coming out of our schools should be able to write a decent paragraph, letter, or essay. And most people probably can, given the motivation to practice and something significant to say. But that doesn't mean everyone can become an expert writer. The novice-expert analogy does not work quite so well for writers as for social scientists or mathematicians. Someone who masters the subject matter of mathematics to the extent of earning a doctorate and doing research and teaching in the field will qualify as an expert. Knowing subject matter in and of itself is far from enough to make an expert writer, for an expert writer must control style as well as content. This is where the intervention of a writing teacher, particularly one who shares the writer's knowledge of subject matter, may do the most good.

The Ways We Write

Just as writing instruction has traditionally undervalued the writer's knowledge, it has until very recently ignored the ways writers go about writing. One common injunction of writing teachers to their students is "Plan your work." This usually means that students are encouraged before they write to decide on a specific, narrowed-down topic, as well as the manner in which they will treat it. We tell students their essay must begin with a thesis statement that predicts what the finished product will be about. We may further expect that each of their paragraphs will have a similarly binding topic sentence directing the focus of each major unit of text. Particularly with longer works like research papers, we may go so far as to require that students create outlines that they will expand as they write, and we often ask that these be handed in together with the final draft as a check to ensure that the essay keeps the promise of the outline.

Such methodology proceeds from an instructional model that works backwards from the finished piece of writing, assuming that the elements of its construction reflect the process of its creation. Such an approach, we are only now discovering, is naive. Just as movies are edited to give the illusion that they proceed from start to finish, when in fact scenes and sequences may be shot out of order, sound dubbed in, and special effects added even later still, so too, the process of writing seldom goes smoothly from beginning to middle to end. Many writers do not start at the beginning and have only a dim idea at the outset of what the end product will look like. It is in the juxtapositions created in the final cut of a film that the illusion of continuity is created, and it is only after what may be extensive revision, cutting and pasting that many an essay finally takes on form.

Lately, writing research has focused on the process of writing and revising. It has become quantitative and cognitive, relying heavily on the reconstruction of the writing situation by the writer or an observer. Unlike composition specialists, who have come to this method of analysis only recently, professional writers have always been naturally interested in process: they tend to discuss their particular writing quirks whenever they get together. And from such discussion, informal and statistically invalid as it is, there emerges a portrait of two distinct types of composition which the more empirically oriented cognitive specialists might be able to confirm.

Most writers I have talked to—let us call them *speculative* writers for want of a better term—discover their subject as they write. Of course they have some idea of general topic, of some of the examples they will use, and of other aspects of development, and they may even have sketched an outline of their work. But their plans invariably change with the writing, and it may be no exaggeration to say that like a good mystery they do not know what the outcome will be until the task is done. For such writers, the sequence of construction confirms the uncertainty of composition. Outlines, like weather forecasts, must be discarded or continually reworked. Thesis statements and the introduction itself are written last (or, if written earlier, they must be revised to reflect the new direction of the content). And topic sentences may be absent from many or most paragraphs. For these speculative writers, structure is imposed in some degree through revision, which creates an outline after the fact rather than before. It is no wonder that so many of these writers, for whom revision *is* writing, have enthusiastically embraced the word processor, which greatly facilitates their arduous task of shaping and polishing the text.

Other writers, perhaps fifteen or twenty percent of those I know, do things just the opposite: they plan everything in their heads before pen ever touches paper. According to Iryce Baron (personal communication), these *mnemonic* writers, as I call them, lay out the work to be composed very carefully in their minds. They require more time than speculative writers to do what we call prewriting: to assimilate their source material, and to etch into their minds the key aspects of their organization, argument, and style. But once the mental planning work is done, the sentences of mnemonic writers flow onto the paper with some spontaneity. The mnemonic writer is so familiar with the material and the plan of attack that revision comes before writing, editing is accomplished as the writing is done, and little else is needed later. First draft is virtually the same as final draft for these writers. In addition, although mnemonic writers need more planning time, they can write more in a single sitting than speculative writers. While a speculative writer may produce three pages a day, and then spend several hours revising and editing them, a mnemonic writer may write ten pages and have little or no clean up work to do until the entire piece is finished.

This division of writers into speculative and mnemonic seems fairly decisive. Although I have nothing empirical to back this up, the types seem to represent two incompatible ways of processing written language. Each kind of writer is incredulous that the others can write the way they do, and each seems unable to adapt to the other's method with any ease, particularly when they are producing long documents like research papers, dissertations, or book manuscripts. Most important from the perspective of the writing teacher is the fact that neither type fits the usual model of writing instruction. Speculative writers know that all their attempts to plan ahead will ultimately be ineffective, that they will never manage to flesh out those outlines the way their teachers encouraged them to do. On the other hand, revision, for mnemonic writers, is a strange concept, encompassing little more than minor tinkering and proofreading, and they wonder why writing teachers place so much stress on the revising process. Mnemonic writers see little use for expensive word processors: self-correcting typewriters are sufficient for their needs.

Much of today's writing research focuses on how novices go about their chores. As these last examples show, we must look just as closely at what writing experts—that is, professional writers—do. Examining the differences between novices and experts, as well as those between speculative and mnemonic writers, might give us some much-needed clues about how better writers come to be, and this in turn will help us not only to make basic writers into passable ones, thus satisfying the demands of minimal competence, but what is an even more important and much neglected social goal, it will help our best writers to become experts.

II Language Usage

8 Declining Grammar

> Most of the occasions of this world's troubles are Grammatical.
>
> —Montaigne, *Essayes*

Language change is generally considered a gradual process. In some cases, such as the almost imperceptible shift in the way we pronounce our vowels, it may take a century or more for a change to become widespread enough to attract any attention. More immediately visible are changes in our vocabulary. These sometimes occur almost overnight, for example when a new word catches on like wildfire. With virtually instantaneous global communication by means of satellites, television, radio, and the press, such a word, like a popular song, can be on everyone's lips in a matter of days. A few years ago, *Yuppie* had to be explained every time it appeared in print (formed by analogy with *hippie* and *yippie*, it is an acronym standing for "Young Urban Professional," or perhaps "Young Upwardly mobile Professional," although some prefer *Yumpie* for the latter). Now the explanation is not so necessary. Perhaps by the time you read this, *Yuppie* will have faded from the firmament of our vocabulary.

Not quite so sudden, but still fairly noticeable, old words can change meaning too—sometimes for the better, sometimes for the worse. When a word takes on positive connotations, we say it ameliorates (from the Latin, 'to make better'): *nice*, at first 'ignorant,' is now a positive term, as is *glamour*, which once meant 'witchcraft.' If a word takes on a negative sense, it pejorates, or gets worse: *knave* first meant 'boy,' then 'servant,' and ultimately 'a deceptive or evil person.' A word's meaning may widen: it can become more inclusive or general. For example, *virtue* has shifted from the original 'manliness' to the generalized 'good quality.' Or it may narrow: *meat*, once 'food of any kind,' now refers to animal flesh, or more narrowly still, to 'red meat,' that is, beef, pork, and lamb as opposed to fish and poultry. (Recent attempts by the pork industry to connect their product with lower cholesterol meats like chicken and turkey by calling it "the other white meat" have failed to fool consumers.)

It is an unfortunate reflection of the generally negative attitude toward women in our culture that many of our words relating to the female sex have become pejorative over the years (chapter 22). Many terms relating to knowledge are subject to pejoration in popular usage as well. We may respect knowledge, but we are suspicious of those who do not wear their knowledge lightly, and we have little tolerance for those who merely pretend to know. As a result, an *academic* matter is not a subject for learned discussion but an unimportant one. A *question of semantics* no longer refers to meaning, which is the essence of language, but to insignificant hair-splitting instead. Scholars learn soon enough that *school* means not the ivory tower but the lower levels of instruction.

Great as well is the fall of *rhetoric*, which together with grammar and logic formed the trivium, the lower branch of the seven liberal arts, in the middle ages (the quadrivium, the upper branch, consisted of arithmetic, music, geometry, and astronomy). Now a rhetorical question is one whose linguistic force has been vitiated; rhetoric itself commonly signals devious, insincere, or inflated language. The *OED* records negative senses of *rhetoric* from the seventeenth century on, as well as *rhetorculist* (1609), 'a petty rhetorician' and *rhetoricaster* (1591), 'a poor rhetorician.' And nowadays a *trivial* matter has nothing to do with the trivium, the font of human knowledge. It is not surprising then that *grammar* and *grammarian* now share in this depressing fate.

The Ugly Grammarian

Grammar, which climbed from humble beginnings to encompass the whole of human knowledge, has fallen upon hard times. While it still refers to linguistic structure, of course, and to the standards of usage, outside of these technical senses it is often used to indicate an inappropriate, if not a niggling concern with the minutiae of language. Similarly, a practitioner of grammar, once an all-knowing polymath, possibly a magician, is now a pedant, perhaps a harmful drudge. The grammarian's trade has declined, and while our experts in the English language may admit to studying grammar, few of today's linguists and usage critics choose to call themselves grammarians.

Our standard dictionaries generally do not record the unhappy fate of today's grammarians. Some call a grammarian 'a philologist,' though that meaning is probably obsolete. Most dictionaries sidestep the problem by defining grammarian as 'a specialist in grammar' or by listing the variant *grammarian,* without any explicit definition, at the end of their entries for *grammar.* So to understand what a grammarian does we must first decide what grammar is.

As we mentioned in the introduction, grammar has two related but sometimes conflicting meanings in Modern English. As a science, it can be the formal, descriptive study of the facts of language, its phonology, syntax, and semantics. As an art, grammar refers to the rules of language use, the prescribed standards of good speech and writing. However, anyone who has taught English will attest that *grammar* is a word charged with emotion. And everyone knows who has studied English—and that is a large group indeed—that *grammar* can also be a dirty word. Its very mention frightens those who are insecure about usage, and, as the philosopher Montaigne reminds us, grammar can produce conflict and misunderstanding as well as fear. Both sides in the never-ending debate over the health of English employ it as a slogan word, one arguing that grammar determines good usage, the other vilifying grammar as a false standard that none but grammarians observe.

Though it is a basic part of the back-to-basics movement, for all too many of us grammar has come to represent an unpleasant or odious school subject, just as grammarians take on negative if not insidious connotations ignored by most of our dictionaries. The existence of Greek and Latin *grammaticomastix,* 'a scourge or reviler of grammarians,' suggests that the image of the ugly grammarian is nothing new.

The Rise of Grammar

The meaning of *grammar* has widened as well as narrowed over the centuries. Those who equate grammar with linguistic purity may blush at the irony that grammar itself is an "incorrect" or "corrupt" variant of Latin *grammatica,* a derivative of Greek *gramma,* 'letter.' According to the *OED, grammatica* refers initially to the art of letters, or literature. In the medieval period, *grammar* acquires a curious additional sense that has now been lost. Since it referred to learning in general, and since learning included magic and astrology, grammar came to stand for the occult as well as the natural arts and sciences. Such English derivatives as *gramarye,* still current in the nineteenth century, and *glamour,* which has strayed somewhat from its original sense, initially meant 'magic, enchantment, or spell,' and a grammarian could be a fortuneteller or a witch.

After the classical period, grammar becomes restricted to the linguistic aspects of philology. The word enters English from French during the fourteenth century, and its meaning narrows further to signify the study of Latin as a second language. In fact grammar is so completely tied to Latin, for centuries the only language taught formally in the schools, that references to French or English or even Latin grammar do not occur until the seventeenth century. Before that, anything called a grammar was a Latin textbook. Moreover, the unflattering senses of *grammar* were first applied not to our language, but to Latin, for English was initially considered too primitive and too devoid of inflection to have any grammar at all.

The first English grammars, following Latin models, treat their subject in both a prescriptive and a descriptive fashion. They define grammar as the art of speaking and writing correctly, a notion which persists to this day. And they also employ a second, more scientific, sense of grammar, 'the study of the formal features of a language'—what the early grammars called orthography, etymology, syntax, and prosody, the equivalents of our phonetics, morphology, syntax, and metrics.

The earliest citations in the *OED* exemplify both the descriptive and prescriptive senses of grammar: John of Trevisa (1398) reveals an impatience with prescriptive notions of correctness when he proclaims, "Holy writ will not always be subject to the rules of grammar"; while Lanfranc (ca. 1400) takes the opposite position in advising a physician to "study . . . in grammar, so that he [may] speak correctly." Both William Caxton (1485) and Francis Bacon (1605) call grammar a science, though most eighteenth-century grammarians consider their subject an art.

As an element of the trivium, grammar was part and parcel of a liberal education. Certainly the early connection between learning and grammar is maintained in our *grammar* schools. However the practitioners of grammar are not always thought worthy of emulation. Grammarians may be serious students of language, but they are frequently caricatured as pedants. Chambers's *Cyclopedia* (1727–41) comments, "The denomination grammarian is, like that of critic, now frequently used as a term of reproach; a mere grammarian; a dry, plodding grammarian." And Robert Browning, in "A Grammarian's Funeral" (1855), characterizes the deceased, who " ground . . . at grammar," as "dead from the waist down." Ben Jonson (1601), one of the first grammarians to use the phrase *English grammar,* speaks slightingly of the *grammaticaster,* 'a petty or inferior grammarian.' This pejorative still occurs in the nineteenth century, along with the similarly disparaging *grammatist,* and *grammar monger,* one whose language is like "a sluggish monotonous canal." The appearance of such words as *grammar-grinding* and the related *gerund-grinding* in wider contexts shows that by the nineteenth century grammar had come to embrace not just linguistic pedantry but pedantic instruction generally (*OED*, s.v.).

De Casibus, or The Fall of Grammar

Two factors affect the derogation of grammar in the mid-nineteenth century: its position in the school curriculum, and the rise of modern linguistics. By 1850 English grammar had become a widely taught and generally despised subject in American elementary and secondary schools. Students considered it too hard, and many instructors resisted teaching a subject that they themselves had not mastered. Writing in 1870, usage critic Richard Grant White, for one, takes a dim view of grammar and its professors. His conviction that the rules of grammar are "mere make-believe" is firmly grounded in his own childhood punishment for "a failure to get a lesson in English grammar." Some twentieth-century usage critics also characterize grammar as harmful rather than beneficial. In his *Practical Handbook of Better English* (1944), Frank Colby complains of the "unintelligible, medieval nomenclature of the grammar books."

While in present-day English *grammar* may refer either to the little-loved school subject or the cutting edge of linguistic theory, *grammarian* retains little of its once positive significance. We have found an alternative to refer to the student of linguistic structure. By the mid-nineteenth century the impact of Indo-European studies had begun to change the shape of English philology. In order to indicate the modern, scientific status of the field as well as to differentiate it from earlier grammatical study, the nouns *linguistic* and *linguistics* (parallel to the French *linguistique* and German *Linguistik*) began to appear in place of *grammar*. It took *linguist* a bit longer to replace *grammarian*.

Linguist, which first occurs in English in the late sixteenth century, originally meant 'one skilled in the use of languages,' a sense that remains current to the chagrin of theoretical linguists. From the seventeenth to the early nineteenth century *linguist* also meant 'philologist or grammarian.' The *OED* marked this sense as obsolete, but the *Supplement* to the *OED* (1976) records its revival, along with the competing *linguistician*. In 1922 Otto Jespersen uses *linguist* for 'a student of language,' though he feels the need to define the term for his readers. The *OED Supplement* records a proposal made in 1949 to supplant *linguist*, because of its ambiguity, with *linguistician*, together with a response to this proposal labeling *linguistician* as pretentious

rather than precise. Despite the insistence of the *OED* that both terms
are current, *linguist* has clearly become the word of choice: it occurs
twenty-four times in the Brown Corpus, which contains over one
million words of edited contemporary English prose, while *grammarian*
occurs only once, and *linguistician* does not appear at all.

The manner in which experts on language discuss one another can
best be described as terminological warfare. Usage critics, though
always eager to censure the catch phrases of others, have lately taken
to calling linguists *permissive* to underscore their contention that the
diplomates in the study of language do not care a fig what happens
to our tongue. Linguists have responded with the equally opprobrious
usageaster, on the analogy of *poetaster* and *criticaster* (not to mention
grammaticaster), alleging the usage critics' inferior knowledge of the
history and structure of the language they profess to judge.

Grammarians would seem to be caught in the middle, but their
responses to the naming struggle are difficult to chart because it is
rare nowadays to find a self-confessed grammarian. We use the term
for other people, not ourselves. Nowadays, a grammarian is someone
considered in a more or less unflattering way. Thus in *The New
Grammarians' Funeral: A Critique of Noam Chomsky's Linguistics* (1975),
Ian Robinson calls the transformational theorists grammarians in order
to show his contempt for their approach, while he characterizes their
work as linguistics, not grammar.

In fact, in the minds of many linguists and usage critics, *grammarian*
has degenerated to such an extent that it has become synonymous
with *purist,* a word which derives from the untarnished adjective *pure*
but which has always indicated an unhealthy concern for the small
points of language etiquette, and a zeal for linguistic reform which
exceeds the bounds of good taste. Purists are pedants insisting on the
letter—the "grammatical" meaning—rather than the spirit of the text.
Although the dictionaries have been slow to pick up on it, grammarians
are now the bad guys. *Grammarian* and *purist* are ugly epithets to hurl
at one's enemies, not professions to identify as one's own.

Negative Future

Pejoration may be a transitory phenomenon for some words, but we
should not expect the immediate future to bring a new dispensation
releasing grammar and grammarians from their obloquy. After all,
grammar has been entwined with the negative aspects of education
for so long that all our grammarians have gone underground, and it

is difficult to imagine either word regaining much of its initial stature. It is reassuring, however, that although linguistic terminology may have its ups and downs, language itself continues as a topic of interest for scholars and amateurs alike. Nor can it be altogether negative that language still arouses in us so much passion. For some people words will always be more important than things and, when it comes to language, terminological issues may never be settled once and for all. As William Camden put it over three centuries ago in his *Remaines Concerning Britain,* "It is a greater glory now to be a linguist than a realist."

9 A Literal Paradox

Confound it, Hawkins, when I said I meant that literally,
that was just a figure of speech.
—Lorenz, *New Yorker* cartoon (February 28, 1977, p. 54)

English is a language so rich in like-meaning words that it is common for us to say the same thing many different ways. We may even go so far as to use apparently opposite constructions synonymously. For example, with *Is this true?* and *Isn't this true?* we use both a positive and a negative question to elicit the same information. And there is the popular exclamation *I could care less!* which is stigmatized by many critics because it is used not literally as a positive, but as a synonym for its negative, *I couldn't care less!* But the most striking, and perhaps one of the more exasperating, confusions of our language occurs when we use a single word to mean both itself and its opposite.

For example, *restive,* which originally meant 'standing still,' from Old French *rester,* came to mean 'stubborn' and now is the equivalent of its apparent opposite, *restless.* *Let* normally means 'permit, allow,' but in tennis a *let* is a serve that has been hindered or obstructed. *Ravel* means both to tangle and untangle, to knit up and, as we know from Macbeth, who calls on sleep to knit up "the ravelled sleeve of care," it means to unknit as well. *Fast* refers to immobility ("The car was stuck fast in the mud") as well as speed, and *dust* can mean 'to sprinkle with dust' and 'to remove the dust from.' Both *head* and *tail* can mean, respectively, 'to add a head to, or to behead, to remove the tail of, or to supply with a tail.' The preposition *with* means both 'accompanying, together' (*grow old along with me*) and 'opposing, against' (armies fight *with* one another). *Oversight* means both looking closely at something (from *oversee*) and ignoring or forgetting it as well. And there is *sanction,* which sometimes means 'to forbid,' sometimes, 'to permit or encourage.'

Curiously, there is no exact name for this phenomenon of self-contradiction, though the rhetorical terms *ambiguity, amphibology, equivocation,* and *oxymoron* come close. Furthermore, we generally pay little mind to this *autoantonymy,* assuming perhaps that such lexical instability

73

must be rare and temporary, the sort of ambiguity that language should not tolerate for very long. In fact, these lexical oxymora crop up regularly, and some have a long and stable history. For example, the double meanings of *dust* have coexisted peacefully since the sixteenth century, and *ravel* and *unravel*, which both enter the language in the 1600s, are with us still today. We have tolerated the paradox of *sanction*, whose double meanings derive from the original legal sense 'to ordain, decree, ratify,' almost as long, while we have suffered *cleave*, both 'split apart' and 'cling to,' for even longer. But some new wrinkles in the universe of opposites are causing trouble. Some usage critics are scandalized that *scan*, which has always meant 'to examine closely,' has now been used for at least thirty years to mean 'skim, examine hastily or superficially,' as well, a sense accepted without comment by the major dictionaries. In a more interesting, and much more controversial shift of meaning, we find *literally* used both in the old-fashioned way to mean 'literally,' and in the newfangled but quite opposite sense to mean 'figuratively' (*He was literally climbing the walls*). This the critics of usage univocally condemn.

To dissolve lexical paradoxes, their conflicting senses must interfere sufficiently with one another to create an intolerable situation. Unfortunately, it is often difficult to determine when or why users of English have had enough of double meaning. Take the case of *egregious*. Initially it meant 'prominent' in both a good and bad sense (the earliest cited by *OED* are 1534 and 1573, respectively), but the positive sense of the word became obsolete by the nineteenth century, except in humorous contexts. Similarly, the adjective *mere* exhibits two potentially conflicting senses from the sixteenth to the early nineteenth centuries: a positive group of meanings revolving around the notions 'pure, absolute, entire, and downright' (*Things rank and gross in nature possess it merely*), all of which have become obsolete, and a negative signification, 'having no greater extent or importance than the designation implies; that is barely or only what it is said to be' (*OED*, s. v.), the one sense which survives today. It is more than likely that disambiguation has played some role in the loss of the positive connotations of *egregious* and *mere*, though it is not clear why this occurred after English tolerated their ambiguity for so long.

In some cases fear of confusion rather than actual ambiguity can bring about a lexical shift. This may have happened with *annul*, which since the early fifteenth century has signified 'to abolish, cancel.' A second negative, *disannul*, used as the equivalent of *annul*, first appeared some years after, perhaps because *annul* was not clearly negative enough. The creation of a clearer distinction between negative and positive is certainly behind the coining of *flammable*. *Inflammable* always means 'capable of burning,' its sense since it came into the English language in the seventeenth century. By the nineteenth century, however, the notion that someone might carelessly take *inflammable* for nonflammable, a sense not actually recorded by dictionaries but whose misreading would prove disastrous, prompted the clarification *flammable* for the unambiguous incendiary sense of the word. *Inflame, inflammation,* and *inflammatory,* whose meaning is never in doubt, remain unmodified. *Inflammable* itself continues to be used, though it may occur less frequently than the newer, derived form. A similar process of clarification produces *debone* (1944) alongside the older *bone,* all but one of whose verbal senses clearly refer to the removal rather than the addition of bone matter.

The prefix *un-* presents an opportunity for the creation of apparent rather than actual autoantonyms. Redundant *un-* gives us *unloose* and *unloosen,* which have survived in standard English alongside the synonymous *loose* and *loosen* since the 1300s. *Unthaw,* a less-authorized form used as a synonym for *thaw* rather than *freeze,* is still commonly heard. In addition, the *OED* records *unbare, unsolve, unstrip, unempty* and *unrid,* all used in the same sense as the simple positive. In the sixteenth and seventeenth centuries it was common to prefix *un-* to words also suffixed with *-less,* creating such redundancies as *unboundless, uncomfortless, undauntless, uneffectless, unhelpless, unmerciless, unremorseless, unrespectless, unshameless,* and *unquestionless.* Despite the apparent double negative, such words—which are no longer current—were treated not as positives but as negatives, much in the way some people today use the stigmatized *irregardless* to mean 'regardless.'

The resolution of many lexical paradoxes involves the loss of an existing word rather than the creation of a new one. Competition existed in the seventeenth century between *queen,* 'female monarch,' a word with positive connotations, and the homonymous but derogatory *quean,* 'prostitute'—both ultimately from the same root meaning 'woman.' The situation was exacerbated during the rule of Elizabeth I: while the opportunity for punning proved irresistible to the literary wits of the age, the need to stay on the sovereign's good side was also clear. Some historians of the English language go so far as to argue that the decline in frequency of *quean* in favor of *whore* and *harlot* is directly attributable to the political exigencies of the time.

The negative sense of *ravel* and the morphologically explicit negative *unravel* appear at about the same time in the history of English and have continued to coexist without causing significant entanglements of sense, though *unravel* may now be a slightly more common form.

Similarly with *cleave* we have a lexical paradox of long standing that has not been resolved. *Cleave* represents the conflation of two verbs whose form, pronunciation, and spelling were once distinct, and whose meanings, 'to cut, flay, separate,' and 'to stick fast, adhere, or cling to,' are virtually opposite. Yet the intertwining of these words, which began as early as the fourteenth century, seems never to have presented much of a problem for us. We can attribute this to the fact that neither word is very common (the participles *cleft* and *cloven* are more familiar to us, though not necessarily frequent in occurrence), and the latter sense of *cleave* in particular has an archaic flavor to it that further restricts its use.

The Letter and the Spirit

We come now to a fairly common paradox that has attracted a good bit of attention of late. The use of *literally* to mean its opposite, *figuratively,* as illustrated in our epigraph from a *New Yorker* cartoon of some years back, first appears in the nineteenth century. A look at the complex of *letter*-related words may throw some light on this spreading English amphibology.

Just as *gramma*, the Greek word for 'sign, something written,' gives us English *grammar,* Latin *littera,* 'alphabetic letter,' furnishes not only English *letter* but a set of related words whose meaning turns on letters, including *literal, literate, literature* and their derivatives *literally, literacy,* and *literary.* Since the development of the alphabet, and even more so since the invention of printing, letters have become the key to learning and serve as metaphors for our knowledge.

As today's concerns with the level of student reading and writing illustrate, the ability to manipulate letters remains indispensable to survival in our society. Claims that the print culture of the past several centuries is being displaced by our dependence on television are not supported by our continued and frequently irrational faith in the written representation of speech. We still feel uncomfortable with a new word, particularly a new name, until we see it spelled, and while our word is still our bond, most spoken affirmation must be quickly followed up by a written confirmation. Except for some few aspects of legal or religious ceremony, or gambling, a signature rather than an affirmation remains our strongest guarantee. Students, who still ask if spelling counts, seem particularly unwilling to question let alone outright disbelieve what they find between the covers of their textbooks. And legal and evangelical fundamentalists are ever louder and more insistent that interpretation of the civil and moral code be bound by the letter and not the spirit of the written text.

Of course our attitude toward the configuration of letters, language, and knowledge has a negative side as well: we may respect the scholarly mind, but as we saw in the preceding chapter, we also tend to suspect those who know too much. Moreover, our acquaintance with the many pretenders to knowledge has caused us to confuse and debase terms associated with learning. We have already seen how *grammarian* acquired a negative sense. Words derived from *littera* can reveal the abuse of learning as well. *Literator,* now more or less obsolete, once meant 'a pretender to learning,' and *literose* signified 'studiedly or affectedly literary,' referring to that surfeit of words aptly styled *literosity.* Other *letter*-words specify lack of learning: *illiterate* is used in the seventeenth century as it is today—either objectively or as the insulting 'generally unlearned.' An eighteenth-century citation in the *OED* specifically ties illiteracy to ignorance of the learned languages, Latin and Greek. We might do well to revive the related term *illiterature,* which for many centuries meant a general want of knowledge.

By the 1800s, with the spread of mass public education, *illiteracy* had come to refer more narrowly to an inability to process letters: someone unable to read is called *totally illiterate* by the *OED.* And while we continue to use *illiterate* as a synonym for *uncultured,* by which we mean 'someone who doesn't know what we know,' we restrict it as a technical term to the context of reading. Now that the ability to read is widespread, a new term has inserted itself in the literacy spectrum. Between the inability to decode and encode letters (reading and writing, to use language that is freer of jargon), and the exemplification of wide and impressive knowledge (a *literate* speech, or essay, or person), we see the use of *functional illiteracy* to indicate that the ability to read and write is present but inadequate. A functional illiterate is variously defined as one who cannot follow simple written instructions (for example, a recipe) or fill out common forms (applications for employment or a driver's license); whose literacy is beneath a designated standard; or is insufficient for a given task.

We also commonly specify literacy by extension as knowledge of a particular area or subject. Though we may fear *literacy* to be on the decline, *literacies* are ever on the rise as we discover new things to be ignorant about. Thus over the years it has been customary to speak of *psychological* literacy, *musical* literacy, *economic* literacy, *natural science* literacy, *quantitative* literacy, 'familiarity with statistics,' *geoliteracy,* 'knowledge of geography,' *oracy,* 'fluency in speaking,' and even *tele-*

vision literacy, which hypercritics might take to be a contradiction in terms. To this list we have now added *critical literacy,* 'ability to read, write, and think critically,' and the phrase popularized by E. D. Hirsch's book, *cultural literacy,* together with both *computer literacy* and *computeracy.* The association between letters and knowledge is so strong we even extend the word-formation pattern to numbers: *numeracy* refers to 'knowledge of arithmetic or math,' while *innumerate* and *innumeracy* indicate the arithmetical equivalent of our reading-writing failures. This metaphorical extension of letter-words has never been seriously challenged, with one ironic exception in the case of *literally.*

By some quirk of idiom, *literal* and *literally* are almost always used not in literal reference to the alphabet, but figuratively to refer to meaning. According to the *OED, literal* first appears in English in the fourteenth century in a theological context, referring to the interpretation of a text in terms of the ordinary rather than the mystical or allegorical sense of its words. It is not used about the letters of the alphabet until the fifteenth century. By the end of the 1500s *literal* had acquired another extended meaning, 'verbally exact,' in the context of the translation or reproduction of a text, as well as its most common meaning, 'the sense expressed by the actual wording of a passage,' in contrast to figurative or metaphorical meaning. The adverb *literally* places a similar stress on the common, ordinary, or basic sense of a word or phrase, for example Hume's *He had the singular fate of dying literally of hunger (OED,* s. v.).

Literal can also be associated with the misinterpretation of language. A literal, or literal-minded person is one who takes seriously or at face value what is meant either figuratively or in jest. As the epigraph for this chapter shows, this sort of literality is frequently the source of humor. But the epigraph also illustrates a use which the *OED* labels as a mistake, despite the number of examples cited in its most recent supplement: the use of *literally* as an intensifier to mean 'figuratively,' as in the words addressed to poor Hawkins at the head of this chapter.

This figurative use has become a bugbear for language critics. While they tolerate the two-faced *ravel* and *cleave,* they draw the line at *literal* because it is a word directly tied to the interpretation of words. Opponents of the change in *literally* would restrict the word to its literal sense, forgetting for the moment that what they take to be the letter is itself a figure. Many of today's commentators on language join the *OED* in calling figurative *literally* incorrect. In their usage handbook, Marius and Wiener (1985, 592) call the new *literally* misleading or ridiculous. Crews and Schor (1985) maintain, "If you write *I literally died laughing,* you must be writing from beyond the grave." Donald Hall (1985, 434) sees in it a misguided attempt to vivify dead metaphors. And Harry Shaw (1981, 305) charges that we overuse both the figurative and the literal meanings of *literally*. *Webster's New World Dictionary* (1959) acknowledges the new *literally*, tagging it as colloquial and commenting, "regarded by many as an erroneous usage." The *American Heritage Dictionary* (1982) finds the error common, and Claire Cook (1985, 185) warns against it from a practical point of view: "Abuses of the word can seem ludicrous, and those who recognize them enjoy pointing them out."

Word for Word

The fact that authorities grudgingly acknowledge the increasing paradoxical use of *literally*, even though they disapprove of it, provides further evidence that a semantic turnaround has taken place. It is not unusual for words to undergo such antonymic transformation. *History* once meant 'factual account,' but eventually acquired the opposite meaning, 'fictional account,' as well, no doubt because many factual accounts prove unreliable. *History* now generally indicates nonfiction, while the clipped form of the word, *story*, developed a stress on fictionality (similarly, French *histoire* and *conte*—the latter from Latin *computus*, 'exact account'—can mean both 'true account' and 'lie'). In addition to the examples cited earlier, the change is common for a whole set of expressions which once meant 'right away.' *Anon, by and by, in a moment, presently,* and *soon* once meant 'instantly,' but now they refer to an unspecified time in the near future. Even *directly, immediately,* and *right away* have come in certain disappointing instances to mean 'in a little while.' In some cases, opposite meanings coexist so subtly that we do not notice them. *Incidentally* refers to matters indirectly connected with what has gone before, though *incident* originally means 'naturally appertaining to,' a sense quite opposite. And even *à propos* means both 'having direct reference to the matter at hand' and, when used in the absolute, 'incidentally, by the way.'

In other cases, the oppositions are both blatant and tolerated. Both *bad* and *good* can be used in slang to indicate their opposites. *Terrible* does not retain much connection with *terror,* though it still means something negative, but *terribly,* as in *terribly entertaining,* has become a positive intensifier. Many such intensifiers are words stripped of their original meaning, and three of these, *really, truly,* and *very* (the last from Latin *verus,* 'true'), are words which, like *literally,* once signified truth and exactness but are now frequently used instead to indicate an extreme state, often a figurative one at that.

The fate of *literally* will ultimately depend not so much on the classification of one of its uses as an error, but on the actual ambiguity generated by the literal paradox. Our opening illustration from the *New Yorker* notwithstanding, the use of *literally* to mean 'figuratively' does not seem to interfere significantly with comprehension. For one thing, the literal sense of the word is largely restricted to formal, written contexts, while the loose sense tends to occur in less formal speech and writing. It may be that not enough people use *literally* in conflicting senses to cause a problem. On the other hand, the frequent complaints that the new meaning of *literally* is common may indicate the form has already stood the test of time.

Unlike *cleave, quean, ravel,* and *inflammable, literally* has become a fairly common word (it occurs twenty-six times in the Brown Corpus). If communicative interference does result from competing meanings of *literally,* we can be fairly confident that some lexical or semantic change will occur to dissolve the paradox and restore comprehension. Whatever form it takes, this change will certainly be boosted by the complaints that have been lodged against the construction. But, as we will see in the next chapter, complaints alone are not going to be enough, for revamping the ways we use *literally,* like most of the reforms that have been advocated for English at one time or another, will take quite a bit more than simply pointing out the illogicality of the construction in question.

Opponents of the new *literally* may draw some consolation from the fact that it and other intensifiers such as *really* and *truly* eventually lose their intensity and become candidates for replacement. So it may be that while we are stuck with the literal paradox for now, speakers and writers of English will insist on using *literally* in its new sense only until something better comes along.

10 Academies of One: The Critics and English Usage

> No one who has once taken the language under
> his care can ever again be really happy.
> —Thomas Lounsbury, *English Spelling and Spelling Reform*

When a furor arose some years ago over the "incorrect" use of *like* for *as* in the advertising slogan, "Winston tastes good like a cigarette should," the tobacco company management decided to tough it out, figuring perhaps that those who were picky enough to object to their catchphrase would not respond to advertising anyway. Winston weathered the storm by depicting its foes as unrealistic purists. Capitalizing on the publicity with yet another slogan, "What do you want, good grammar or good taste?", the firm toughed it out and smoked all the way to the bank.

The Winston to-do was a once in a lifetime opportunity to cash in on a usage controversy; advertisers remain leery of notoriety. The fear of making a Winston-like faux pas probably lies behind the effort a couple of years ago of a group working for the McDonald's Corporation to ascertain, by writing to heads of university English Departments and editors of language journals, the correct plural for *Egg McMuffin*.

Had they asked me, which they did not, I would not have recommended the obvious *Egg McMuffins*, which like blueberry or English muffins is just a tad too plebeian for an advertising ploy. Besides, if McDonald's was content with a normal plural, why the survey? I would not have chosen *Eggs McMuffin*, either, because that gives the product too much the air of *eggs Benedict*. The analogy here is imperfect, since eggs Benedict has no singular, the dish typically consisting of two eggs, while an order of Egg McMuffin contains, by definition, only one. There is no such thing as an *egg Benedict*, and besides, how could McDonald's come up with the requisite number of truffles?

Taking into consideration the requirements both of correct English and effective public relations—of good grammar *and* good taste—I would strike a blow for one of our less-popular but certainly no less-authorized plurals. Why not pick the double plural, *Eggs McMuffins*, on the analogy of *children*, which shows an *-en* plural (as in *oxen* and *brethren*) added to an obsolete plural in *-er*? Curiously enough, *egg* once had an *-er* plural in English, *eier*, much like the modern German, but *Eier McMuffins* would probably affect the product recognition factor adversely. Double plurals are more common than we think. Quite a few of our singulars were actually once plural, including a number of French borrowings that developed new plurals once they came into English: *apprentice* is from the French plural, *apprentis* (sg. *apprenti*), *invoice* from *envois* (sg. *envoi*), *quince* from *quins* (Old French sg. *coin*), and *lettuce* from *laitus* (sg. *laitu*). Our *penthouse* is the French plural *appentis*, literally 'hanging from.' *Tweezers* comes from the French *etuis* (sg. *etui*), 'case,' and was originally (a pair of) *twees*. Native English *breeches* (from Old English singular *broc*, plural *breech*) is a double plural, as is *bodices* (*bodice* is actually *bodies*, plural of *body*).

More dramatic than the English double plural and certainly more euphonic is the zero plural, *Egg McMuffin*, on the model of *fish* and *sheep*. Ablaut, or vowel shift, as in *mouse/mice*, is unfortunately not an option in this case. But all in all, it is not likely that the hamburger chain would have heeded my advice on the correct naming of its *breakfast sandwiches* (that in itself is a new generic term). If McDonald's ever did decide on an appropriate plural, it is certainly one that has brought little attention to itself. In contrast, some products dare to walk the fine line of the peculiar singular or plural, perhaps hoping to draw additional attention to the trademark. *Life Savers* is a candy which, according to its recent television commercials, takes the same form in the singular and the plural, for example, "I'll have a Life Savers." One recently introduced candy bar called *Kudos* presents an even more interesting problem in terms of number. The word comes from the Greek for 'praise, glory,' and has been a minor usage issue for a number of years because, while it is a singular noun, its final *-s* frequently leads us to treat it as a plural instead. This in turn can lead to a new singular form, *kudo*. Exactly the same process affected *pease*, a word, now found only in the nursery rhyme beginning *pease porridge hot* (the proper Middle English plural of *pease* was *peasen*), and *shay*, a false singular of the plural-sounding *chaise*. But when *-en* plurals began to disappear from English, enough people construed singular *pease* as a plural to produce the new singular, *pea*. *Kudos* is still too new on the market to have run into such grammatical tangles, but it is a bar that bears watching, and its manufacturers should be prepared to deal with the purists.

The Law of Usage

Like McDonald's, we are all concerned in one way or another with the question of correctness in language. The poet Horace, discussing vocabulary change in his *Ars Poetica,* notes that *usage* is the determining factor in issues of linguistic correctness. By usage Horace means custom; however, just whose custom and how much weight it carries remain vexed questions to this day.

In its nonlinguistic senses, *usage* may be informal, describing a habitual or customary action, or it may be a prescribed practice, one determined by law. Though our standard dictionaries are silent on the matter, a similar polarization is inherent in the linguistic sense of the word. For some language experts, usage is a descriptive term referring to the forms and tendencies of language, while for most it is normative, prescribing exactly what we should or should not do with words. Indeed, the first citation for linguistic usage in the *OED* comes from Daniel Defoe's *Essay Upon Projects* (1697), which recommends that usage be subordinated to reason through the legalistic intercession of a language academy.

Although it has been proposed many times, the idea of an English Academy to regulate usage remains no more than a dream. In its stead, though, many individual commentators have assumed the task of guarding our language against degeneration and barbarism. Setting themselves up as academies of one, these usage critics form a loose network of collegiality and attract both vast and vocal followings. They play fast and loose with usage: when it suits their purpose, usage is none other than English 'as it is spoke and writ,' a body of sacred precepts which we must protect from harmful error or innovation. At other times, usage is viewed as something to be stamped out, the untamed, uneducated practice of the masses which requires direction and regulation, if not exorcism.

We not only listen to the critics of usage, we often seek out their advice, for our own uncertainty about what is right and wrong in English worries us. Some of the critics, in turn, derive a dizzying sense of power from their mission to reform the language and educate their readership. While most remain in awe of English, writing over-carefully and at times dully to avoid making the very mistakes they declaim against, or admitting their own fallibility when it is pointed out by the vigilant followers of their books and columns, a few usage critics veer dangerously toward the idiosyncratic in their judgments. The majority of language commentators pay some homage to Horace's doctrine of usage, but a few in this lonely crowd go so far as to reject the force of custom altogether—at least the force of anyone's custom but their own—in the establishment of language standards. In the final analysis, usage for these critics is whatever their personal academy decrees.

A Higher Law

Ironically, many of these unaffiliated academicians, who see themselves as experts on language, reject the formal study of language as inimical. Robert Baker (1770), author of one of the first English usage handbooks, boasts of having left school at the age of fifteen with small Latin and less Greek, and of never having seen a copy of Samuel Johnson's Dictionary (1755), perhaps the most important language treatise of his time. Just a century later, the journalist Richard Grant White (1870) proclaims his ignorance of the rules of grammar, and again in our own day John Simon (1980), the art critic turned usage monitor, celebrates the ignorance of linguistic theory that allows him to be objective about the mismanagement of our language.

Such know-nothing-ism is only half the story, however, for these language critics frequently reject the legitimacy not only of language theory, but of linguistic data as well. At their most extreme, the usage critics honor Daniel Defoe's prescription to subordinate tradition, even the linguistic tradition of the best and the brightest, to reason. Thus Richard Grant White maintains that language, like morality, is subject to a higher law than usage, and he finds no inconsistency in writing that "the 'authority' of eminent writers . . . does not completely justify or establish a use of words inconsistent with reason."

The irresistibility of reason for the usage critics lies in its apparent objectivity. Linguistic custom, on the other hand, is fraught with human error; and idiom, which is by definition resistant to logical or grammatical analysis, is treated with suspicion by the language academicians. More specifically, reason-oriented usage critics search out so-called illogicalities of expression and mark them for extinction. For almost three hundred years, multiple negation has been one of their chief targets.

Though two wrongs do not make a right, and a *no-no* is not a yes, critic after critic repeats the slogan that appears in the sixteenth century in Sir Philip Sidney's *Astrophel and Stella*, and two centuries later became a staple of grammar books, that two negatives cancel each other out to make a single positive. This may be true in logic, and in some arithmetic operations—in multiplication two minuses make a plus, though in addition they produce an even greater minus—but it is not always true in morality or in language. A not unkind remark does not have quite the same effect as a kind one. Even double negatives like "They don't like no grammarians," proscribed in standard English though common enough in speech, are neither intended nor interpreted as positives.

Usage critics frequently confuse logic with literal meaning, and many of them delight in finding paradox in the literal reading of popular expressions. Thus the commentator Alfred Ayres (1882) maintains that one cannot have a *bad cold,* for colds are never good; the poet and spelling reformer Walter Savage Landor opposes the label *bad orthography* because *orthography* literally means 'right spelling'; and the grammarian Josephine Turck Baker (1907) contends that since *grammar* refers only to 'correct English,' the expression *bad grammar* is a contradiction in terms. The suspicion that *bad* does not go with certain words continues to plague us. Recently Malcolm Forbes, the editor of *Forbes* magazine, complained that the phrase *a bad mistake* is redundant because there are no good mistakes (Safire 1986). While a few critics insist on limiting the range of *bad* according to a narrow view of meaning and logic, for the rest of us the word continues to serve a useful, indeed a necessary, function in reference to language, health, and human behavior in general.

This is not to say that there is no room for logic in language. Unfortunately, in usage criticism as in usage, logic may be subjective, existing only in the eye of the beholder. For example, while almost every commentator who deals with it rejects the idiom *to create a Frankenstein* on the grounds that Baron Frankenstein was the patentee and not the monster, the usage critic Wilson Follett (1966) sees in the expression the same logical and orderly transfer of meaning that gives us the eponymous *Ford, sandwich, mackintosh,* and *malaprop.*

Even more extreme is the usage critics' occasional insistence on literality at the expense of all good sense. In this vein, the critic Edward S. Gould (1867), arguing from etymology, limits *journal* to daily publications. More wrongheaded still is the debate over time-telling idioms that occurred earlier in this century.

In his *Desk-Book of Errors in English* (1907), the pronunciation expert Frank Vizetelly proscribes the common horological phrase *a quarter of seven* on the grounds that it literally means 'one and three quarters,' that is, 'seven divided by four.' Vizetelly only accepts *a quarter to seven* as correct. Taking an opposite though equally absurd position, Josephine Turck Baker (1907) contends that since *to* is a preposition indicating 'direction toward,' *a quarter to seven* is really 'one quarter of an hour in the direction of seven on the clock dial,' or 'six fifteen,' and she mandates the very form Vizetelly rejects. Neither mentions *a quarter till seven*, a variant that is generally snubbed as dialectal, although it alone satisfies the demand for logical rigor. This leaves the unfortunate follower of these hyperliteral language experts to select between two equally illogical expressions. Better to say "six forty-five" and have done with it, especially today, when digital time telling is rendering the analog variety obsolete.

Only in rare cases will a usage critic exempt an idiom from the rule of logic. For well over a century *mutual friend* has been castigated as an error for *common friend*. The language commentators Richard Meade Bache (1869), Alfred Ayres (1882), and Henry W. Fowler (1926) all take up arms against *mutual friend*, attributing its popularity in part to Charles Dickens's novel *Our Mutual Friend*. Fowler tersely explains the offense in a pseudo-mathematical style designed to lend weight to his opinion: "The essence of [mutual's] meaning is that it involves the relation, x is or does to y as y to x; & not the relation, x is or does to z as y to z." Wilson Follett (1966) and dictionary editors William and Mary Morris (1975) reluctantly admit that *mutual friend*, despite its illogicality, has now become well-entrenched in the language, though according to the *OED*, *mutual* in the sense 'common' occurs as early as the mid-seventeenth century, and was already an entrenched phrase (or, more neutrally, an English idiom) when Dickens was casting about for a title. But for the linguists and usage critics Bergen and Cornelia Evans (1957), the even higher law of clarity takes precedence over logic, and they judge *mutual friend* to be clearer than the ambiguous *common friend*, which may signify either a friend that two people have in common, or a vulgar, commonplace one.

Creating a Shibboleth

As part of their mission to impose order where chaos once ruled, usage critics may invent grammatical rules to regulate our behavior, providing language with a logical structure that it actually lacks. For example, both *that* and *which* can serve in restrictive relative clauses: "The book which [that] you recommended was stolen from the library." However, only *which* occurs in nonrestrictive ones: "The book, which you returned just last week, is now missing." In the late nineteenth century, some usage critics sought to neaten things up by limiting *that* to restrictive clauses, and *which* to nonrestrictive ones. Although this distinction is advocated by Ayres (1882) and is elaborately discussed by H. W. and F. G. Fowler (1906), its status as a tentative and arbitrary innovation is most clearly stated in Henry Fowler's *Modern English Usage* (1926):

> The relations between *that, who,* & *which,* have come to us from our forefathers as an odd jumble, & plainly show that the language has not been neatly constructed by a master builder. . . . If writers would agree to regard *that* as the defining relative pronoun, & *which* as the non-defining, there would be much gain both in lucidity & in ease.

With the exception of Evans and Evans (1957), who observe that most speakers and writers remain oblivious to this distinction, those twentieth-century usage critics who treat the issue favor this rule, despite the fact that—or perhaps, because—general practice probably still reflects Fowler's assessment of the situation as a jumble. (s.v. *that* rel. pron.)

Linguistic usage has traditionally functioned as a caste mark, a determinant of membership within a group, and in at least one case a rule imposed by the usage critics has become a shibboleth. Since the eighteenth century, many guardians of our speech have insisted that the correct differentiation of the auxiliary verbs *shall* and *will* is a trait inbred among certain classes of the English, though not generally accessible to the Scots, the Irish, provincials, colonials, and other unfortunates. To Richard Grant White (1870) the proper use of *shall* and *will* is found only among those Americans who qualify as "fairly educated people of English stock," while the Fowlers (1906) drastically limit its range to "the idiomatic use [which] comes by nature to southern Englishmen [but which] is so complicated that those who are not to the manner born can hardly acquire it." Despite this expression of despair, the authors present twenty-one pages of detailed explanation for readers seeking to master the shibboleth.

The shall/will rule was stated somewhat more succinctly than the Fowlers choose to do it in Bishop Robert Lowth's extremely popular *Short Introduction to English Grammar* (1762):

> *Will,* in the first person singular and plural, promises or threatens; in the second and third persons, only foretells: *shall* on the contrary, in the first person, simply foretells; in the second and third persons, promises, commands, or threatens. . . . When the sentence is interrogative, just the reverse for the most part takes place. (41–42)

But for Lowth the distinctions are innovative rather than inbred: he remarks in a footnote that they are not observed in the King James translation of the Bible (1611), and his aim is clearly to introduce a rule to cover a new linguistic development.

Historical evidence supports Lowth's feeling that the distinction was an innovation, though the exact significance of auxiliaries is often impossible to pin down. According to the *OED*, the functions of *shall* and *will* have varied considerably over time. During the mid-seventeenth century the two start to sort themselves out by person: *shall* becomes the standard first person future auxiliary, with *will* serving in the second and third persons. This differentiation, however, applies largely to standard British English, and is subject to a myriad of conditions and qualifications upon which historical grammarians and lexicographers, not to mention the actual speakers of English, have never been able to agree.

Whatever the exact nature of this seventeenth-century innovation may have been, Lowth and his contemporaries were extremely successful in their efforts to formalize the change. Since the eighteenth century the shall/will rule has received widespread institutional support on both sides of the Atlantic. Noah Webster (1784) prescribed the differences between *shall* and *will* in an elaborate treatise on auxiliary verbs. Richard Grant White and the Fowler brothers subscribed to it, as we have already noted, and Wilson Follett devoted twenty-four pages of his *Modern American Usage* (1966) to a tortuous discussion of a rule that "can be coped with by anyone minded to take the pains without which expression can be accurate only by chance."

In the case of *shall* and *will*, the academician's opinion has become a higher law than usage, or logic, or even clarity. Nonetheless, a bold observer occasionally perceives a mismatch between paradigm and usage. According to Evans and Evans (1957), an American grammarian insisted as early as 1784 that *will* had always been the universal future auxiliary. The American diplomat and linguist George Perkins Marsh echoes this opinion in 1859, as do the British-born Evanses themselves a century later.

Today we find signs that the official stranglehold of the shall/will rule is weakening, at least outside Britain. The *New York Times* editor and language critic Theodore Bernstein (1965) calls *shall* too formal for general use, and William and Mary Morris (1975) hold that the "so-called" rule has been dead at least since MacArthur expressed his determination to retake the Philippines with "I *shall* return." Recent college writing handbooks are either silent on the matter of these auxiliaries, or advise that most writers use *will*. Their comments often reveal an incorrect belief that the shall/will distinctions were not innovations whose spread was encouraged by the language establishment, but a rule of English syntax that has always been with us, and that has only recently begun to decline. Thus the scholar and critic

Sheridan Baker laments the decline of *shall* in *The Complete Stylist* (1981), "The older distinctions . . . have faded," and H. Ramsey Fowler remarks in 1983, "*Will*, originally reserved for the second and third person, is now generally accepted as the future-tense auxiliary."

Despite these concessions to the universal *will*, the shall/will rule is still frequently regarded as necessary in exact or formal writing. The scholar and writing critic Thomas Kane (1983), who explains the matter as a question of usage (in its prescriptive sense) rather than grammar, hints his disapproval of those who do not indulge when he says, "The rule . . . is often ignored by modern writers. A careful, formal stylist observes it; most others do not." (672)

There are indications that Kane is correct in assuming the rule still functions as a powerful shibboleth. According to the Brown Corpus, *will* is about ten times more common than *shall* in edited prose. In contrast, H. L. Mencken (1937) reports a count of 1,305 *wills* to only 6 *shalls* (less than one half of one percent) in a study of transcribed telephone conversations. Although these word counts ignore context, they do suggest that *shall* is twenty times more common in writing than in speech. This in turn probably indicates that we perceive *shall* as a formal word, and that many writers and editors still follow some version of a rule now classified by most of our academies as obsolete.

Against the Tide

Usage critics not only attempt to impose rules on language, they may also urge us to forget a rule that has become invalid in their eyes. This too is not an easy task. Just as recent attempts to counter the effects of the shall/will rule have not been altogether successful, official efforts to suppress *an* before an aspirated *h* show every sign of failing.

The rule, according to Josephine Turck Baker (1904), requires *an* rather than *a* before a word beginning with an *h* that is pronounced, if the initial syllable of that word is unaccented: for example, *an historic*, but *a history*. The practice, which Baker favors, dates from a time when the initial *h* of words borrowed from Latin and French was always silent. However for most of these words aspiration has long since been restored, rendering *an* phonetically inappropriate. As early as 1882 Alfred Ayres opposes this use of *an* as obsolete. Henry Fowler (1926) agrees, calling *an historic* pedantic. Evans and Evans (1957) label the usage archaic; Theodore Bernstein (1965) claims it is improper on both sides of the Atlantic; and Morris and Morris (1975) find it one of the commonest mistakes in English today. Yet the form, perceived by many to be stylish, if not mandatory, persists despite requests from the usage critics that we relax our guard. Surveying a panel of teachers, writers, business executives, and linguists, the linguist Sterling Leonard (1932) reports *an historical* ranked as the most correct of two hundred thirty examples of disputed usage. Even Jimmy Breslin, whose journalism and fiction generally reveal a keen ear for colloquial English, writes jarringly in a recent novel of "an Hasidic Jew."

Ain't Misbehavin'

One linguistic form that is definitely not perceived as stylish is *ain't*, though curiously enough usage critics go against the tide on this issue just as they do on *an historic*. They are more likely than either lexicographers or the general public to defend *ain't*. Traditionally, *ain't* has been stigmatized by dictionaries, and a great cry of dismay went up when *Webster's Third New International Dictionary* (1961) dropped the labels 'colloquial' and 'illiterate' in its entry for the word. Although the dictionary's editors acknowledged that the form was generally condemned—it has in fact been called the most stigmatized word in English—critics objected to *W3's* contention that *ain't* is "used orally in most parts of the U.S. by many *cultivated* speakers esp. in the phrase *ain't I.*"

The *OED* derives *ain't* and its variant *an't* from *are n't, are not* (*r* being lost in standard British pronunciation during the eighteenth century). However, H. W. Fowler's comment is representative of the general feeling among usage critics that *ain't* is instead a contracted form of *am not*, and has a definite place in the language so long as it is restricted to the first person singular: "*A(i)n't* is merely colloquial, & as used for *isn't* is an uneducated blunder & serves no useful purpose. But it is a pity that *a(i)n't* for *am not*, being a natural contraction & supplying a real want, should shock us as though tarred with the same brush."

Alternative contractions for *am not* are generally rejected by the language critics as coming from the dialects of speakers who are considered inferior. Thus Richard Meade Bache (1869) condemns *amn't*, which he attributes to Negro minstrels. Other critics object to *amn't* as being Irish, although each generation of American children of all races and ethnicities seems to invent the form anew. In his *Comprehensive Guide to Good English* (1935), the linguist George Philip Krapp calls the variant *aren't I* "a kind of kittenish feminine English." Frank

Colby (1944) also condemns *aren't I,* while the language historian Arthur G. Kennedy (1935) sees *ain't,* though in disfavor, as the logical contraction of *am not.* Forgetting for the moment that *ain't* and *aren't* are probably the same word, Kennedy labels *aren't I* illogical.

In spite of these objections, *aren't I* seems to be less stigmatized than *ain't I* for the inverted first person singular negative contraction of *to be.* Although they treat *ain't* as nonstandard, Evans and Evans (1957) complain that the uncontracted *am I not* "is much too stiff for ordinary conversation and *amn't I?* is practically impossible to say." The Evanses are the only usage critics to relate *ain't* and *aren't* as British and American variants of the same word:

> In England *aren't I?* is considered acceptable spoken English. But in England the *r* in *aren't* is not pronounced. What is actually said is more like *aunt I?* The difference between the English *aren't I?* and the American *ain't I?* is simply the difference that we have in the two pronunciations of *tomato.* However, some Americans who would not say *ain't I?* feel that *aren't I?,* pronounced with its full American *r,* is very respectable. Others consider it affected. (s.v. *ain't*)

Of recent commentators, William Safire (1986) comes most actively to the defense of *ain't I?,* though he opposes any other use of *ain't.* The *New York Times's* resident language columnist rejects *aren't I,* citing Jacques Barzun in his support, because it is grammatically wrong, and because the uninverted form, *I aren't,* cannot exist. The insistence of usage commentators on limiting *ain't* to the first person, and to the negative, interrogative first person at that, is unrealistic since people who use *ain't* regularly use it for all persons and numbers, for positives and declaratives as well as negative questions. What the usageists ask is that only a tiny bit of *ain't* be welcomed into standard English, while the rest of *ain't* is to keep what they unanimously regard as its well-deserved stigma of illiteracy. Standard English users are already so conditioned to avoid *ain't* that they are not likely to change, and *ain't* users will not readily divest themselves of 98 percent of their paradigm just to please someone who is going to object to much of the rest of their usage anyway.

The *ain't/aren't* usage debate is interesting because it sets the critics of language and the users of language in uncustomary roles. The attempts by the critics to defend, or at least explain, a form that is treated by the general public as illiterate, together with their efforts to condemn as illiterate expressions which are favored by educated English writers and speakers, suggest a certain perversity. While the most conservative of the usage critics seem to think whatever is, is wrong, the *ain't* issue is only one of many indications that the usage critics do not always look closely at the present state of the language when they make their lists of preferred and proscribed phrases.

The Usage Index

Arthur Kennedy (1942) has claimed that "there is a well-defined and relatively unchanging list of questions of good usage," and the linguist John Algeo (1977) has demonstrated that the usage critics tend to feed on the work of their predecessors, rehearsing a canonical list of errors in English while ignoring the actual variations and changes that affect our language. Certainly a number of items have remained on the critical list since usage commentaries began. We repeatedly find discussions of *none is/are, different than/from/to, everyone ... their,* and *between you and I.* But there are a surprising number of words that seem to us perfectly innocent and acceptable, such as *lengthy, reliable, scientist,* and *ice cream,* which at one time or another were anathema in usage circles.

Now and then a new form is added to the usage index. *Alright,* which flourished in the twelfth and thirteenth centuries before it became quiescent, reappears in the late nineteenth century and quickly draws the attention of critics. Fowler treats it as a nonword: "There are no such forms as *all-right, allright,* or *alright,* though the last, if seldom allowed by the compositors to appear in print, is often seen . . . in MS." This paradox of denying and affirming in the same breath the existence of a stigmatized word is common among usage critics, who do not always find logical behavior convenient. So a panelist for the *Harper Dictionary of Contemporary Usage* claims that " 'irregardless' is not only a non-word but it is wasteful of breath," and the editors of that dictionary proclaim that "the words *grevious* and *grieviously* simply do not exist, although they turn up all too often in popular speech."

A few of the usage critics admit the existence of *alright,* and some are even willing to give this common spelling of *all right* a chance. While critic Frank Colby (1944) opposes it, his colleague Porter G. Perrin (1939) labels *alright* as informal and marks it as a form which bears watching. Evans and Evans (1957) find *alright* theoretically justifiable, on the analogy with *already,* though they warn that most people prefer the two-word alternative. The panelists of the *Harper Dictionary* reject *alright* by a margin of three to one, which means that a surprising twenty-five percent of these generally conservative usage arbiters are willing to permit it, compared for example with only seven percent who will allow *critique* to be used as a verb.

Another recent object of the usage critics' concern is *hopefully*. Though it was originally limited to the unobjectionable sense 'in a hopeful manner,' in the 1960s *hopefully* began to serve as a sentence adverbial meaning 'it is to be hoped.' If this new usage, sometimes called "dangling *hopefully*," existed earlier, it did not draw enough attention for inclusion in Evans and Evans (1957) or *Webster's Third* (1961). But once dangling *hopefully* was noticed, its rise to success, and to controversy, was rapid. By 1973 the *Barnhart Dictionary of New English Since 1963* is able to claim that, despite criticism, the new meaning of *hopefully* is thoroughly established.

The faults charged against *hopefully* are various, a sure sign that its detractors are grasping at straws. Apparently the form fills a lexical need, though some opponents of *hopefully* maintain that no such need exists, because we can always resort to the phrasal *it is to be hoped*. Others contend that *hopefully* cannot be used in its new sense because it already means something else. They may go so far as to coin even more objectionable alternatives to the neologism they oppose.

Of course it is all right for some words to have several meanings or uses. In *The Careful Writer* (1965), Theodore Bernstein allows *fortunately* and *luckily* to mean both 'in a fortunate or lucky manner,' and 'it is fortunate or lucky that,' and he notes that the German cognate *hoffentlich* conveys both sorts of meanings as well. Nonetheless Bernstein charges that "*hopefully* is not equal to the burden sometimes placed on it." There is no attempt to explain why *hopefully* is not as capable of multiple signification as other adverbs, but Bernstein concludes with a tacit recognition of the lexical gap that dangling *hopefully* fills: "What is needed is a word like *hopably*, which is not here being nominated for the job." Wilson Follett also condemns *hopefully* in his *Modern American Usage* (1966) as un-English and eccentric, "strain[ing] the sense of *-ly* to the breaking point," but like Bernstein he concedes that those writers who feel the need for such a word might make one up. He suggests *hopingly*.

The few defenders of the word among the *Harper Dictionary* panelists argue for its utility, but most of the opposition take a less than rational tack, resorting to hyperbolic epithets like *bastard, barbarism, jargon* and *sleazy,* equating the use of dangling *hopefully* with chalk squeaking on blackboards. But the more heated the objections become, the more speakers and writers of English seem to ignore them. While the laws of usage may at times accord with the opinions of the usage expert, more often than not usage and its critic are at odds.

The Laws of Usage

Although language does not readily lend itself to analysis in terms of concise formulae, this has not stopped language commentators from attempting to formulate the laws of usage. In his *Philosophy of Rhetoric* (1776), the Scottish rhetorician George Campbell defines acceptable language as that which is national, reputable, and current. As he explains it, for an expression to be standard it must not be confined to dialectal or provincial use, or to the language of unworthy speakers and writers, and it must be neither old-fashioned nor innovative. Many of Campbell's successors have adopted these criteria, despite the problems they entail. For example, national usage frequently turns out to be that of a prestige dialect which may be localized either geographically or socially; the repute of speakers and writers is often a matter of contention; and the very fact that some of us are always older or younger than others means a current form for some speakers must be either archaic or innovative for the rest.

Less hopeful than Campbell's theorem is Theodore Bernstein's assumption that we have an inescapable attraction to the linguistically incorrect. Bernstein does not think *whatever is*, is necessarily wrong. Rather, he feels that whatever is may become wrong given half a chance. This he formulates as Bernstein's Second Law, an analog of Gresham's law of economic theory that bad money drives out good. Bernstein's Second Law states simply, "bad words tend to drive out good ones." Bad words are defined as "secondary meanings that diverge from the true or primary meanings of words, and that come into use because of ignorance, confusion, faddishness, or the importunities of slang." Dangling *hopefully* would be for Bernstein a secondary, divergent, ignorant, importunate, downright bad word.

In "The Word Police" (1982), the critic Hugh Kenner warns us to "beware of any statement [about language] containing the phrase 'the real meaning.' " Since the academicians of usage invariably concern themselves with real meaning, it is with some degree of skepticism that we must approach the laws of a Campbell or a Bernstein. The intent of usage guides, which contain the laws of usage, is to regulate language behavior. In some cases they are effective. Some people may in fact successfully regulate their own practice according to the requirements of one or another of the language authorities. But on the broader, historical scale, it would seem that language users as a whole are unwilling or unable to submit to the tutelage of the reformers and guardians of our tongue.

This is not to say that we have no regard for correctness in language. If anything, we may be too much concerned with what is right and proper, too afraid that our misuse of a word, like our inability to remember which fork is for salad, will reveal our true ignorance, expose us to our audience as frauds and pretenders in matters of culture. The existence of usage guides is one more example of a concern for etiquette that is the hallmark of the socially insecure.

We look upon the usage guide, however, as a patent-medicine remedy, a quick fix for what may or may not be ailing language. It treats only symptoms, not causes, and even then only partially. Too many of the usage admonitions of the past have shown themselves to be ineffective. Often, by the time a usage critic complains about a form, it has become so much a part of the language that nothing can be done about it. It is ironic that we can treat usage guides as testimonials to the success of the aspects of language they seek to stigmatize. But, like a patent medicine, the usage guide is relatively cheap, easy to get, and easy to swallow. No thinking is necessary when taken as directed. It should be no surprise that the most popular treatment is also the least effective.

As something to lean on, the usage guide will continue to be necessary for the linguistically perplexed. It will calm to some extent their fear of being incorrect. But the usage guide also exacerbates that fear, encouraging language hypochondriacs to become even more reliant on its authority, thus assuring the success of future generations of guides. As far as language regulation goes, however, the guides often backfire. Readers, unable to follow the confusing or oversimplified recommendations of the critic to the letter, may make new mistakes, coming up, in their attempts to do the right thing, with new species of error, mutating the language to assure its adaptability, and giving the usage commentators still more to complain about.

This complex situation leads me to found my own academy of one in order to authorize my own law of language usage and change. Bernstein's Second Law followed a first one which had nothing to do with language, but concerned what happens to things like cufflinks when they are dropped. Baron's First Law, as I now offer it, presupposes, like the now popular expression, *first annual,* that others will follow. And the law, like others of its kind, must be approached with a healthy smattering of distrust. The law states, simply, that when a language change occurs, some people will—obviously—adopt the change, and others will oppose it; but most will either ignore or misunderstand those who comment on it. As a result, we can safely predict that efforts to control our language use are likely to go awry.

This law is clearly not as powerful as the fourth law of thermodynamics, which is also applicable both to usage critics and their critics, and which posits that the heat of the discussion is inversely proportional to the square of the knowledge, but until I can come up with Baron's Second Law (chapter 25), it will have to do.

11 Thank You for Sharing

> I'm thirty-three years old, went to college once and can
> still speak English if there's any demand for it.
>
> —Raymond Chandler

Chandler put these words in the mouth of his hard-boiled yet literate detective, Philip Marlowe, in his novel *The Big Sleep* (1939). The movie version more of us are familiar with, casting Humphrey Bogart in the lead, ages the *shamus* five years and changes his words slightly, but Marlowe's underlying message is the same: "proper" usage is something we turn on and off as the situation requires. Were *The Big Sleep* a more philosophical tome, Chandler might go on about the native speaker's ability to shift styles to accommodate both audience and purpose. But the book is a mystery novel, and Chandler practices an economy of style not generally found in language treatises. What Marlowe is saying, simply, is that real men and women don't always have to split their infinitives.

Were Marlowe looking for cases today, he would find that the demand certainly exists for speakers and for writers of English as well. But with that demand comes the obligation to control language just as it controls us. Philip Marlowe controls his patter. He may lack the explicit knowledge we get from studying language formally. For example, he probably does not know that *patter* comes from *Pater Noster,* the Latin 'our father' of the Lord's Prayer. But his intuitions are keen. He is used to choosing whether or not to split his infinitives. When he disguises himself as a bibliophile to sniff out a pornographer who is masquerading as a rare book dealer, Marlowe affects an academic tone, minces his words in a "polite falsetto," and, in the movie version, mispronounces *ceramics.* Implicit in this portrayal is a feeling that linguistic correctness can go too far.

It is easy, and as Marlowe shows, it is often fun, to criticize the critics of language. Their very subject, correctness in usage, opens them up to the closest of scrutiny on the part of their readers. William Safire's correspondents take great pleasure in pointing out his mistakes, and Safire is one of the few language commentators graceful enough to admit when he is wrong. Cannibalism is not unknown among the critics themselves. In *Paradigms Lost* (1980), John Simon, one of our sterner and less-forgiving authorities on correctness, includes an essay called "Guarding the Guardians," which enumerates in triumphant and merciless detail the graceless mistakes of those he regards as his less-adept, language-commentating colleagues.

It is almost a given that when a writer complains long and hard enough about a particular usage, you will be able to discover that stigmatized form in his or her speech or writing if you are very patient. But it is also true that even the most descriptive of linguists, who have ranged themselves against the language critics for a century or more, have pet peeves, kinds of language use that make them lose their professional objectivity and literally drive them up the walls. At the risk of committing the very sins I condemn, I must admit that my own usage peeves are as strong as anyone's. To put matters bluntly, I strongly censure *share, plans for the future, more importantly, between you and I,* and *fulfillment,* this last a new example of marketing doublespeak.

First, *share.* To me, sharing is what children do, or refuse to do, with their toys, or nations with their wealth. Or what St. Martin did with his cloak. Sharing means giving a piece of something to someone else. It comes from an Old English word meaning 'to cut,' and is related to the cutting tool, *shears.* The thing shared—whether material object or abstract idea or emotion—is something valuable to the giver and something the receiver desires to have.

Lately, however, sharing has become diluted in meaning (a more forgiving, neutral, or objective commentator would note that the meaning has become extended). According to the *OED Supplement,* the word first appears in the work of the Oxford Group (founded in 1921) and Moral Re-Armament (1938) as the equivalent of confessing one's sins or imparting to others a spiritual experience. Today *share* is rampant in religion, and has spread to psychology, and education. Indeed, it can be found in any almost any situation as a synonym for *tell.*

It is one thing for my four-year-old daughter to come home from nursery school and proudly tell me, "I shared very badly again today." But it is now commonplace for a host or moderator to acknowledge a speaker's words with "Thank you for sharing." I recently received a memo that began, "As I *shared with* you last year, this summer we've been busy installing new local area networks in residence hall sites." And an administrator told me, "I want to share with you that I went to a meeting last week." *Share* is even being used as a noun, for example, "I really enjoyed your share," as if the recitation were an actual portion of something profitable, like a corporation. But when *share* is used this way, I sense that no one has given anything to anybody, except perhaps a junk bond. So, when someone announces they are going to share something with me, I know they are going to tell me what I do not particularly want to hear, and I either look for a handy escape route, or settle in for the duration of a boring narrative. Imagine Julius Caesar saying to the Roman equivalent of a nightclub audience, "I want to share with you a funny thing that happened to me on the way to the forum."

As for *plans for the future,* my complaint is a simple one. The phrase is redundant. Planning implies the future. You cannot plan for the present or the past. Of course my objection is illogical, since language is full of repetition and redundancy. *Time and tide wait for nobody* is redundant because *tide* is really the Old English word for *time.* Similarly, grammatical concord is a redundant feature of language: the *s* with which we end the third person present tense of our verbs, as in *He goes; she thinks; it exists,* is redundant, since the subject of the verb has already announced that the noun in question is singular. None of our other verb forms requires this sort of number concord, yet we insist on that third person singular *s* so fervently that violations are severely condemned as nonstandard, ignorant, decadent, or even worse.

Linguists also know that all information systems—and language is an information system par excellence—require a certain amount of redundancy in order to combat those features which tend to disrupt communication, and which are called noise. But even though I know all this, I still find *future plans* noisy and objectionable. After all, we don't say *I watered the lawn with water,* or *Sally ate food for dinner.* Enough, if you will excuse the repetition, is enough.

More importantly is a phrase that should bring out the opponents of *hopefully* in full battle dress, yet it has sneaked by in apparent obscurity to replace *more important* as a sentence modifier. According to the *OED Supplement, more* and *most important* began to function as sentence adjectives in the early 1960s. The *OED* cites as typical, "More important, a carbon atom in a molecular configuration hardly resembles a free carbon atom." We find the adverbial form of the phrase functioning at the sentence level as early as the 1930s: "Most importantly, when the particles of a pair are brought together, they annihilate." This might initially suggest that the adverbial form is primary, and the adjective derivative, but I suspect that the dates are misleading, and that we did not begin collecting the earlier adjectival form until the adverbial form of the expression began its annoying spread.

The *OED* observes that in these expressions, *importantly* and *important* are interchangeable, and that *importantly* functions not adverbially but as a quasi-adjective. Randolph Quirk, et al. (1985) represent the grammatical consensus in classifying *most important* as a supplementive adjective clause, the equivalent of *What is most important is.* . . . As further evidence that the expression is an adjective and not an adverb, we see that all three degrees of the adjective, absolute, comparative, and superlative, can function in this fashion as sentence modifiers, either in full or in some kind of elliptical form:

1. What is (more, most) important, too, is that when the particles of a pair are brought together, they annihilate.

2. (More, most) Important, too, when the particles of a pair are brought together, they annihilate.

However, the absolute form of the adverb cannot stand alone sententially:

3. *Importantly, too, when the particles of a pair are brought together, they annihilate.

Such grammatical evidence would suggest that we are correct in analyzing the structure as adjectival rather than adverbial, and the few usage critics who comment at all on the problem prefer *more important* as the "grammatical" construction, though some find the adverb "acceptable" as well. Similarly, the *American Heritage Dictionary* rules *important* to be grammatical, though half of the *AHD* usage panel accept *importantly*. Edwin Newman (1974) complains, assuming textual evidence that does not in fact exist: "Why, after centuries, has more importantly, misused, begun to replace more important?" Three quarters of the panel of the *Harper Dictionary of Contemporary Usage* (Morris and Morris, 1975) prefer *important*, though some panelists strongly defend the adverbial construction, and the *New York Times* editor and usage critic Theodore Bernstein (1977) argues that both constructions are just fine.

I myself began noticing *more importantly* a number of years ago, and I must admit that while I side with the purists and grammarians favoring the adjective version of the phrase, I almost never encounter it anymore—certainly never in speech, and rarely, if ever, in writing. The rise of *more importantly* parallels almost exactly that of *hopefully*; they share the same grammatical function and spread at about the same time and pace from relative obscurity to near universality. Yet while *more importantly* draws only a few half-hearted objections from the random observer, *hopefully* is everywhere condemned and stigmatized.

Next in my current list of the cardinal sins of usage we come to *between you and I*. You cannot imagine how much it grieves me to find myself aligned with the prescriptive naysayers on this one.

In the best of all grammatical worlds, we would say *between you and me,* because the preposition *between* takes the object form of the pronoun. Explanations for the common deviation from this practice have not been entirely satisfactory. One popular theory has it that *between you and I* is a hypercorrection. According to this argument, some of us react with confusion to grammar-grinding schoolteachers who drilled generations of children in the evils of "Her and me went to the store," changing every *me* to an *I.* But it is unfair, and probably inaccurate, to blame this on the schools. In fact, the usage does not occur in speakers who were the objects of their teacher's derision. Rather it occurs in the speech of people whom we would otherwise characterize as well-educated users of standard English. Many of these people never said "Him and me went," and never received the grammatical admonition so vital to this explanation of the phenomenon, which is more or less restricted to the first person singular pronoun. They would never be caught dead saying "Between he and she," or "Albert gave the money to my sisters and they." Nor will these speakers be guilty of "Between you, I, and the lamppost." In addition, they can generally explain with some precision why such phrases are ungrammatical. Yet "between you and I" rolls off their tongues as surely as *e* follows *i,* except after *c.*

More convincing is the explanation that *you and I,* or the more general formula *(noun or pronoun) and I,* has simply become for many speakers an English idiom, a phrase whose order and inflection do not change no matter where it appears in a sentence. Idioms are notoriously resistant to the requirements of logic and grammar that affect ordinary language use. Claiming this usage as an idiom may simply beg the question, but it is clear that many items arousing the ire of the usage critics have in fact become idioms, words and phrases which through their frequency of use, have fossilized. They have found a kind of sanctuary, a place in our speech where they are immune from attack.

It may be that the true explanation of *between you and I* lies in a combination of hypercorrection and idiom. It is clear that many of us avoid *me* even when it is mandated, perhaps because we suspect it to be tainted with inelegance. This has led to an increase in the use of the reflexive, and it produces such ungainly expressions as "She gave it to Phil and myself." "She gave it to myself" occurs rarely, if at all, and no one says "She gave it to I." The problem presents itself only when the first person pronoun follows another noun or pronoun. "She gave it to Phil and I" is just another attempt to find a pronoun that sounds right in an object sequence.

The Doublespeak Award

Finally, to risk another sentence adverbial, we come to a new example of doublespeak, the *fulfillment* departments that are replacing *order* departments in businesses around the country. Doublespeak is a deceptive use of language—frequently a euphemism masking a truth or protecting an evil-doer, for example, when a war is called a police action, killing becomes termination with extreme prejudice, or a missile is named the Peacekeeper.

On a less life-threatening level, we find doublespeak in most areas of modern life. Freshmen use doublespeak, though without malice or intent to cover up, when they refer to the present in their essays as *the fast-paced modern world of today.* Here, wordiness takes the place of significance. More significantly (or is it *more significant?*), marketeers use doublespeak to help us over difficult buying decisions. *Cultured pearls* are real pearls, which is to say they are made by real mollusks, though human interference induces their formation, and it is not wise to drop them in wine. *Cultured marble,* however, is faked to look like the real thing, as is the latest product of our industrial culture, *cultured gold,* which is actually a kind of brass. *Virgin wool* has not been previously spun, woven, or used, and the expression is common in the advertising of fabric, but *100% virgin polyurethane foam,* which recently appeared in a newspaper advertisement for pillows, seems to have little real meaning, since the recycling of polymers is not yet a major consumer worry.

One national chain of discount stores, convinced that a house is not a home, speaks double when it calls its housewares department *homewares* instead. A similar derangement of the vocabulary helps sell goods that are no longer new. Clothes are not old or even recycled, and certainly not cast-off; instead they are *pre-worn.* Tape rental stores when they cull their stock now sell off *previously viewed* videos. And houses (or homes) and cars, particularly expensive ones, are no longer used, but *pre-owned* and *pre-driven.* An inspired local dealer advertises *renewed cars,* which suggests a freshness of purpose even new car dealers find difficult to imbue the product with.

The National Council of Teachers of English (NCTE) has waged war on doublespeak these many years, presenting annual awards, greeted with some fanfare by the press, for the most egregious of these all-too-common linguistic transgressions, usually committed by American government officials seeking to hide their ignorance or evade responsibility for their mistakes. It is only fitting then that my own small doublespeak award be presented to the NCTE (of which I am a member in what I hope will continue to be good standing) for its own brand of substantive abuse: replacing its order department with a fulfillment department.

Fulfill is an old and honorable English word, going back to Old English, and it literally means 'to fill full,' which, like *plans for the future*, is a pleonasm, since just as *plans* implies futurity, *fill* implies *full*. For most of its history, *fulfill* could serve as a synonym for *fill*, though so far as I know, no hypercritic ever complained about that redundancy. Now, however, most dictionaries consider the synonymy archaic, and in this century *fulfill* has taken on a certain amount of psychological baggage. *Fulfillment* has gone beyond *filling*—the mere acquisition of material goods—to a higher semantic plane. We seek fulfillment, that is, completion, a sense of achievement or wholeness, in our work, our hobbies, our families, our lives; we speak of experiences as being *fulfilling*—emotionally satisfying—or not. The opposite of fulfillment is frustration. But now, thanks to NCTE and other organizations engaged in direct mail advertising, we can find fulfillment as easily as picking up the phone and dialing toll-free. The publishing firm of Harper and Row now has a Book Fulfillment Department, as does rival Random House. Although the second edition of *The Random House Dictionary of the English Language* (1987) does not tell us that *share* can now mean 'tell,' it comes as no surprise that this company's lexicon is the first to record the new meaning of *fulfillment* as "the process in business of handling and executing customer orders" (s.v., sense 3).

It is clear that order departments became fulfillment departments by a simple chain of reasoning: because these departments are charged with *filling* orders, it was only a simple hop, skip, and doublespeak from *filling* to *fulfilling* for some bright marketing manager *cum* neologist. Besides delivering the goods, one major responsibility of order departments is to create satisfied customers and attract repeat business, or at least to discourage returns. Furthermore, the marketing psychologist would argue, customers will be less likely to return purchases to a fulfillment department, since such returns would imply a failure on the part of the buyer to produce the correct emotional response to the product. Besides, since *ordering* sounds so authoritarian and militaristic to today's sensitive ears, why not replace it with the one word that has come to signal the quintessence of satisfaction?

The reason not to do this is probably clearer to customers than it is to sellers: opening that box ordered from Pandora's latest catalogue or even from NCTE may indeed bring some degree of satisfaction, but it just doesn't go that extra mile from satisfying to fulfilling, at least not for me. It does however suggest somewhat impertinently that the order department clerks and the operators waiting at 800 numbers round the clock are concerned with my emotional well being—and I know that just is not true. They may want me to like the product, the speedy delivery, and the return policy. But so long as my credit card is good, they could care less (*sic*) about the state of my frustrations. NCTE is supposed to fight the good fight for English teachers, but when that organization abandons clear, precise, plain language for the obfuscating presumption of *fulfilling* the dreams and not the orders of the membership, then it is time to bring the Doublespeak Award home where it belongs.

A Contradiction in Terms

It is my job to collect language variants and explain them. But it is not my job to like everything I find. I may not be bothered by dangling *hopefully* but I dislike *between you and I* and the constellation of analogous expressions. I notice them too much. They make me wince and I must consciously suppress a desire to correct the speaker who utters them. If this is inconsistent with my stance as a maddeningly noncommittal descriptivist, so be it. Walt Whitman contradicted himself with impunity, and his mentor, Emerson, covered his own tracks by calling foolish consistency the hobgoblin of little minds.

Perhaps my own positive reaction to *hopefully* and negative response to *more importantly* are conditioned by a desire to side with the underdog and even the odds. Or perhaps I am as inconsistent as all language observers ultimately prove to be. If language is a law unto itself, operating by turns logically, illogically, and psychologically, then critics too must be permitted their unreasonable preferences. More important (not, if you please, *more importantly*), even permissive linguists may be human, and I have a life as a writer and editor as well, occupations that require me to worry long and hard in search of the right word.

One locution I have been worrying over recently is new to my ears, and I can't decide whether or not I like it. So far, I don't think I have used it. The phrase is *What I'm hearing is,* the reciprocal of *What I'm saying is,* and it is used by committee chairs or other group leaders to summarize what the leader surmises the group consensus to be, or what the group wants the leader to do. I'm not sure it originates with committees—it may very well come from talk shows or religious discussions, where it connects with *I hear you,* a popular expression which means 'I understand where you're coming from,' or 'I agree.'

Ron Butters, editor of *American Speech*, suggests that *what I'm hearing* derives from clinical psychology. In any case, it is synonymous with *in other words*, but has in addition an intimation that action is to follow summary. What makes the phrase positive is its refreshing stress on the role of the chair not as independent actor but as interpreter of the committee's will. What makes it negative is the air of false democracy it may suggest: what the chair hears in the committee's presence does not have to be what the chair does after the committee has gone home. Perhaps my experiences both as a committee member too often ignored and a committee chair too impatient with the members have left me too cynical to recognize the change in group dynamics that *what I'm hearing* suggests. Nonetheless, I suspect that *what I'm hearing* will sooner or later come to mean, not a true summary, but 'what I want to hear.' As such, it will make a handy complement not to *What I'm saying*, but to *share*, which has come to mean 'that which I don't want to hear.'

All of us who live in this busy postmodern age of today (and *postmodern* is itself a contradiction in terms) must realize we can no longer pretend to true objectivity, whether in language or anything else, for as Woody Allen suggested in his film *Love and Death*, objectivity is really subjectivity in disguise. Let others share their future plans with myself. I would prefer not to. What you should be hearing from all this is, to paraphrase the coach, that language isn't everything, and it may not be the only thing. But it won't be over till it's over. Fulfillment cannot occur at least until a large soprano, or perhaps a tenor, sings.

12 Dialect Notes

[handwritten margin note: It's like closing your eyes ... when you speak ... accent can't until he speaks]

Although it is generally agreed that English in the United States and Canada is much less varied than it is in Great Britain, we have all come in contact, to our delight and occasionally to our dismay, with some of the regional and social differences in American English. We encounter dialect variation when we travel, or when we move to a new community, or simply when we turn on our television sets.

Despite this exposure to the varieties of English in the New World, there are some common but false assumptions about dialect variation that we should correct. In effect, dialect has become a loaded word. For one thing, we often think of dialect in the United States in terms of north and south, and it is commonly asserted that there is no dialect in the Mid- or far west. The north/south division is a gross oversimplification of language patterning in this country, and while midwesterners may claim that they use pure English rather than a dialect, linguists know such claims are downright wrong. The linguistic map of Illinois shows why. It is a solidly midwestern state that crosses three major geographic dialect boundaries (northern, north midland, and south midland), and that contains significant urban, suburban, and rural populations as well as a great mix of ethnic and racial settlements. In short, Illinois, in the heart of the Midwest, presents about as complex a dialect picture as you can expect to find.

In addition, we generally think of dialect as something negative, or nonstandard. Dialect speech is loosely considered inferior or at least very informal language, deficient in its ability to convey information. We also presume that it reveals the poor education and low social status of the user. Actually there are formal and informal dialects (*registers* may be the better term), as well as standard and nonstandard ones. Furthermore, standard English is no less of a dialect than any other variety of the language. It is no better and no worse, no more expressive or flexible or beautiful, than any other English dialect. It simply is the variety of English that found itself in the right place at the right time, the dialect that happened to be used by "the right people," those who came to direct the political, economic, and literary affairs of England and eventually, the United States. Because *dialect*

107

is a word with so many negative associations, some linguists have come to prefer the more neutral term *variety* to describe the types of language used by the different speakers of English around the world, though I use both dialect and variety interchangeably here.

We also wrongly assume that dialect is a feature of other people's language, not our own. This is only natural. Our language sounds perfectly normal to us, while the language of strangers or "foreigners" sounds accented. In fact strangers regard our speech as accented or unusual as well, for everyone's language is a dialect of sorts.

We also tend to think of dialect differences simply in terms of accent, or pronunciation, when variation actually extends to vocabulary and grammar as well. Differences in accent are perhaps the most noticeable features of dialect, and if pronunciation is different enough from what we are used to, we may have some initial difficulty separating out the words a speaker is using. As a result speech may sound more rapid or more drawn out than it really is, and this in turn can provoke some embarrassment.

I remember traveling through Kentucky and stopping at a small convenience store. (I am convinced they are called convenience stores ironically, for nothing in them is easy to find, the service is slow, and the prices are inconveniently high.) When I got to the checkout the clerk said to me something short and staccato that sounded like "Biáfya." He repeated this puzzling motto several times, each time a little louder (a futile tactic we use with children and speakers of other languages when they don't seem to understand what is crystal clear to us), and I realized that what I took for a word was actually a complete sentence. Listening carefully for word boundaries, on the third or fourth go round I finally pieced out enough for the message to come together as, "Will that be all for you?" Once I understood what was being said, I felt about as stupid as the clerk had begun to assume I was. The words didn't sound rushed and breathless, but more or less normal.

As the foregoing anecdote illustrates, differences in pronunciation are generally only temporary barriers to communication. Lexical differences exist as well, and in some cases these may cause embarrassment if a taboo term is involved. An American complimenting someone's *vest* in England is actually praising an undergarment. The British call our erasers *rubbers,* and when *they knock someone up* they mean to call for, or visit them.

In most cases, however, lexical variation merely requires that we learn new terms for familiar things. Water coolers are *bubblers* in Rhode Island and Wisconsin. A carbonated beverage is *pop* in Michigan, *tonic* in Massachusetts (where ordering *soda* will get you club soda) and *soda* in New York (where calling for *tonic* produces quinine water). For many in the south, south midland, and southwest, the trademark terms *Coke* or *Coca-Cola* (sometimes *Co' Cola*) now refer to any bubbly soft drink no matter what the brand.

Frequently the less common of two synonymous words will receive a distinct or specialized meaning. In the north we put our purchases into *bags* at the grocery store, while in the south the containers are called *sacks*. To a Northerner, *sack* may have a narrower connotation, for example, 'a large bag to store feed, or flour,' while a Southerner may think of *bags* in some other restricted or metaphoric fashion. Similar distinctions apply to *pail* (the more northerly term) and *bucket* (more common in the south).

I have moved around quite a bit in my academic career, from New York to New England to the Midwest, and I have both studied and been affected by the language of each area. I still say *idear* for *idea* and I stand *on* line while everyone around me stands *in* line. But I have learned to stretch out the vowel of *that* and *hat* in order to make myself understood; I can respond when I am called *Dinnis* instead of *Dennis*; and I never pronounce *coffee* the same way twice.

Speaking of coffee, there are three dialect items that I have encountered since coming to the Midwest which altogether fascinate me: *coffee and, might could* (an item linguists call the double modal), and *anymore* used in a positive sense.

Coffee and

Coffee and is an expression I have only heard in parts of the Chicago area, or the Chicagoland area, as it is known on the local radio and TV stations. For readers unfamiliar with this phrase, it is a deliciously incomplete invitation, either spoken or written. "Come over Sunday for coffee and" means coffee and whatever food might be appropriate for the occasion or the time of day: coffee and cake, coffee and ice cream, coffee and doughnuts, coffee and bagels. According to the *Dictionary of American Regional English* (*DARE*), the expression is not limited to Chicago. It goes back to the early 1900s, and in the past was frequently associated with cheap hash house or skid row diner meals of coffee and a roll. The phrase may also refer to coffee with cream and sugar, what is called regular or light coffee, or *coffee with* in other parts of the country. This sense is similar to that of *cider-and*, 'cider mixed with spirits or some other ingredient' (*OED*).

The Double Modal

The double modal, or double auxiliary, is a feature of some southern speech, though it is found in the north as well. Modal verbs are ones like *can, may, might, shall, should, will,* and *would,* and in standard English we generally use only one modal per verb phrase, for example "You might read that if you have some time." There are many kinds of double modals, some of the commonest being *used to could, may can,* and *might could,* as in, "You might could do that" (triple modals have also been reported by dialect observers). The double modal is a fairly stigmatized form, and users who become conscious of it may try to eradicate it from their speech. It was not long after coming to central Illinois that I first read about double modals, and not much after that when I encountered my first *might could* from someone who had lived in Danville, Illinois all her life. My excitement at this little bit of linguistic fieldwork was doubled because this same woman also used a positive *anymore.*

Anymore

Though double modals may sound strange if you are not accustomed to them, their meaning is generally clear. However, the use of *anymore* without a negative constraint makes no sense at all to someone not familiar with the construction, and many refuse to believe it can occur in English. *Anymore* means 'at the present time,' and every English speaker recognizes its appropriateness when accompanied by a negative: "You can't trust what people tell you anymore." But when we encounter something like "Anymore people are wanting no-wax vinyl in their kitchens," where the word still means 'nowadays,' quite a few of us will balk and reject the sentence as meaningless as well as ungrammatical.

On the other hand, in areas where positive *anymore* occurs it is considered perfectly normal in both prestige and nonprestige speech. The positive *anymore* has a long history and, while it may have originated in northern Ireland, it is found across a wide expanse of the United States, being rarest in New England and most common in a wide band stretching from upstate New York through Tennessee, Indiana, Illinois, Iowa, Oklahoma, and Oregon, as well as Southern California. Usage critics generally frown on this kind of *anymore,* finding it incorrect. Theodore Bernstein, in *The Careful Writer* (1965), calls positive *anymore* "an unacceptable though not uncommon casualism," and the generally liberal usage guide, the Reader's Digest *Success with Words* (1983), finds only the negative *anymore* acceptable.

I myself have not integrated double modals or positive *anymore* into my speech, although linguists do run the risk of unconsciously adopting the forms they study, and I may eventually succumb to *anymore,* at least in speech. Nor do I use *coffee and,* for the simple reason that we seem to invite people over for full-fledged dinners or for tea. But I am strangely enamored of these three dialect terms, and discuss them whenever the subject of variation in English comes up.

One final dialect story shows the degree to which linguists can become entangled in their work. A colleague of mine, born and bred in New Orleans, where the *r*'s that occur in written words are left elegantly unpronounced in speech, once asked me in the strictest of confidence to enlighten him on a matter that had troubled him for years: "Dinnis," he said, raising the vowel in my first name to new heights, "I can ask you without embarrassment because you are a linguist, and you'll understand." And then came the question: "Where (or more exactly, /hweah/) is the *r* in *Harvard?*" He was shocked to find that there was not one *r* but two, or as I put it rather indelicately, "They is two of 'em," but he was relieved again to learn that, just like folks from Louisiana, his New England counterparts dropped both of the *r*'s in speech anymore, and they might could have some trouble spelling the name of the college as well.

III Language Trends

13 The Etymology Trap

> Man is an etymologizing animal.
>
> —A. S. Palmer, 1883, *Folk-Etymology*

Word coiners, and critics of language in general, often rely on etymology to justify their efforts. But there is a lot of guesswork in etymology, and reliance on it can produce some unanticipated effects. Etymology is the study of the original or literal meanings of words. The etymology of *etymology* reveals that the word itself comes from Greek *etymos*, 'true,' (which is actually related to the English word *sooth*, as in *soothsayer*) and *logos*, 'discourse.' When it is on target, etymology illuminates relationships between words quite different in appearance. We can show for example that English *hemp* and Latin *cannabis* are one and the same, explaining the differences in terms of regular and predictable sound shifts. When we *etymologe* (this rare verb was last recorded by the *OED* in 1611—*etymologize* is a bit more current) we learn that *nostril* comes from a descriptive compound meaning 'nose-hole'; that *skirt* and *shirt* are synonyms, or doublets, from Old Norse and Old English, respectively; that *a nickname* was originally *an ekename*, 'an also or extra-name'; or that the *h* in *hangnail* has grown upon an original Old English *angnaegl*, where *ang* means 'painful' (as in *anguish*), and has nothing whatever to do with hanging.

The eighteenth-century philologist Rowland Jones exhibits a naive faith in the derivation of words when he predicts in 1771 that etymology might be useful to prevent a war between England and the American colonies. But not all opinions of etymology have been so sanguine. Its critics are only too happy to portray etymology as an enterprise which is frequently unscientific if not completely frivolous.

Ben Jonson parodies etymology when he traces *breeches* to *bare riches*, "when a gallant beares all his Ritches in his Breeches" (1599). Jonathan Swift does much the same in his *Discourse to Prove the Antiquity of the English Tongue* (1765), deriving *Mars*, the war god, from "Kiss my a—se." Perhaps the granddaddy of all false etymology is the serious attempt to derive words from their opposites, for example

115

Latin *lucus*, 'a grove,' from *non lucendo*, 'having no light.' After all, it was argued, no light can penetrate a dense clump of trees.

Some popular explanations of words are difficult to snuff out. The source of Latin *sincerus* remains unknown, but I vividly remember one of my high school English teachers, eager to impress upon us his familiarity with the ancient languages, recounting the derivation of *sincere* from the Latin *sine cera*, 'without wax.' He told the class that the word served to authenticate used (or for those more upscale models, *previously owned*) Roman statuary that had not been patched up with the classical equivalent of body lead. Another false derivation frequently accompanies *bloody* (as in, "You're a bloody liar"), a common intensifier in Renaissance English which later became taboo in Britain. Although Weekley (1946) clearly demonstrates that the word is nothing more than the adjectival form of *blood*, the myth persists that the taboo derives instead from a condensation of the epithet *By our lady*, just as *zounds* comes from *God's wounds* and *'sblood* is from *God's blood*. Similarly while *cabal* derives from the Hebrew *kabbala*, which refers to mystical interpretation of the scriptures, it is often and inaccurately thought to be an acronym for Clifford, Ashley, Buckingham, Arlington, and Lauderdale, five ministers of Charles II known for their secret plots and intrigues. *Beefeater*, the name applied to a Yeoman of the Guard, is routinely explained as an Englishing of the French *buffetier*, supposedly one who waits at the sideboard, or *buffet*. However, *buffetier*, which exists only in Old French, means 'wine merchant,' and has no apparent connection with the British usage. According to Weekley, *beefeater* is a transparent term, simply referring to someone like a modern football player who is fed beef for strength.

Even when an etymology is correct, it may provide misleading information about the word's source. For example, *dandelion* (*taraxacum officinale*) does come to us in the early fifteenth century from the French *dent-de-lion*, 'lion's tooth.' Interestingly, though, the standard French word for the weed (or flower, if you insist), has always been *pissenlit*, reflecting not the physical description of its sawtooth leaves, but the plant's well-known diuretic powers. *Dent-de-lion* is the plant's "vulgar" name in French, as the *Grand Larousse Universel* informs us. In English, the status of these two terms is exactly reversed, which may say something about the role of euphemism in our language: while *dandelion* is perfectly good English, *pissabed* is a stigmatized form firmly rooted in dialectal folk speech.

Many writers, influenced by the existence of such etymologically transparent words as *dandelion* and *pissenlit*, have adopted the popular notion which goes back to the Greeks, that language is always transparent, that spelling and pronunciation must reflect a word's origin and meaning. They are easily convinced that words which look or sound alike really are alike. Since we do not analyze language in a vacuum, our prejudices and cultural assumptions may further steer our thoughts about English into error. For example, *girl*, which originally referred to a child of either sex, is derived by the great dictionary maker Noah Webster from Latin *gerula*, "a young woman employed in tending children and carrying them about."

Girl has also been derived over the years from other words that reflect the sexual preoccupations of the etymologue more than the true history of our language. Although the actual origin of the word is clouded in history, one influential commentator saw in *girl* the Greek word for whore. Others erroneously relate *girl* to Latin *garrula*, 'talkative,' because girls were presumed to talk more than boys, as well as to the Italian for weathercock, *girella*, because girls were supposed to be fickle. Other incorrect sources for *girl* are *girdle* (a belt worn by brides, to be removed by their husbands, so the explanation goes), *gull*, 'a gullible person, one easily cheated,' and Old Norse *gaurr*, 'a clumsy, stupid person.'

The word *woman* suffers similar degradation at the hands of the etymologists. *Woman* comes from the Old English compound *wifman*, literally 'female person,' but even today's more enlightened linguists disagree over the original sense of the Indo-European ancestor of *wife*. At best, modern opinion finds the origin of *wife* to be unknown. However, both *woman* and *wife* have received from English word sleuths an astonishing number of incorrect interpretations, most of them based on the presumed sexual or domestic function of women. One school of thought derived *woman* from *womb-man*, that is, 'person with a womb,' even though *womb* originally meant 'belly' and was as such an anatomical feature of men as well as women. Another group correctly traced *woman* to *wife-man*, but then incorrectly derived *wife* from *weaver*, assuming that spinning and weaving were the primary occupations of early woman. Yet a third tradition steeped in fundamentalism read *woman* as *woe to man*, alluding without linguistic basis to the Judeo-Christian story of the Edenic expulsion and its consequences. These explanations may sound far-fetched, but they are still noised abroad by the linguistically naive.

Such serious but wrongheaded analyses of words prompt the bad reputation of etymology over the centuries. The dialectologist Samuel Pegge wrote, "Nothing in the world is more subject to the power of accident, of fancy, of caprice, of custom, and even of absurdity, than etymology" (1818), and the linguist Max Müller warned that "the etymology of a word can never give us its definition" (1860). Perhaps the most familiar attack on etymology is that attributed to Voltaire, who is said to have called it "a science where the vowels mean nothing, and the consonants very little at all."

The mistakes of earlier generations of etymologists are fruitful in that they tell us something of the prevailing attitudes toward language. But language is an interest all of us share, and nonprofessionals are in the business of explaining words as well. Often we take an unfamiliar word or name, one whose origins have become obscure, and recast it in a form that means something to us, thus rendering it familiar. This process is called folk or popular etymology, and it results in such expressions as *hangnail*, mentioned above, and *winding one's way*.

The original phrase in the latter instance is *wending one's way*, the verb *wend* coming from Old English *wendan*, 'to go.' In Modern English *wend* doesn't seem to mean much of anything (far from being transparent, its connection with *went*, the past tense form of *go*, is not apparent to those unschooled in the history of English), and it is only natural to replace *wend* with *wind*, a word similar in form, whose association with *winding roads* reinforces the substitution. In the same way the virtually obsolete *wreak* in *wreak havoc*, which comes from Old English *wrecan*, 'to harm, punish, inflict,' frequently appears as the related but still current *wreck*, producing *wreck havoc*, a phrase used by the Harvard-educated former head of my own department.

Folk etymology also gives us the town Bob Ruly in Arkansas, not named for a founder or early settler, as is so often the case with American place names, but Englished from the original French (the area was part of the Louisiana Purchase) Bois Brûlé, which means 'burnt woods.' Place names are often associated through the "folk" process with products or foods. The French do not eat French fries, but they do of course eat *frites*, or fries, nor do Belgians sell Belgian waffles though *gauffres*, or waffles (the terms are etymologically identical), are commonly sold on Belgian city streets. In these cases, the place name identifies for outsiders what the locals take for granted. But in some cases, we associate a place with a thing when residents of that place do not. There is no *New York cut steak* to be found on menus in the Big Apple, though you will find there the *Kansas City steak* absent from the restaurants of the heartland. Panama hats actually come from Ecuador, and Stilton cheese is not made in that English town, though it is sold there.

Additionally, folk etymology is responsible for a restructuring of certain words which in turn facilitates the formation of new words. For example, *helicopter* is a modern coinage based on the Greek combining form *helico-*, 'spiral,' from *helix*, and the root *pter*, 'wing,' as in *pterodactyl* and *archeopteryx*. Since no native English words begin with *pt*—we couldn't begin to know how to pronounce them—we sensibly interpret the first part of *helicopter* as the prefix *heli-*, which allows us to produce the clipped form *'copter* and the compounds *heliport* and *helipad* (surely *helicoport* and *helicopad* would be ridiculous in English). A *helideck* is where helicopters land on offshore drilling rigs. Similarly *amphibian*, composed of *amphi*, 'both,' and *bios*, 'life,' referring to a creature (later a craft as well) that can function on land or in the sea, has spawned *airphibian*, referring to a combination ground-air vehicle. And *bikini*, the two-piece bathing suit which derives from the name of the Pacific atoll which was the site of early atomic bomb tests, has been reinterpreted as beginning with the prefix *bi-*, 'two,' making possible the names for the even briefer *trikini* and *monokini*.

We treat as a prefix or removable element the *ham* in *hamburger*, though it is really just the first syllable of the German city *Hamburg*, whence the original name of the delicacy, *Hamburg steak*. During World War I, and again in World War II, when *hamburger* revealed its geographic origins only too well, the British and Americans, reluctant to give up the food though equally reluctant to pronounce its Germanic name, switched the label from *hamburger* to *liberty sandwich*. The freestanding bit of chopped meat became a *Salisbury steak*, but not after the English cathedral city. Instead it is named for the nineteenth-century British physician who advocated a diet of well-cooked ground beef with an accompanying beverage of hot water thrice daily as a cure for tuberculosis, gout, atherosclerosis, and just about anything else. Today the geographical reference of *hamburger* is lost, and the root has become *burger*, to which we freely add almost anything palatable that comes to mind: *cheeseburger, baconburger, tacoburger, fishburger, pizzaburger, soyburger*, even *Burger Bits* (a kind of dog food).

But just as our names can be pliable, so are they often conservative reminders of what our language used to be. The name of the *falcon*, the hunting bird made famous in *The Maltese Falcon* as the stuff that dreams are made of, is generally pronounced as it is spelled, with an *l*. Many words containing *al* come to us from French, where they are rendered without that letter: *falcon/faucon, palm/paume, almond/amande, salmon/saumone*. But while the tendency nowadays, at least in American English, is toward the pronunciation of the *l*, particularly in *falcon*, the name *Faulkner* still resists the shift to a spelling pronunciation.

Likewise the *th* in words like *theater* and in such names as *Anthony* and *Elizabeth* was pronounced as if it were a simple *t* (in earlier spelling the *h* did not occur), and while these words have long since adapted their pronunciation to their written form, the nicknames *Tony* and *Betty* recall for us the original pronunciations. *Thomas* and *Theresa* (known familiarly as *Tom* and *Terry*) and the river *Thames* did not succumb to the fashions of this particular sound change, and there is no indication they will do so in the near future.

14 At a Loss for Words

There is nothing so hard to kill as a word.

—Arthur Gilman, *Short Stories from the Dictionary*

Folk etymology produces new words like *sparrow grass* for *asparagus*. One characteristic of new words in English is that they are highly visible. We spot them in the press, we hear them on radio and television, or in conversation. Their newness is often striking, though it may also be subtle—new words can creep up on us or jump out at us. Sometimes we are pleased, sometimes annoyed, by these innovations. But we do notice them. We are not aware of all of the several thousand new words which enter English every year, of course. Most of these are technical terms: we encounter them only if they impinge directly on our lives. Only a few hundred become part of the standard, or everyday, language available to all of us. Other neologisms are ephemeral. They arise out of a particular need; their impact is brief; and they fade from use when the need for them fades. Many of us never even knew they were around.

There are lots of reasons why new words are born—advances in technology, new discoveries, social and political changes, borrowings from foreign languages, and of course our continual urge to play with English, to combine and recombine its parts just for the fun of it. But how and why do old words drop from use?

Just as words can be born, so they can die. They die when we stop using them, but we are seldom aware enough of their loss to pinpoint the moment of their disappearance. It is far easier to notice a neologism, a strange or interesting newcomer to our vocabulary, no matter how temporary its life may be, than to notice that we have stopped using a word or phrase. Ironically, we cannot mark the absence of a word until we encounter its presence: we hear it revived, or find it in an old book or magazine, or we dredge it up from memory. Only then do we notice that we haven't seen that particular word for some time, and we may wonder if anyone still uses it. There is often no easy way to find that information out.

Sometimes word death is not complete: a living fossil survives the catastrophe. This is the case with *piecemeal*, which retains the once-active suffix *-meal*, 'measure.' Words in *-meal* included *cuclermeal*, 'by the spoonful,' *cupmeal, dropmeal, flockmeal, footmeal, gobbetmeal, heapmeal, inchmeal, jointmeal, limbmeal, littlemeal, lumpmeal, parcelmeal, pennymeal, poundmeal, sheafmeal, stemmeal, stickmeal, tablemeal* and *yearmeal*, as well as the jocular nineteenth-century nonce-coinage *pagemeal. Answer* retains the Old English prefix cognate with the still-active German *ent-* and the Latin *anti-*, 'against.' And *with-*, 'away, back,' now found only in *withdraw, withhold,* and *withstand*, once produced such words as *withbear*, 'carry away,' *withbuy*, 'redeem,' *withcall*, 'recall,' *withchoose, withfare* (also, *withscape*), 'escape,' *withgo*, 'disappear,' *withhave*, 'resist,' *withlie* (also, *withfight*), 'oppose,' *withnay* (also *withtell*), 'deny,' *withspeak*, 'contradict,' *withstay*, 'withstand,' *withtake*, 'withdraw,' and *withturn*, 'avert.' The *wan-* of *wanton* is a prefix that is basically extinct. Equivalent to the negative *un-*, it was productive in Old English and produced a number of northern dialect terms and is responsible for *wanbelief, wanbode, wancheer*, 'grief,' *wancouth*, 'uncouth,' *wandeedy*, 'mischievous,' *wanearthly, wanease, wanfortune, wanhap, wanlit, wanluck, wanuse* and *wanweird*, 'bad fortune.'

Is It Dead?

When lexicographers prepare a new edition of a dictionary, they must classify words that are on the wane as either archaic (found only in old texts) or obsolete (not in current use except for intentional antique flavoring). They must further decide which such words they can safely discard, for obsolete words do occur in works familiar to today's readers, for example, the King James translation of the Bible, or the plays of Shakespeare, and dictionary readers will need to know about them.

Indeed, an influential text can act as an artificial life support system for the obsolete words it contains. Old but widely read books preserve some words in fossilized or mummified form which otherwise would have died. Such words, when they occur outside the framework of their source text, tend to allude to its original context. According to Margot Lawrence (1986), the popularity of the *Book of Common Prayer* (1662) in the English-speaking world is responsible for the continued life of two words: *vouchsafe*, which does not appear in the King James Bible (1611), and the verb *to wed*, a rare form in the King James version, which prefers *marry* instead. The marriage service in that prayer book has also fostered the continued use of *plight* and *troth*, two otherwise uncommon words. And John Moore (1961) suggests that we owe the survival of *damsel* and *raiment* to the Authorized Version.

The decision to mark a word as disused is not always simple, for lexicographers cannot always agree on the interpretation of the written record of our language. Some kinds of writing are intensely conservative (traditionally law, religion, and poetry), and as we have seen with the Saxonists, during periods of antiquarian interest in the Renaissance and again in the nineteenth century, old and disused words are revived, some only for a time, others for a much longer cycle of life.

Moreover, in many cases only one particular sense of a word may be on the wane, while others retain varying degrees of currency. Although *Webster's Second New International Dictionary* (1934) labels *vouchsafe* as archaic, the *OED* marks only certain of its senses as such, and many more recent desk dictionaries do not question the word's currency at all. Nonetheless, it is clear that *vouchsafe* cannot occur in a text without conjuring up an antique or specialized flavor. In the same fashion, *plight* and *troth* generally occur together, and always have some allusion to marriage, but the *Random House College Dictionary* (1980) marks *troth* as archaic, while it gives the verb to *plight*, 'pledge,' no such classification (the verb is not related to the noun *plight*, 'trouble, fix, predicament,' which comes from *plait*, 'fold, braid'). *Webster's Second* marks only one sense of *plight* as obsolete, while the *OED* is probably closest to the mark in calling *plight* "now chiefly poetic or rhetorical."

Changing Times

In a few cases, not just individual senses or whole words but entire groups of words disappear from our language. In Old English, there were a variety of synonyms for man and woman. *Mann* did not initially mean 'adult male' in Old English, but referred instead to human beings in general. The most common words for man in the 'male' sense were *wer* (the first element in the compound *werewolf*, or 'man-wolf') and *wæpmann*, literally 'weaponed person,' a sexual rather than a military allusion. In addition we find *esne* (indicating a male of low status), *guma, secg,* and *beorn* (the last two occurring only in poetry).

For 'woman' the common terms were *wif* and *wifmann* (corresponding to modern English *wife* and *woman*), as well as the less-frequent *fæmne, meowle,* and *ides* (the last being poetic). But as we see from Modern English, with its occasionally embarrassing richness of verbiage, only *man, woman,* and *wife* survive. It is true that other words have been borrowed or co-opted to fill the synonym gap: *person, individual, lady* (an Old English word, true, but one which, like *lord,* referred at the time specifically to the nobility), and *gentleman* serve more or less adequately, as well as *guy, boy,* and *girl,* though the last two generally connote youth or servility.

The inevitability of changing times may be the basic force that dooms our words. It is not entirely clear why we lost a few of our Old English words for people, or why other words took their place. More striking, perhaps, is the loss of the massive number of Old English words for war and death. Thomas De Quincey, writing on the English language in 1839, characterized Anglo-Saxon as a language with a vocabulary of only six to eight hundred words, "most of which express some idea in close relation to the state of war." Of course this is an exaggeration, but according to Janet Aiken (1930), a more objective student of our language, there are more than fifteen separate terms for war or battle in the Old English epic, *Beowulf.* In addition, *guth,* the primary word for war, compounds with over thirty other terms to produce words such as war-song, war-strength, and war-avoider (that is, coward). So complete is the loss of most of these terms today that we cannot begin to guess at the fine distinctions separating *guth* from its synonyms *beade, fyrd, gewinn, heathu, hild, orlege* and *wig.*

Of the dozen or so Anglo-Saxon words meaning *kill* or *die,* few survive into Middle English, and four which still occur today have lost some of their connection with death. *Shoot,* from *sceotan,* can now simply mean 'to wound,' and must generally be supplemented (*shoot to kill, shot to death*) to indicate fatality. *To fell* is used nowadays more for trees than people. *Quell,* from Old English *cwellan,* now means to quieten or subdue (it is not clearly related to Modern English *kill,* which does not appear until Middle English and means at first 'to strike or knock'). One word, *sweltan,* has completely lost its warlike connection: *swelter,* which meant at first 'to die,' and later, 'to faint or be near death,' now means only 'to be very hot.'

Unfortunately for the inhabitants of the English countryside, the loss of our native war terms was not triggered by a long period of peace. Aiken does argue that the hundred or more Anglo-Saxon military words declined by the tenth century because the war-oriented nomadic Germanic peoples who migrated to England in the fifth century had finally settled down and become more interested in agriculture than fighting. However, we can also blame much of this vocabulary shift on the ninth-century Danish invasions and the Norman conquest of England in 1066, which fostered the later swing of our military terminology from a native to a French model. There may be fewer words in general circulation today for war and killing, but war persists and accident and murder rates are still a public concern. Furthermore, violence and death are major features of our entertainment industries: movies, television, and children's toys.

Technological change affects virtually all aspects of our lives. In addition to words of war and death, we count upwards of fifty obsolete Anglo-Saxon terms for various kinds of military equipment. While many of these were overthrown for continental battle fashions, the changing technology of war itself has had an even greater effect on our vocabulary. We are no longer conversant with the complexities of medieval arms and armor, and few of us can tell a hauberk from a cuirass, let alone define *greave, gorget, cuisse,* and *poleyn.* In their place we have *Uzis* and *Kalashnikovs, cruise missiles* and *star wars.*

A more recent, and generally a more benign change resulting in the death of words was the invention of the automobile. The shift from horse-drawn to horseless vehicles led to the abandonment of the terminology of the carriage trade, and while we read of *broughams, stanhopes, victorias, gigs,* and *chaises* in period novels, pictures of these vehicles do not readily spring to mind.

When change occurs, there are a number of words that adapt rather than die. The *visor* of the knight's helmet became the modern brim of a cap. The *Brougham,* named after Lord Brougham, was a closed, boxlike carriage with the driver's perch outside. It became in the early days of motoring a limousine with an open driver's compartment, and now sometimes appears as a model name for an elegant motor car. The *landau,* originally a carriage with a fold down roof, became a motor car with a similar feature, though *convertible* has become the generic term today. *Car* itself experienced a revival. An old word, by the eighteenth century it had developed an exclusively poetic coloration, and was generally applied to some opulent imaginary vehicle like the *Car of Phaeton.* Car was preserved in some dialect use as the equivalent of the ordinary *cart,* from which it developed into the *horse car* and *tram car,* ultimately transferring with the introduction of internal combustion to the *motor car.* In popular use it triumphed over the more formal coinage, *automobile,* though the clipped form auto remains common as well.

Planned and Unplanned Obsolescence

There are a number of areas in our speech where we can expect lexical obsolescence almost as a matter of course. In fashion and food terminology, and in sport, the life of a word is often severely limited by "what they're showing this season," as well as by public whim and fancy. And in the area of slang, new words are little more than cannon fodder. Slang is a form of speech where going out of style is the name of the game. We frequently replace words in a number of slang categories: terms characterizing 'nonsense' (*blarney, baloney, stuff, rot, tripe, bunk, crap, bull*), positive labels (*swell, cool, neat, groovy, intense, tubular*), ways to refer to a 'boring person' (*pill, stick-in-the-mud, square, creep, nerd, dork*), or an 'attractive male or female' (*beaut, babe, dish, fox, hunk, looker, peach, ten*).

Change is nothing new in the fast-paced and competitive world of slang, but change occurs with even greater force—perhaps because it is less common there—when it affects the core of our speech. In rare instances a word of great centrality will be lost, or set aside. This happened with our former second person singular pronoun, *thou,* and its oblique forms *thee, thy,* and *thine,* which were replaced by *you, your,* and *yours,* forms originally signifying the plural. *Thou* still appears in pronoun paradigms and verb conjugations in nineteenth-century grammar books, though it had long since dropped from standard English speech and writing. Were it not for the preservation of the older pronoun in Shakespeare and the King James version of the Bible, and in the earlier practice of the Quakers, *thou* would now be completely obsolete, not just a lexical antique.

Earlier upheavals occurred in the pronoun system as well. *They* and *she* are both newcomers that gradually drove out older forms which began with *h* (we still preserve that initial *h* in *her*). At one time we could pluralize nouns by adding *-er* or *-en* (*eyer,* 'eggs,' *schoon,* 'shoes'). The *-er* plurals have all disappeared, and only a few *-en* plurals remain (*oxen, brethren,* and *children,* which itself contains a fossilized *-er* as well). Gone too (or going, depending on which dictionary you believe) are a number of basic words whose continued existence we might have counted on by virtue of the derivatives they leave behind. For example, the obsolete *gust,* both noun and verb, meaning 'taste,' produced the no longer current *gusty,* 'tasty' (not related to the homonym referring to the wind), as well as the long gone pair, *gustful* and *gustless.* Of this little remains but *disgusting,* but then in language, as in other matters, there is no accounting for taste. Similarly, both *commodate* and *discommodate* became obsolete, though *accommodate* persists. We lost *bash,* 'daunt, destroy the confidence of,' which gave us the obsolete *bashless* as well as the original and still current *abash* and its derivative, *bashful* (the resurgence of *bashing* in our vocabulary, for example, *teacher-bashing,* is from the unrelated *bash,* 'to hit').

Many of our lost root words are positives which leave only negatives as clues to their former existence. Most obvious perhaps is *uncouth*, a word that has survived its more positive root, *couth*, though that root is revived from time to time as a slang antonym for *uncouth*. *Disgruntle* leads us to the no longer current *gruntle*, whose meaning originally relates to the noise of pigs (and which survives in this sense in British dialect speech). There is no record of a base form *pellent* from which *repellent* is built. We probably get the word directly from Latin *repellere*, 'to repel, drive back,' though the obsolete English verb *pell*, 'to drive,' certainly rounds out the paradigm. Also in this category of lost roots we find *kempt*, 'combed,' which produced the current *unkempt*; *ruth*, source of *ruthless*, marked "now archaic" by the *OED* but not by other dictionaries; *parage*, 'lineage, worth,' producing *disparage*, originally 'make an unequal match or marriage'; habille, 'to dress,' which gives us *dishabille*; and *delible*, which has faded, though *indelible* remains to mark its passing.

Time Out of Joint

When a word is used outside of its historical frame it is called an *anachronism* (from the Greek, 'without time'), a word whose time is literally out of joint. Shakespeare's mention of striking clocks in *Julius Caesar* is an anachronism (as it were), because the sort of renaissance clock he is referring to did not exist in Roman times. Getting the dates right is one of our favorite historical fetishes, and our vocabulary reflects this. An *anachronism* is any mis-assignment of time, either too early or too late. More specifically, *parachronism* occurs when a person or event is given a date later than the actual one, and a *prochronism* is the assignment of a date that is too early (technically, Caesar's striking clock is a prochronism). William Safire (1986) has now given the label *chronism* to words no longer in use (standard as well as slang) which may be used to evoke the flavor of a historical period. *Plight* and *troth*, outside of weddings, are chronisms. Safire's chronisms include *milk bottle* (now rare in American refrigerators if not in American English), *slide rule* (replaced by the pocket calculator), and *watch fob*, as well as *uptown*, 'ritzy,' peachy, keen, and *grippe*, which we now call *flu* (no longer written *'flu*—and never written *'flu'*—to indicate the clipped form of *influenza*). To illustrate the flavor of chronisms, *hi fi* (now *stereo*) evokes the 1950s, as does *atomic* (it has now generally been replaced by *nuclear*), *the bomb* itself, and of course *strontium 90*.

Before Safire, there was never a word *chronism* to counter *anachronism*. Not all negative words presuppose the existence of a positive, a sign that language and logic do not always go hand in hand. There is no lost word *combobulate* from which *discombobulate* might have been taken. But speakers of English hate a semantic vacuum, and it is reasonable to suppose that, like *chronism, combobulate* has been uttered, or at least thought of, from time to time.

When a word is coined to fill a void predicted by the existence of another term that apparently derives from it, we call the process *back formation*. For example, it is likely that the verb *beg* comes from the *Beghards,* a medieval European mendicant order of laymen whose reputation was not the best. The English for *Beghard* became *beggar,* and the final syllable of this word could have been erroneously interpreted as an agent suffix, the *-er* which in English generally indicates 'one who does' (*thinker, baker, weaver*). The unsuffixed form indicates the action done: as a *baker* bakes, so a *beggar* must *beg*. *Burgle,* a nineteenth-century back formation, is based on *burglar,* a word of clouded origin whose suffix probably was not agentive in origin.

Some recent innovations have triggered words that might qualify as intermediate rather than back formations. In these instances, the base term is rendered vague and generic by our advancing technology, and a new specific term must be found to fill the lexical void created by the new invention. For example, the widespread use of *videotape* forces us to change what used to be just plain *tape,* or sometimes *recording tape,* into *audiotape*. In the same way, the preponderance of electric instruments in today's popular music has turned the old, unamplified guitar and piano into "new" instruments, the *acoustic* guitar and piano, though their sound and shape are unaffected by these new names. A feature that has been standard on many imported cars for some time, a lever mounted on the steering column that allows the driver to flash the headlights, is being referred to as an *optical horn* now that it has become an option on domestic vehicles.

One word whose meaning requires it to be in continuous flux is *modern*. Since the sixteenth century *modern* has referred to 'the present time,' whatever time that happens to be, as opposed to the past, which is characterized by *ancient* or *classical* and their synonyms. But from time to time an era has found the term *modern* insufficient to differentiate itself from the immediate past. Thus the Renaissance, which called itself the Renaissance to emphasize the self-image of giants standing on the shoulders of dwarfs, coined the term *middle ages* to signify that vast, dark period between classical and modern where—according to the inhabitants of the Renaissance—nothing in particular happened. The modern age, by which I mean today's modern age, has felt a similar need to set itself off from the earlier *modernism* that has come to include 'the twentieth century up to the end of World War II.' Bookstores in the 1960s found the need to set up one section for 'modern literature' and another for the more recently produced *contemporary literature*—not to be confused with the *avant garde,* the *nouvelle vague,* 'new wave' or perhaps more appropriately, 'new vague,' or any other sort of *cutting edge.* In addition, since the late 1940s the *OED Supplement* chronicles the steady rise of the term *postmodern,* particularly in reference to literature, art, and architecture. I have come across one indication that *postmodern* is poised to break out into more general lexical usage: a recent campus newspaper advertisement hyperbolically lures future tenants to inspect a block of "new post modern luxury apartments" that feature "one of a kind architectural design."

I doubt that *tape, piano, horn* and *modern* will become so vague as to be rendered useless, but it is always possible for a term cut free from specific meaning in a culture to die a quiet death in a dark corner. In any case, however, we need not fear a net shrinkage in our lexicon, for we never run out of our need for more and more words, and we still import, invent, or revive more than we abandon in our vocabulary.

15 What's in a Name?

Many English words are loaded with history. This is particularly true of eponyms, words derived from people's names. Rome is an eponym based on Romulus, one of the supposed founders of the eternal city. According to legend, Britain comes from Brutus, not Julius Caesar's false friend but an earlier and more obscure Brutus who fled the burning city of Troy (as did the legendary Aeneas, who is also associated with Rome) and went on to settle the land named after him. *Guy* comes from the effigies of Guy Fawkes carried about by the English on the anniversary of the Gunpowder Plot (November 5, 1605). We know that *boycott* is the name of a nineteenth-century Irish overseer who was the original recipient of that treatment, while *lynch* or *lynch law* has been traced to something like a dozen different historical Lynches who took the law into their own hands, including Captain William Lynch (1742–1820) of Virginia and South Carolina, the most likely source of the word. *Lynch* has also been attributed to Charles Lynch of Virginia, as well as to Lynche's Creek, in South Carolina, apparently a place where rough justice was often done.

Some eponyms are easier to pin down: the sandwich refers to the Earl of same, who is reputed to have spent twenty-four hours at a gambling table without taking any refreshment except meat between sliced bread. *Macadam* was developed by the engineer John L. McAdam. Animals and plants are often named after their discoverers: *guppy* (the fish) and *gardenia* are eponyms, as is *Frankenstein* (or as purists insist, *Frankenstein's monster*), the brainchild of the fictional Baron F. in Mary Shelley's novel. The *leotard* was designed and worn by the nineteenth-century French acrobat, Jules Léotard, who urged other men to follow his example and wear "a more natural garb that does not hide your best features" (Hendrickson 1972). However the leotard has become most popular as a woman's garment, and we have forgotten the eponymic origins of the word, assuming instead that it is composed of a prefix, *leo-*, affixed to a base, *tard*. In 1959 an attempt to reinterest men in the leotard led to ads for the *he-o-tard* in the *New York Times,* and a recent ad for a new version with built-in tights is called the *unitard*.

Sometimes eponyms are false, or at least illusory: the individuals in question either never existed, or they came on the scene long after the appearance of the word popularly supposed to bear their name. *Scrimshaw*, or whalebone carving and decoration, is generally traced to French *escrimer*, but there is a tradition which derives the art from an expert carver named Scrimshaw, who has left us his or her mark, but no biographical trace. According to the *Dictionary of American English* (*DAE*), *bogus*, whose origins also remain obscure, originally designated a machine for counterfeiting coins. As one popular account has it, the word is a corruption of *Borghese*, the name of a swindler who papered the American West and Southwest with worthless securities and rubber checks in the 1830s. However, like Scrimshaw, no evidence of Borghese's existence has come to light. Similarly, the *bowler hat* has been credited to one London milliner named Bowler, and another named Beaulieu, though we have no direct proof of either's existence, and the hat's name may simply be descriptive. *Marmalade* has been incorrectly traced to Mary Queen of Scots who, when out of sorts was supposed to have tolerated only orange jam. According to this story, the jam was therefore called *marie malade*, 'sick Mary,' which later elided to its present form. *Marmalade* actually comes to English from Portuguese, where it simply means 'quince preserves.'

Although few experts accept this derivation of the term, *fudge*, a word of uncertain origin, is traced by Isaac D'Israeli to an actual Captain Fudge, a British merchant seaman known for his ability to embroider the truth. There actually was an officer named *Martinet* in the French army, but *martinet* does not appear in French in the sense 'tyrant,' and occurs in English at least a generation before Martinet's reorganization of the infantry. *Hobson's choice*, which is no choice at all, is commonly said to derive from Tobias Hobson, a Cambridge stablekeeper who made his customers "choose" the next horse in line, no matter what their preference might be. John Milton celebrated Hobson, as did Richard Steele in *Spectator* 509, and the *OED* accepts the eponym with a 1660 citation. While Ernest Weekley (1961) finds an earlier reference to *Hodgson's choice* (1617) which suggests that Hobson may simply have fit into an already existing idiom, origin unknown, Robert Hendrickson, in his extensive study of eponyms, *Human Words* (1972), finds the evidence for Hobson overwhelming.

However, Hendrickson does find the stories behind *booze* suspicious. According to the legends, an American distiller named either E. S. or E. G. Booz, operating out of Kentucky or possibly Philadelphia, sold whiskey in log-cabin-shaped bottles. The story goes that when William Henry Harrison, who was born in a log cabin, ran for president in

1840, his supporters found *Booz's Log Cabin Whiskey* effective in getting out the vote. Now the word *booze* had been around in English since the fourteenth century, but the fortunate coincidence may certainly have appealed to early political strategists and the voting public, as well as to etymologists, who see it reinforcing the earlier slang term for alcoholic beverage. However, the vagueness associated with Mr. Booz's initials and his place of business, and the absence of any traceable biography, further suggest that Booz was not a real person but a marketing strategy, an imaginary character like Betty Crocker, but a brand name as well that deforms an English word, just as today's dog treat, *Bonz*, is based on *bones*, or the antacid *Chooz* comes from *chews*.

Another well-known reinforcing eponym comes from Thomas Crapper, designer of the float and siphon mechanism used in flush toilets, which items of household furniture are therefore often said to bear his name. In fact, *crap*, meaning 'husk, dregs, residue,' is found as early as the mid-fifteenth century, and has long signified excrement as well, and Crapper's firm produced not just toilets but all manner of plumbing pipe and fixtures. Nonetheless, the coincidence of *crap* and *Crapper* affords both humor—Crapper's biography is titled *Flushed with Pride*—and serious linguistic discussion: Hendrickson (1972) suggests that American doughboys brought both the term and the flush mechanism home with them after World War I. It might not be going too far to imagine that Crapper's name even influenced the line of work he went into. Though I have not seen that suggestion made before, it is not as far-fetched as it may sound: consider the professional connections of these actual people, English the English teacher, Paper and Pencil the linguists, Filler the pharmacist, and the aptly named medics Dr. Ei (rhymes with 'eye'), the ophthalmologist, Dr. Neucks, the radiologist, Dr. Kwak, in the emergency room, and the inevitable Dr. Doctor.

Is There a Doctor in the House?

Two English words are commonly traced to names of physicians, Dr. Latan and Dr. Condom, whose existence cannot be proved. The word *charlatan*, 'a medical quack,' comes from an Italian root meaning 'to babble.' However Brewer, who accepts the standard Italian derivation, recounts in his popular *Dictionary of Phrase and Fable* the story of a French medicineman and tooth extractor whose name is also associated with the word:

> It is said that one Latan, a famous quack, used to go about Paris
> in a gorgeous car, in which he had a traveling dispensary. A man

> with a horn announced the approach of this magnate, and the
> delighted sightseers used to cry out, "Voilà! le char de Latan."
> When I lived in Paris I often saw this gorgeous car. (s.v. *Charlatan*)

Despite this personal testimony any connection between Dr. Latan, if there really was one, and *charlatan* is purely coincidental.

Just who engendered the *condom* is another matter which is certainly obscure. There is a strong tradition dating from the eighteenth century, when the word first appears, crediting the invention of this prophylactic device to a Dr. Condom, or Condon, or possibly a Col. Condom or Cundum. This traditional etymology is still rehearsed in a number of current dictionaries, though the *OED Supplement* (1972) finds no trace of any such eighteenth-century English doctor. In an exhaustive monograph on the subject, William Kruck (1981) fails to locate any candidate, surgical or military, whose name could have transferred to the condom. Other derivations for *condom* include a place name, the village of Condom in France, a set of Latin words (*condus*, 'receptacle,' and *conduma*, 'house,' as well as *quondam*, which means 'former,' but which might be a sexual pun as well), or a Persian word for 'seed container.' None of these speculative derivations can be borne out by evidence either, and any sensible dictionary must mark the term 'origin unknown.'

What Is It?

Whenever we encounter something new, one of our first responses is to ask, "What is it?" Giving a name to the new or unknown enables us to deal with it. Even if we don't know the name of something, or the name slips our mind for the moment, we can fall back on *thing*, or some such word. In the movie version of Dashiell Hammett's *The Maltese Falcon*, the detective Sam Spade (once again played by Humphrey Bogart) calls the statue of the bird a *dingus*, a pseudo-learned slang variant of *thing*. In addition, we find the concise *whatsis* or the more colorful *whatchamacallit* (the *OED* lists variants of this under *What-d'ye-call-'em*). And Chaucer's Wife of Bath uses Latin *quoniam*, literally 'since, therefore, that,' but serving here as the equivalent of *whatsis*, to refer to her genitals. In at least one case, a synonym of *whatsis* became the actual name of an object. Apparently lacking a ready term for the architectural feature that we refer to in American English as a transom (short for *transom window*), in the later eighteenth century speakers of French borrowed the German "Was ist das?"— which means, "What's that?" The borrowing was initially jocular, but *le vasistas* has since become the standard French word for transom.

There is a similar story about *kangaroo* recounted by lexicographer Charles Funk (1950). *Kangaroo* was recorded by Captain James Cook, the Pacific explorer, and by the naturalist, Sir Joseph Banks, who accompanied him on a voyage to Australia in 1770. Later European visitors to Australia were unable to connect the word *kangaroo* with the animal in question, although they did encounter the term *patagorong*. From this the theory arose that in response to Cook's question, "What is it?" the aboriginal reply *kangaroo* actually meant, "I don't know." This explanation was never proved, however, and the editors of the *OED* suggest *kangaroo* may simply have been a local term, or an obsolete one, for the animal. John Moore (1961) asserts *kangaroo* is an aboriginal word meaning 'the jumper,' but lexicographers today are still uncertain about the word's origin. Whether or not Cook's linguistic observation was based on a mistake, the common word for the marsupial in question is now *kangaroo*.

A Word Is Born

The origins of most of our words tend to be cloaked in obscurity. Sometimes, too, they are dressed in myth. Once in a while in the annals of wordlore we come across a story purporting to describe how someone created a particular word. Such accounts may be true, particularly those that concern scientific or technical terms whose history has been well documented. Or they may simply be entertaining. The word *sirloin,* for example, which comes from the French and describes a cut of meat taken quite literally from 'above the loin,' has been incorrectly attributed to at least three hungry English kings, Henry VIII, James I, and Charles II. Each of these monarchs was thought to have taken his sword and knighted a roast beef he found particularly pleasing with a phrase on the order of, "I dub thee Sir Loin." *Schooners* were initially popular in America, and there is an account reported by Logan Pearsall Smith (1948) that links the name of the sailing vessel to a spectator at its initial launching, at Gloucester, Massachusetts around 1713. Seeing the boat skim through the water, the spectator is said to have exclaimed, "Oh, how she scoons!" upon which the builder, a Capt. Andrew Robinson, replied, "A scooner let her be." *Scoon* is a dialect word from Scotland and the north of England meaning 'to skim or skip along the water, like a stone,' and while there is no evidence *scoon* was used in New England, the *OED* finds the etymology plausible. However, it regards the story of the word's origin as an invention.

In contrast to such fancies, we do know that the Dutch chemist J. B. Van Helmont (1577–1644) created *gas* as it were out of thin air (he was actually describing water vapor), though he admitted being influenced in his naming by the Greek *chaos*, whose pronunciation in Dutch makes it sound very much like *gas*. Joseph Priestley, the English grammarian and chemist who discovered oxygen, was unaware of Van Helmont's Greek analog and presumed the word came from Dutch *geest* (similar to German *Geist*), which means 'spirit.' Van Helmont also coined *blas* to signify the motion of the stars that was thought to influence the weather. Presumably Van Helmont formed this unsuccessful term to rhyme with his more popular creation, though had we known about sunspots in the seventeenth century *blas* might have endured.

Seeking a feminine correlative of *patrimony*, and finding *matrimony* already locked into a somewhat different meaning, the anthropologist Sir G. Campbell proposed *matriheritage* in 1876 for the social system in which inheritance passes through the mother's rather than the father's side. Like *blas*, the term is little used today. Other technical innovations have been more successful. The mathematician John Napier (died, 1617) applied the term *logarithm* (actually, *logarithmus*) to a class of numerical relations that he discovered, although we do not know what he viewed the literal sense of the word to be. In 1848, the meteorologist Henry Piddington coined *cyclone*, from the Greek word which means, among other things, 'the coil of a serpent.' Although his Greek was apparently a bit shaky, Piddington's word did catch on as a designation for a storm with circular winds of great force.

We can trace the naming of some inventions as well. The *kaleidoscope*, invented in 1817, was named by its inventor, Sir David Brewster, from the Greek elements meaning 'beautiful' and 'form.' More down to earth, *linoleum* was named in 1878 by Frederick Walton, its inventor, after the linseed oil used in its formation. Earthier still is the *bazooka*, initially a comic musical instrument made from a length of gas pipe by Bob Burns, a radio humorist. Only later did *bazooka* become, by transference, the name of a weapon. According to Burns, the word consists of *bazoo*, 'mouth,' and the suffix *-ka*, as in *harmonica* and *balalaika* (Funk 1950). And *copesetic*, 'fine, o.k.,' was claimed as a childhood invention by the tap dancer Bill Bojangles Robinson, though Funk finds it a common expression in the South and Wentworth and Flexner trace it to Yiddish.

Though we cannot always trace a word directly to its maker, we are able to attribute the creation of many words to our literary artists. Thomas More made up the word *utopia* (1516) from Greek elements that literally mean 'not a place.' Edmund Spenser coined *blatant* to name the thousand-tongued beast representing 'calumny' in the *Faerie Queene* (1596). He is also responsible for *derring-do*, a noun he created inadvertently in the *Shepherds' Calendar* (1579) through his misreading of a passage in Lydgate. John Milton created *pandemonium*, the home of 'all-demons,' in *Paradise Lost* (1667). One edition of his poems credits Milton with the word *joking* as well. But *joke* is a seventeenth-century slang term, a clipped form of Latin *jocus*. Neither *joke* nor *joking* occurs in Milton's works, though he does use *jesting*, a term that had been around for a century or more. *Namby-pamby* is the creation of Henry Carey (1726), though this play on the name of pastoral poet Ambrose (*Amby*) Philips was made popular by Alexander Pope in his "Dunciad" (1733). Jeremy Bentham coined *international* in 1780. In a note, the *OED* explains that the word is included in the dictionary, although it is so new, because it is "sufficiently analogous and intelligible." Samuel Taylor Coleridge first used *homesick* in 1798 to translate the *Heimweh* which had recently become endemic among the German romanticists, and the *OED* suggests that his less popular coinage *esemplastic* (1817), incorrectly formed from Greek roots to mean 'molding into one, unifying,' was influenced by the German *ineinsbildung*. In his poem *Don Juan* (1819), Byron employed the backformation *darkle*, a new verb based on the well-established adverb *darkling*. George Bernard Shaw introduced *superman* in 1903 as a translation for Nietzsche's *Übermensch* (compare also French *surhomme*, *superhomme*). Robot, from a Czech word meaning 'slave,' first appears in Karel Capek's play *R. U. R.* (Rossum's Universal Robots), which premiered in London in 1923. And we owe *quark* to James Joyce. The word appears in *Finnegans Wake* (1939) and was adapted in 1963 by physicist Murray Gell-Mann to replace his own coinage, *quork*, as the name for a subatomic particle.

Then there is the case of *halitosis*. This word for 'bad breath' (from the Latin *halere*, 'to breathe,' plus -*osis*) was dredged up from an obscure medical dictionary by Gerard Lambert, the manufacturer of *Listerine*. Named after Joseph Lister, though in no way connected with his work, *Listerine* was first promoted as a surgical antiseptic, later as a gargle for sore throats. In the 1920s, Lambert and his copywriters, seeking to widen their market share, put out a series of ads striking at our deepest fears, and creating almost overnight a need for their product as a mouthwash. The popularity of their ad campaign soon turned *halitosis* into a household word, though it has never generated much medical interest.

As *gas* and *blas* illustrate, most coined words are influenced by the analogy of earlier words or forms. Occasionally a derivation is misleading. H. L. Mencken reports in *The American Language* (1937) that

Pyrex, a trademark for the heat-resistant cookware made by the Corning Glass Company, comes not from Greek *pyr,* 'fire,' but English *pie:* the first Pyrex utensil was a pie plate. Only very rarely do we find a word with no source, one created as it were out of whole cloth. Spenser's *blatant* may be such a coinage. Today's names for artificial fibers often seem to be such root creations, or zero derivatives. *Rayon* is a generic term adopted in 1924 for the fibers once known as artificial silk. It has its source in the older *rayon,* 'a ray or beam of light,' but other artificial fibers pattern after it: *nylon* (first used in toothbrush bristles; nylon stockings were introduced in 1939), *orlon,* and *dacron.* The origins of *qiana* and *ramie* are not immediately clear. For all intents and purposes, these may be root creations as well.

Kodak, coined by George Eastman in 1888 for his invention, a portable camera using roll film rather than plates, is a word without a derivation, though according to his biographer, Eastman took the *k,* a letter he considered "firm and unyielding" as well as unique, from the first letter of his mother's family name. The inventor used a formula of sorts to come up with a name for his product. He sought for his camera an arbitrary combination of letters not related to any other existing word. The name had to be short, easily spelled and pronounced, vigorous, and distinctive, and it had to qualify as a trademark under the laws of several countries. For some time *kodak* was a synonym for camera, and the verb *to kodak* meant 'to take pictures (with a Kodak).' Today, however, the *Kodak* trademark no longer doubles as a generic in the way *Coke* and *Xerox* do. Incidentally, *Xerox* owes its significance to a coinage based on Greek: *xerography,* or 'dry-writing,' is a copying method based on a "dry" electrostatic process, replacing the older "wet" copiers such as *Photostats,* which used chemical developers and required special photographic papers.

Root creation is also claimed for the familiar word, *quiz.* Interesting to the modern reader is the fact that the earliest meaning of *quiz* (ca. 1782) is 'an odd or eccentric person' (*quoz* also appears in the same sense). This meaning is preserved in *quizzical,* 'odd or amusing,' usually said of a look or facial expression. Other early meanings include 'a practical joke or hoax' (1807); and, as a verb, 'to make sport or fun of, ridicule, mock' (1796). The modern notion of *quiz,* 'an act of examining or questioning,' is probably an Americanism dating from the 1860s.

According to the *OED, quiz* is of obscure origin. It is sometimes suggested that *quiz* comes from *question* or *inquisitive,* though the original meaning of the word, 'odd or eccentric person,' does not support such an explanation. There is also a story that *quiz* was invented in 1791 by a Dublin theater owner named Richard Daly, who, like John Montagu, the fourth Earl of Sandwich, was a betting man.

As Frank Thorpe Porter, a magistrate and head of the Dublin police, tells it, on August 21, 1791, Daly and a man named Delahoyde got into a discussion concerning the French word *fagotin*, which they defined as "a low, vulgar mountebank." Delahoyde regretted the absence of a suitable English synonym. Daly challenged him to coin one, but Delahoyde demurred. Then Daly bet twenty guineas "that within forty-eight hours there shall be a word in the mouths of the Dublin public, of all classes and sexes, young and old; and also that within a week, the same public shall attach a definite and generally adopted meaning to that word, without any suggestion or explanation from me. I also undertake . . . that my word shall be altogether new and unconnected with any derivation from another language, ancient or modern" (Porter 1875, 32). The word was *quiz*, though the sources are silent on how Daly thought it up.

To accomplish his goal, Daly enlisted the help of his stage crew, who chalked the word on doors and shutters all over Dublin during the night. One homeowner feared *quiz* was a nickname for him thought up by a neighbor. The suspicion that it was a personal attack or a religious or political slogan was dispelled when people realized the word appeared almost everywhere, indiscriminately. After a few days it was generally agreed the mystery word was a hoax, but *quiz*, with its initial meaning 'clown, low vulgar fellow, *fagotin*,' stuck in the language and spread throughout the English speaking world.

Although Porter claims to have heard his account directly from several of the principals, this legend, while intriguing, seems to have no historical basis. For one thing, the story reeks of the apocryphal. There is no explanation of how Dubliners managed to decipher the meaning of the mysterious word. More to the point, however, is the fact that *quiz* appears in a diary of the writer Fanny Burney some nine years before Daly's supposed invention.

Some analogous word situations come to mind. One involves the invention of *Kilroy*, the mythical American soldier whose name appeared on walls and other appropriate writing surfaces all over the world during and shortly after World War II, either alone or in the phrase *Kilroy was here*. Hendrickson (1972) mentions a theory that Kilroy was a Quincy, Massachusetts shipyard inspector who approved war materiel by chalking his name on crates that were then shipped around the world. There are many candidates who could serve as the original *Kilroy*, but as yet no one has been able to pinpoint him (or her) with any accuracy.

Ron Butters, the editor of *American Speech* (1987), reports that Harry Miller, of New Jersey, wrote to the *Dictionary of American Regional English* (*DARE*) detailing the origin of the term *hubba hubba*, another expression popular in the military during World War II. According to Miller, the term was first applied to a marine sergeant who used it in double-time drills. Miller claims responsibility for first using *hubba hubba* as a wolf whistle, a sense which was later picked up and popularized by comedian Bob Hope. Other sources trace *hubba hubba* to baseball or to Chinese, and despite Miller's first-hand account, the origin of the expression remains uncertain.

Writing in *American Speech*, Fred R. Shapiro (1987) debunks the commonly repeated story that *bug* came to mean 'defect in computer hardware or software' only after Grace Murray Hopper, the computer pioneer who developed COBOL, found a moth inside an early computer at Harvard in the 1940s. While Hopper apparently did find a literal computer bug, which is taped to her computer log for September 9, 1945, it is clear from the log entry, "First actual case of bug being found," that the figurative use of *bug* was already well established. Shapiro notes that as early as 1878, Thomas Edison employed *bug* to refer to 'a mechanical defect,' and Edison's use of the term suggests he was not its inventor.

Then there is the claim made for *humongous*. According to dictionary editor Fred Cassidy, another letter in the files of *DARE* describes how two fraternity brothers at the University of Kansas made up the word from *huge* and *tremendous*, with some fiddling for euphony, and promoted its use on campus around 1975. As the story has it, the word quickly spread to the town and beyond, and of course it is now in wide circulation. Dictionaries record citations of *humongous* starting with 1973, though we do not have independent evidence corroborating this account.

Whether they are visible, invisible, or apocryphal, the word coiners among us continue to be active. They are seeking to fill the semantic gaps in our language, some of them trivial, others a bit more important. The humorist George Carlin once lamented the absence of words naming the c-shaped stretch of anatomy located between the thumb and forefinger or the little depression twixt the nether lip and chin. There are other lexical black holes as well: no common gender third person singular pronoun, no adult-sounding word for an adult's boy- or girlfriend. There is no agreed-upon term for the perforated tear strips that border computer paper. And no doubt there are neologists out there trying desperately to find the right combination of sounds and syllables that will produce another *quiz* or *humongous*.

Short Circuits

One kind of neologism serves as a shortcut, a quicker way of saying or writing something. We commonly clip words, removing beginnings or endings to produce terser speech. Clippings are common in slang. For example the now perfectly standard terms *bus* from *omnibus*, *taxi* from *taximeter*, *varsity* from *university*, and *mob* from the Latin *mobile vulgus*, 'the fickle crowd,' were once considered less than acceptable. *Tache* or *tash*, the clipped form of *moustache*, was popular in the British armed services in the 1920s. More recent, on American college campuses, are the clippings 'za, 'pizza,' 'roni, 'pepperoni,' 'ski, short for *brewski*, 'beer,' and 'rents, 'parents.'

Acronyms, words formed from the initial letters, or groups of letters of a set of words, provide another kind of short circuit. Names of groups or organizations are commonly reduced to acronyms: NATO, UN, GM, NBC, CIA. So common are acronyms in government circles that agencies and their regulations are sometimes referred to as *alphabet soup*. There is some indication that many organizations develop their acronyms by first finding a suitable word, then assigning an appropriate meaning to each of its letters, for example, *MADD*, 'Mothers Against Drunk Driving,' and *SAD*, 'Seasonal Affective Disorder,' which describes a depression syndrome associated with the coming of winter.

Some common words actually began as acronyms: *radar*, 'radio detection and ranging,' *scuba*, 'self-contained underwater breathing apparatus,' and *snafu*, the military acronym for 'situation normal, all fucked up.' However, the derivation of *posh* as an acronym from 'port outward, starboard home,' the preferred, shady-side stateroom locations of the Pacific and Orient boats heading from England to India, turns out to be just another bit of language folklore.

In one extreme case, a man seeking to adopt a new identity actually took an acronym as his name: Charles Cist, one of the original owners of *The Columbian Magazine*, which published in Pennsylvania between 1786 and 1792, was born Charles Jacob Sigismund Thiel, Jr., in Russia, where he served as a physician at the court of Catherine the Great. Forced to leave his home for unknown reasons, he came to the New World with a name based on his initials, C, I, S, T. (*I* and *j* were considered the same letter, alphabetically, in the eighteenth century, and appear together in dictionaries of the day. The use of acronyms for personal names also occurs in Hebrew.)

So prevalent are acronyms that folk linguists commonly turn popular names into joking acronyms, for example, *GM*, 'generous motors,' *Ford*, 'fuel, oil, and repair daily,' or 'found on road dead.' And of course there is the string of academic degrees, *B.S., M.S., Ph.D.*, 'bullshit, more shit, piled higher and deeper.' Finally, useful phrases tend to get reduced to acronymic status. There are of course the common party terms *RSVP* and *BYO(B)*, *TGIF*, and the business abbreviations *FYI* and *FOB* (that's 'freight on board,' for those of you, like me, who can never remember what the letters in the last one stand for).

Acronyms are common in campus jargon. Our Foreign Language Building at the University of Illinois is universally known as the *FLB*, and David Kinley Hall is always *DKH*. An eatery near campus is called *Home of Gourmet*, which students affectionately reduce to *HOG*. Acronyms can even fall victim to clipping. Travel agents fondly refer to TWA (Trans World Airlines) as *T-Dub*.

Sometimes a phrase is reduced to an acronym and pronounced as if it were a word, as in *RATS*, which stands for 'reduced admission tickets,' or *AIDS*, 'acquired immune deficiency syndrome,' *MEGO*, 'my eyes glaze over,' *KISS*, 'keep it simple, stupid,' *LIFO*, 'last in, first out,' the computer programmers' *GIGO*, 'garbage in, garbage out,' and the recent word-processing phrase, *WYSIWYG*, 'what you see is what you get.' Teenagers go in for acronyms as well, particularly in their writing. They apologize with *S/S/S*, 'sorry so sloppy,' and end their letters with *W/B*, 'write back,' and *LYLAS*, 'love you like a sister.'

But there is a newer, and probably more widespread verbal shortcut making the rounds these days, one so recent that so far as I know it hasn't appeared in print before and consequently has no official spelling. It has several spoken versions, the most common of which I shall represent as the iambically stressed *da da da da da da*, rapidly enunciated in a singsong manner. This increasingly common expression and its variants (*dă dá dă dá; dă dă dá*) serve as synonyms for the Englished Latin *etc.* (*etcetera*), the German *usw.* (*und so weiter*), and the more formal English *and so forth and so on*. The derivation of the form is far from certain. It is imitative, like its equally slangy, more negative, and equivalent *blah blah blah* (which is still current in Australian English). The phonologist James Hartmann, at the University of Kansas, whose ear I trust much more than my own, hears /t/ rather than /d/ in the first syllable of each pair. Another colleague is struck by the resemblance of the phrase to the *dahs* and *dits* of Morse code, though I myself suspect the form derives from the verbalization of the suspension dots we commonly use in print to indicate material left out at the ends of sentences: . . . . , or *dot dot dot dot*, a form I have occasionally heard as well. As it is now used, however, the final consonant is not sounded. *Dă dá dă dá dă dá dă dá* is very informal, and usually functions to complete a summary of reported speech, the last part of which is not particularly important or already known to the hearer, as in the following citation made up for the purposes of illustration:

> The President said on television that the stock market crash was just a mild correction and not to panic about it and, you know, the dollar is strong and dǎ dá dǎ dá dǎ dá dǎ dá.

I am not aware that a term exists to describe such summatives or suspensories—perhaps *summative* is as good a word as any—but it seems to me that it will not be long before an expression as widespread as *dǎ dá dǎ dá* appears in print.

16 Telephone Talk

Just as some inventions contribute their names as lasting parts of our language, others significantly change the way we use language altogether. In 1876, Alexander Graham Bell patented the first telephone, an instrument which did not initially excite much public interest, but which has gone on to have a profound effect on the way we use the English language. Only a few hours after Bell applied for his patent on February 14, Professor Elisha Gray, another inventor specializing in telegraphy, filed his own plans for a telephone. After hundreds of lawsuits, Bell's patent was upheld and he is officially credited with the invention.

The Bell concern with speech communication spanned three generations. Alexander Bell, grandfather of the inventor, was an authority on phonetics and speech pathology. Alexander Melville Bell carried on the family tradition, devoting himself to the education of the deaf by means of "Bell's visible speech," a system of alphabetic characters that taught pronunciation by diagraming the positions of the speech organs. Melville Bell's son Alexander Graham Bell ran a school for training teachers of the deaf, and was a widely respected lecturer and writer in the areas of phonetics and pronunciation (he was also president of the National Geographic Society).

It took a few years after its invention for Bell's telephone to get off the ground, but once its importance became apparent, it spread rapidly. The first telephone switchboard began operation in New Haven in 1878 with twenty-one customers. By 1885 there were over 150,000 phones in use in the United States. And people soon noticed that the telephone made for a different kind of conversation.

In 1884, a writer identified initially as A. E. warns in *Lippincott's Magazine* of some of the linguistic problems associated with the telephone's popularity. For one thing, A. E. complains that the American public is totally unprepared for this particular invention. The telegraph, first publicly tested by Morse in 1844, had always been a vehicle for business communications, or personal messages of a more than social nature. Then, as now, non-business telegrams were formal and serious, bringing news of illness, accident, or death. Furthermore, the tele-

145

graphic message is impersonal in its transmission. According to A. E., "A telegram passes through so many hands . . . that one does not look upon it as the utterance of a friend."

The telephone, on the other hand, is much more humanized (though some people still consider it a strange and unnatural communication device). It allows us to talk freely, and more or less privately. However, the telephone forced us to adapt our manner of conversation. A. E. recognizes the need for developing a suitable code of telephonic conventions to make up for the fact that we are not face-to-face when we speak on the phone. For one thing, he complains that telephone communication is bald and thoroughly unsubtle. Voice transmission in the 1880s was fairly primitive compared to today's advanced sound technology, and it would have been difficult to convey the nuances and tones of ordinary speech on those early instruments. Nor, as A. E. notes, can we convey a smile across the wires. Furthermore, he states that telephone novices feel the need always to say something clever, and they are obliged to juggle their attention, acting as intermediaries between those who are in the room with them, but not on the phone, and the party on the other end.

But worst of all for A. E. is the fact that in 1884 there were no established conventions for beginning and ending phone calls. As a result, he complains, people have drifted into such hideous forms as *Hello* and *Good-bye*, words that are so familiar to us now they seem to have been coined expressly for telephone conversations. But for A. E. they are thoroughly inappropriate. Not much better in his eyes is the more "elevated" greeting, "Who is it?" or the more abrupt "Well?" both of which sound rather cantankerous to our more practiced ear. Sometimes A. E.'s telephone is answered, "How do you do?" a very polite greeting but one which today requires some introductory remark by our interlocutor before we use it.

Though he bemoans our lack of an appropriate greeting term to begin a phone conversation, A. E. dislikes the use of *Good-bye* to terminate calls even more than *Hello* and its feeble substitutes:

> Is this word—which trembling lips and sobbing breaths have found so hard to utter from time immemorial—to be employed to let the baker know that one loaf of bread is enough, and that we are to give no order for cake? (A. E. 1884, 418–19)

In other words, *good-bye* is far too elevated for the mundane telephonic meaning it must convey, which A. E. paraphrases as, "Go, now, about your business, I am going about mine!" In preference, we are asked to choose a less familiar word, perhaps one from another language, or "Hold!" or even "Enough!"—both rather dramatic terminators to today's ears. Better still would be an invented word, for use only in the telephone context. Unfortunately A. E. offers no suggestions for such a coinage.

This diatribe over *hello* and *good-bye* was no doubt a case of too little too late. Today's phone greetings were already firmly established just a few short years after the instrument's invention. The *OED Supplement* (1976) finds Rudyard Kipling using *hello* as an answer to a telephone call in 1892, though the term must have been well established by that time, for Mark Twain in 1889 refers to telephone operators as *hello-girls,* a term that became extremely popular but has now died out. Nonetheless, *hello* may have been viewed as a bit informal even as late as 1903, when an article in *Booklovers Magazine* on telephone switching centers observes, "The use of the word 'hello' is rigorously barred the 'hello girl,' strange to say."

Early phone users were troubled by administrative inefficiency as well as poor sound quality. Operators, under strict orders from their supervisors to keep lines open, regularly interrupted calls to ask, "Are you through?" For variety they would disconnect the call and then ask, "Weren't you through?" *The Critic,* reporting in 1895 about the invention of the automatic telephone (a precursor of the dial phone which like today's touchtone phones used pushbuttons rather than a central operator to connect calls), cheers, "There will be no helloing girl to ask you every minute, 'Have you finished?' while you are straining your ears to hear what the person you are talking to is saying." But worst of all, for *The Critic,* are the attempts people made to behave at the public telephone as if they were speaking in private. He gasps in dismay, "I have even heard people trying to kiss over the wire."

Although advances in telephony now allow us to move the instrument to more private locations than were at first available, and to carry on truly private conversations that may go well beyond some friendly osculation, the instrument still plays havoc with our manners and our expectations. When children first start using telephones they generally assume the person they are talking to is present, so they shake their heads instead of saying yes or no, and assuming their interlocutor can see as well as hear them, they show objects to the receiver. Adults also tend to transfer some of the nonverbal aspects of conversation to the telephone. The linguist Charles Fillmore reports that some elderly Japanese phone users, bound by a strict set of politeness conventions, will end a call by placing the receiver down on a table and bowing toward it, as they would when saying good-bye in person. And I myself have seen the French in phone booths screw their faces up into a moue, shrug their shoulders, and extend their hands in a gesture of hopelessness, just as they frequently do in face-to-face encounters.

Pushbutton Dialing

The telephone has so insinuated itself into our daily lives that we tend to take it for granted. But that is no reason to suppose that telephony no longer influences our use of language in new ways. Recent developments in phone technology require innovative terminology. Among the new words that we need in today's English is a replacement for *dial* when we make a phone call on a pushbutton phone.

According to the *OED*, *dial* probably comes from Latin *dies*, 'day,' and its initial use involves sundials, clocks, and time-telling. From the outset *dial* has been associated with round or circular shapes: time is frequently depicted as a wheel rotating, and the clock face mimics this circular pattern. Instrument dials, or gauges, also started off as round, with rotating pointers like the hands of a clock.

When the dial, or rotary, telephone was invented, it eliminated the need to go through a central exchange, and customers could dial their calls on the round face plate of the instrument. The widespread use of today's pushbutton phone, with its rectangular touch pad or key pad instead of a dial, is making the verb *dial* obsolete in the eyes of many. You don't really *dial* a number on a pushbutton or touchtone phone, you *punch* it, or *press* it, or perhaps you hit it or key it in. My sources at the telephone company (Illinois Bell) say that while there has been no official mandate governing the new usage, operators now *push* a number rather than dial it. However the brochure that accompanies the AT&T credit card instructs users to *enter* their number on any touchtone phone. The competing long distance service MCI tells customers to *dial* the appropriate numbers (the cards only work for pushbutton phones), but to make a second call we are told *"Press '#' button for one second."* And in an all-out effort to avoid ambiguity (or in this case, more properly, *triguity*), the instructions for my G. E. telephone cover all the bases: *"Dial* the desired phone number by *pressing* the numbered *push* buttons" (emphasis added).

Feeling the need to make our language accommodate the new technology, in the fall of 1986 the National Public Radio program "All Things Considered" asked listeners to send in suggestions to replace *dial* for making phone calls, and to name the # button on touchtone phones. (This *double cross* is conventionally referred to as the *pound key,* though the term has been slow to reach the public, perhaps because of the competing *pound sign,* the barred L used to indicate British currency. Both the AT&T and MCI Card instructions refer to it simply as the # *button.*) Needless to say, the words proposed were both plentiful and humorous, but neither a consensus nor a winner for most congenial word emerged.

There is mounting evidence that the days of the dial may be numbered. The instructions on a rotary dial pay phone operated by the GTE system in central Illinois tell the user to *push* the number before inserting any money. And there is a feeling abroad that the dial itself may be on its way out. In the realm of watches, clocks, and gauges, the pointing hands and the round, numbered face are giving way to the digital readout, and the watch dial may soon give way to a new name for the front of a timepiece (*face* is one likely candidate). Like watches, today's radios have abandoned literal dials in favor of linear, and in some cases, digital tuning, and our new televisions find stations not with dials and knobs but with direct access tuning by means of remote control devices that look like little calculators. While there seems to be no move to substitute something more up-to-date for the radio or television dial, there is a sense among industry people that the word is slowly dropping out of use. Phrases like *don't touch that dial* sound old-fashioned, and one now *tunes* a station instead of dialing it. Still, it is difficult to imagine a remake of Alfred Hitchcock's classic film being called *Push M for Murder.*

It is certainly within the realm of possibility that, instead of coining some new word, we will simply disconnect our association of dial with roundness and keep on using the old, familiar telephone term. The continued use of *dial tone* should reinforce this. But it is also very likely that *enter, push, press, touch, key in, punch, ding,* or some new word altogether, may replace *dial* in the near future, and it is virtually certain that as other new developments in telephonics occur, more new phone words will arise.

Of course, words associated with new inventions frequently become the subject of debate. *Telegram* was attacked in 1870 as superfluous, because *telegraph* serves both as noun and verb, and as incorrectly formed as well, because *gram* comes from the Greek word for letter, while *graph* derives from the more appropriate word which means 'to write, writing.' *Cablegram* was deemed even less legitimate—one critic called the coinage downright monstrous—because it combined the English *cable* with the Greek *gram,* and this sort of mixed or hybrid compound brought down the wrath of language purists. *Thalagram,* 'overseas cable,' a combination of the Greek *thalassa,* 'sea,' with the already familiar *gram,* died an early and unlamented death, though both *cablegram* and *telegram* have buried their critics.

Today's inventions have also disrupted or enriched our vocabulary, depending on your point of view. Computer terminology has made its way into everyday speech, and we input and interface and worry about systems going down with gay abandon. A recent late night television news/talk show pointed to creeping computer terminology as an example of the present degradation of the language, though the captions identifying the film clips and the language "experts" (an actor, an essayist, and a political analyst) were computer generated, as were, no doubt, the checks received by the participants in the show.

Interestingly, many of the terms we associate so strongly now with computers have been borrowed by the computer wizards from other areas of our speech. *Glitsch,* for example, comes from Yiddish and was used in electronics for some time before hackers picked it up as a term for 'a problem, or bug.' *Input* and *interface* also go back some centuries, and *hacker,* which refers either to someone who breaks computer security codes for fun, or now more generally to any computer enthusiast, has meant both a cut-throat, or bully, and someone who mangles words and sense.

Phone Tactics

If you have ever been called on the phone by a computer, to tell you your J. C. Penney's order is ready to be picked up, or to remind you to pay a bill you already paid some months before, you know that despite all the improvements in sound quality and gadgetry, despite satellite transmissions, fiber optics, microwave relays, and voice synthesizers, talking on the phone is still not talking face-to-face. Even the long-awaited introduction of phone-a-vision cannot fix that. Nonetheless, professional phone users have worked out some ways to try to get around the artificial nature of telephone conversations.

There is one tactic of modern telephone sales campaigns that I find particularly offensive. The caller asks for me by name, an indication that I am talking to a stranger, or at least someone not expected to recognize my voice. Then, when I acknowledge who I am, the caller immediately asks, "How are you today?" a question which normally presumes a certain degree of intimacy and is no doubt meant to soften me up for the pitch to come.

It may seem churlish of me, but I am not in the habit of telling strangers how I am, unless they are medical personnel. Nor do I take kindly to telephone solicitation, which I consider an invasion of my privacy. And I resent all attempts at overt verbal manipulation. So I'm afraid I respond rather rudely to the solicitous inquiry. Instead of the predictable reply, "I'm fine, how are you?" I ask "What are you selling?" which throws the caller off guard and allows me to direct the conversation, something telephone sellers are not comfortable handling. If I am particularly peevish that day, I simply say, "We don't want any" and hang up. Only once did I get a call back, from an insurance salesman who complained of my rudeness. I was gratified that I got my point across so well on so crude an instrument of communication, and I congratulated him on his perception. He did not call back again.

17 Ending Words

Besides the importation or revival of a ready-made word, one of the easiest ways to make new words for English is to take an old word and tack an ending onto it. Our language abounds in derivational suffixes, endings that can be added to words to give them new meaning or allow them to function in new ways within our sentences. There are common suffixes, like *-ness*, which turns adjectives into nouns (*happy, polite > happiness, politeness*), or *-ize*, which creates verbs (*normal > normalize, final > finalize, burglar > burglarize*). In some cases, the root is clipped before adding *-ize* (*sanitary > sanitize*).

We call the suffixes *-ness* and *-ize* productive because they give us many English words. Other suffixes are rarer. *-Hood*, for example, was never terribly productive, but it is even less active today than it once was. *-Hood* indicates the general state or quality of being of the base to which it is attached. We have a number of well-known words in *-hood* that have been with us a long time: *brotherhood*, 'the state of being a brother,' *childhood, fatherhood, knighthood, likelihood, motherhood, neighborhood*, and *sisterhood*. Newer words don't employ *-hood* very commonly. There are *boyhood, girlhood*, and *widowerhood*, from the eighteenth century, as well as *adulthood, bachelorhood, nationhood, spinsterhood*, and *statehood* (not to mention the less-familiar *grand-motherhood, grandfatherhood*, and *gentlehood*), coined in the nineteenth century.

-Hood has not been active in the twentieth century in terms of standard words, though according to the linguist Hans Marchand (1969), nonce words in *-hood* are fairly frequent, particularly in American English: he records *bearhood, cathood, cubhood, doghood, duckhood, selfhood, tailhood*. Similarly, *-dom*, 'the state or condition of being what is referred to by the base,' is another older suffix whose activity has only seemed to slow down because few modern coinages in *-dom* have any permanence. There have been relatively few common terms added to the venerable old *kingdom, earldom, martyrdom* and *Christendom*, notably *boredom* (1852), *officialdom* (1863), and *stardom* (1865). In the nineteenth century, Thomas Carlyle sparked a revival of the suffix with such coinages as *duncedom, rascaldom, Saxondom*,

scoundreldom, and *tinkerdom.* The suffix was frequently applied to animals: *dogdom, catdom,* and *puppydom,* as well as *horsedom, cattledom, cowdom,* and *micedom. Rebeldom* was common during the American Civil War. *Nazidom* occurs frequently between 1933 and the mid-1940s, and *newspaperdom* is another twentieth-century coinage that has enjoyed some currency. But while -*dom* is still lively in Modern English, most nouns in -*dom* have been jocular, disparaging, and short-lived. This is why many language historians in the earlier part of this century declared the suffix dead or ignored its energetic presence. In 1941 the linguist Harold Wentworth collected some 300 -*dom* nouns coined after 1800, and H. L. Mencken adds a few more: *baseballdom, fandom, hucksterdom, moviedom, parentdom, professordom, stuffed-shirt-dom, suckerdom, wifedom, womandom* (no corresponding *husbandom* or *mandom*), and the unlikely *lawnmowerdom.*

As we see from the liveliness of -*dom* in nonce creation, it is never wise to declare an old form of English dead, even the rare suffix -*th,* forming nouns of action, state, or quality, which gives us such common words as *breadth, depth, length, width, filth, health, wealth, stealth,* and *truth,* and has produced little else recently. *Coolth,* which dates from 1547, is now used jokingly for 'coolness.' Ruskin (1860) used *illth,* 'ill-being,' as the opposite of *wealth,* 'well-being,' and the coinages *greenth* and *lowth* have met with little success. The archaic attraction of -*th* may in part be responsible for the popularity of *couth,* the humorous nonce word revived as the opposite of *uncouth,* where the -*th* is not a suffix but actually part of the root.

In a few instances, a new, productive suffix is invented through the process of folk etymology. We have already mentioned *burger,* the clipped form of *hamburger,* which gives such forms as *Chineseburger, Ikeburger, muttonburger, shrimpburger, sturgeonburger,* and *turkeyburger.* -*Aholic,* meaning 'person addicted to,' is such a suffix. The original *alcoholic,* 'related to alcohol,' was coined in the late eighteenth century as an adjective composed of the base *alcohol* and the suffix -*ic.* Though the phenomenon it refers to is ageless, the noun *alcoholic,* 'person addicted to alcohol,' is a twentieth-century invention. It in turn has led to a series of words based on the supposed suffix -*aholic* (or -*oholic*), beginning with *workaholic* (1971), perhaps the most common derivative, and followed by *beefaholic, bookaholic, chocaholic* ('chocolate lover'), *creditaholic, footballaholic, golfaholic, hashaholic, ice cream-aholic, junkaholic, newsaholic, punaholic, spend-aholic, sweetaholic, wheataholic,* and *worryaholic,* among others.

In other cases we find whole words functioning as suffixes. Here a word will serve as the second element in a large number of compounds.

For example, *proof*, meaning 'able to withstand, impervious to,' has been enormously productive, though many *-proof* words do not have wide currency. In addition to the common *bulletproof, fireproof, foolproof, mothproof, rustproof* and *waterproof,* we find such nonce forms as *babyproof, crapproof, irony-proof, marriageproof, moonproof, pimpleproof, poetryproof, punproof, rageproof, spellproof, twinkleproof, vampireproof, yawnproof* and even *proof-proof.* Rhetoric instructors at the University of Illinois, continually looking for essay topics that will not evoke formulaic religious responses from students, call such topics *God-* or *Jesusproof,* and a European manufacturer of shredders boasts of machines that are *Ayatollah-proof,* a reference to the reconstruction of shredded documents by Iranians who took over the American embassy in Tehran.

It is clear that slang is an area of language where this kind of suffixation abounds. One popular slang formative listed by the lexicographers Harold Wentworth and Stuart Berg Flexner (1975) is *head,* usually applied as a physical description, or an assessment of someone's propensities or mentality. We find everything from *acidhead* and *applehead* to *blockhead, blubberhead, cheesehead, fathead, meathead, pinhead, whistle-head* ('boy'), *weedhead,* and *wood-head* (lumberjack). *Airhead* is noted by the *Barnhart Dictionary Companion,* and *Webster's Second* lists over two hundred forms in *-headed,* many of them clearly not slang, including *fertile-headed, foreheaded, green-headed, rightheaded, single-headed, wagon-headed,* and *wrongheaded.*

Suffixation and compounding sometimes follow social or political trends. A situation or event captures the public fancy, and the terms used to describe it are modified to fit new phenomena. *Deadlock* has been around since the eighteenth century, and was first used to describe a situation of stalemate, and only later to refer to a type of lock. There are not a lot of words in *lock*—some gunnery terms (*flintlock, matchlock*) and a few wrestling words (*armlock, headlock*). But with the coining of *gridlock* (ca. 1980), a situation in which traffic in a city is so snarled that it comes to a complete standstill, or *deadlock,* the combining potential of *lock* revives. *Gridlock* is a provocative new word because it names what has become more and more a fact of modern urban life: in New York City, special traffic controllers are employed to clear midtown intersections in an attempt to prevent gridlock. Having secured a place in our vocabulary, *gridlock* in turn produced phrases such as *corporate gridlock, telephone gridlock,* and *vocal gridlock,* together with the related compounds *boatlock* and *pedlock,* 'pedestrian standstill.' Taking things one step further, *eyelock* was used by a reporter to describe a head-to-head confrontation, or staring contest, between two world leaders.

A popular title can generate numerous "copycat" coinages. W. A. Brewer (1987) collects some fifty ephemeral words in *-buster* resulting from the box-office hit movie *Ghostbusters* (1984), including *alley buster* (a bowling ball), *baby-buster* (abortion advocate), *budget busters*, *coldbusters* (doctors), *fare busters* (travel agents), *linebusters* (queue jumpers), *quotabusters*, *stress busters* (a masseuse service), *taxbusters*, *virus busters* (vaccines), and of course *buster busters*, "persons opposed to the proliferation of *-busters* terms." Sometimes these words are generated by symbols. The universal "not allowed" sign superimposed on an open book served as a notice forbidding study during the lunch hour in the Illini Union cafeteria at the University of Illinois, and produced the predictable *bookbusters*.

I have noticed lately that *bash* and its derivatives have become popular in new formations. Coming from a source like *head bashing*, a term associated with the literal, physical aspects of crowd control, we now find *bash* used as a lively term for 'verbally attacking, abusing,' as in *bureaucrat bashing*, *dissident bashing*, *queer bashing*, *Republican bashing*, *teacher bashing*, *union bashing*, and *yuppie-bashing*, as well as *Paki-bashing* (a British usage for 'beating up Pakistanis'), and my own *Brit-bashing* (chapter 24).

Sometimes notoriety will cause part of a word to become a productive suffix. One current-events suffix, *-scam*, from the slang term for 'trick, deception,' is popular for police entrapment schemes designed to expose corruption and crime: *Abscam* (*Arab* plus *scam*) and *Iranscam* are two that have received national attention. Another such suffix, *-gate*, directly reflecting the Watergate scandal of 1972 that forced Richard Nixon out of the presidency, is even more popular. Used in compounds, *-gate* is stripped of its normal meaning: *Watergate* is the name of a building, and the name in turn means a lock or floodgate used to control the flow of water. There was a flurry of coinages in *-gate* in the American press in the mid-1970s, starting with *Winegate* (1973), and including *Billygate*, *copygate*, *Harborgate*, *Irangate*, *Koreagate*, *Motorgate*, *Sewergate*, even *Gategate*, all spawned by some less than earthshaking story of hanky-panky. The suffix remains productive, at least in the press, though up to now none of the derivative scandals have been as momentous as the original one. The press quickly responded to a recent hubbub among television evangelists with *Pearlygate*. It remains to be seen whether the current *Irangate*, also known as *Contragate*, which looks to be a complex, far-reaching affair, will bear out the promise of its suffix.

By the way, another Watergate-related term, *plumber,* 'a person who tries to prevent leaks of information,' predates the Nixon era by at least a generation. Although the *OED Supplement* calls this usage slang, and dates the earliest such plumbing to 1972, and the White House plumbers may indeed have invented the term independently, the literary scholar and mystery writer Dorothy L. Sayers writes in *Busman's Honeymoon* (1937), that Lord Peter Wimsey was sent on a foreign office mission to Rome "like a plumber, to stop diplomatic leaks."

Reflecting a different kind of politics, words in *-person* have been popping up of late, largely as a result of current concern with sexism in language. Many of these sex-neutral coinages are jocular (*freshperson* and *henchperson*, for example, replacing *freshman* and *henchman*, or such intentional absurdities as *nopersonclature* and *aperson* for *nomenclature* and *amen*), but a few are serious and seem to be sticking around (*anchorperson*, *businessperson*, *councilperson*, even the much-maligned *chairperson*).

Also productive of late, and related to the social and political use of language, is the word suffix *-speak*, which gave George Orwell *doublespeak* and *Newspeak* in *Nineteen Eighty-Four* (1949). Since the 1970s, Orwell's words have become the model for a number of negatively charged, short-lived creations like *nounspeak* to describe a noun-heavy style of writing, *Valspeak* for the speech of teenage girls in California's San Fernando Valley, *computerspeak*, 'the jargon of computer users,' *medspeak*, 'the arcane terminology of doctors,' and *blandspeak*, which describes a dull, unevocative literary style. *-Speak* words, always negative in connotation, are coined to describe the speech of certain well-known people. The *Barnhart Dictionary Companion* records *Connallyspeak*, *Freudspeak*, *Haigspeak* and *Reaganspeak*. Other terms include *discospeak*, *littlespeak*, *Olympicspeak*, *rockspeak*, *safespeak*, *science-speak*, *splitspeak*, *videospeak*, and *warspeak*.

Maybe now that Orwell's prophetic year of 1984 has turned the corner, with no apparent effect on our recurrent crises of language or of politics, coinages in *-speak* will slow down. What is not slowing down, however, is the coining of business names based on puns, a practice that will have many language critics spinning in their graves, if they already have them, or digging graves, if they don't.

18 Nothing Like a Good Pun

Onomastics is not an unspeakable practice forbidden in the Bible, it is the study of names. We have already discussed some eponyms earlier. In this chapter we will consider a new trend in onomastics: the use of increasingly outrageous puns in the naming of businesses and the publicizing of goods and services. Time was, when you surveyed the alluring names of American business establishments, you didn't find much humor in them beyond the level of the *Dew Drop Inn,* the punning title of many a neighborhood bar or roadside rest. Of course there are some unintentional double-meaning business names, like the paradoxical *Vitale Funeral Home,* which I noticed once in New York's Little Italy, and *The World-Wide Exterminating Corporation* (for those radiation resistant ants and roaches, or is its mission somewhat more sinister?). Names like these have been chronicled over the years in the pages of the *New Yorker* magazine.

There may have been a day when life, and puns, were simpler, but today we find kicky eating and drinking establishments like *Just for the Halibut* quickly replacing the *Dew Drop Inns* of yore. The American public is going in for cutespeak in a big way, a predictable outgrowth of the many variants of *Happiness is a warm puppy* and *Love is never having to say you're sorry,* the ubiquitous iconic smiley face, which even appears on municipal water towers, and the new goodbye on everybody's lips, *Have a nice day.* This effusive sentimentality and sense of goodwill has prompted, partly in reaction against, and partly as an extension of, such overt language cuteness, an exaggerated wit in public signboards, both those appearing above business establishments and those of a more idiosyncratic or personal nature.

Corporate Punishment

Just as there are trends in language, there are fads in business names. H. L. Mencken in *The American Language* and Wentworth and Flexner in their *Dictionary of American Slang* discuss the many coinages in *-(a)teria* that follow from the original *cafeteria.* This word, borrowed

into English from American Spanish, spawns such terms as *bookateria,
chocolateria, cleaneteria, groceteria, hatateria, mototeria, restauranteria,
sodateria, washateria,* even *casketeria,* an undertaker's establishment.
The *-orium* of the latinate *emporium* influences *barberatorium, infanto-
rium, restatorium,* and as if these were not unwieldy enough, *hotdo-
gatorium.* One antique store in Chicago calls itself the *Browsatorium.
-Mat,* from *automatic,* produced in its heyday *Automat* (a service mark),
laundromat, and more recently, *Fotomat* (also a service mark). The
Greek *orama,* 'view,' produced two visual inventions, the *panorama* and
the *cyclorama,* in the eighteenth and nineteenth centuries, as well as
the more recent movie technique called *Cinerama;* less literal derivations
include the names of business establishments such as *Bowlarama* and
Cake-o-rama. None of these naming trends seems unusually active
right now, but something new is coming down the pike, or the Interstate,
as we call it in the Midwest, to take their place.

Reviving the tradition of the *Dew Drop Inn,* American business has
turned sharply in the direction of corny humor and outrageous puns
in corporate names. Public cutespeak dictates that bars be called *The
Office* or *The Library,* so you can tell your friends you spent a productive
afternoon at the office or the library. A San Francisco restaurant calls
itself *The Boondocks.* One western saloon bears the name *Belly Up,*
accompanying the literal reading with another, subtler suggestion about
cash flow. Eateries are taking names like *Out to Lunch, The Lunch Hour,
My Choice,* or *My Place* (as in 'Let's go to my place'). A nightclub
exists in Chicago called *Exit,* and there is another, more existential one
called *No Exit.* One drinkery near a Manhattan hospital is called *The
Recovery Room.* There is a Los Angeles clothes store called *The Competition* (check out the competition). More and more common too are
the cute-name restaurants, like *Fritz That's It, Fuddrucker's, TGI Friday's,
P. Eye McFly, T. J. Peppercorn,* and *Guadala Harry's.* The Lender brothers
have a chain of bagel restaurants named after the mythical *S. Kinder,*
a pun on the Yiddish for 'eat, children,' which only a mother could
love. There is a discount clothing chain called *T. J. Maxx,* even a New
York children's clothing store called *O. U. Kidd.* And in Evanston,
Illinois, the still-dry home of the WCTU, you can buy your lingerie at
I See London, whose name evokes naughtiness, not the passion or
romance of lingerie, but the children's rhyme about unmentionables,
"I see London, I see France, I see [so and so]'s underpants."

One aspect of the current outbreak of cutespeak is the deliberate
business pun. There is a tumble-down *Tumble Inn* on the outskirts of
our small Champaign downtown today, an indication that this mildly
reprehensible tradition of naming bars persists uninterrupted. In fact,

the pun phenomenon is making a strong comeback in the Midwest, and there is good evidence that this trend has established beachheads on the coasts as well. Sometimes the names are simple variations or deformations of other words: there is *Tanfastik*, a tanning parlor in Evanston, playing both on *tan fast* and *fantastic* (another such establishment calls itself *Fake 'n Bake*), and Highland Park is the (temporary?) home of a Chinese eatery called *The Meanderin' Mandarin*.

Puns are common in the names of nursery schools, where cutespeak is never out of place: *Babes in Toyland, Captain Kidd, Field Day, Patti's Cakes Nursery, The Next Generation*, and the *Wee Care Day School*. Other services catering to children are opting for these kinds of names: *Space Kiddets* sells clothes, *Yards of Fun* sells children's play structures, and *Bear Feet* deals in youngsters' shoes. And of course there is the *Toddle-In-Nursery*, not to be confused with the *Toddle Inn* cocktail lounge, the *Shoe Inn*, which sells footwear, the *Tucker Inn* of the whipped topping television commercial, the *Yugo Inn*, featuring Yugoslav cuisine, not cars, or the macaronic *Wok Inn* (*wok/walk*, get it?).

This sort of punning is spreading fast among restaurants and beauty salons, and to a lesser extent, in the names of other kinds of businesses. A survey of telephone directories, together with reports from trusted informants, produces the following eateries, which I suspect are just the tip of the iceberg: *Lettuce Entertain You* (the flagship of a chain of Chicago cute-food places), *Annie Tique's, Barnum and Bagel, The Boston Sea Party, The Daily Grind* (coffee shop), *Eaternity, Foggie's Notion, Gables on Clark, Garden of Eatin', Goldie Lox, The Great Impasta, Humphrey Yogart, I & Joy Bagels, Just Desserts, Lawrence of Oregano, Let Them Eat Cake* (a bakery), *Lox Stock and Bagel, Relish the Thought, The Shell Station* (seafood), *Snax Fifth Avenue, Something Fishy, Sweet 'n Counter,* and *Jonathan Livingston Seafood*. There is a Chicago bar called *Rest In Pieces*, a bakery called *The Upper Crust*, and a caterer known as *Quiche Me Lorraine*. There is even a name that puns on the name of another business: *Dogs R Us* (a hot doggery playing on *Toys R Us*). Hot dog vendors seem particularly attracted to the new naming trend. For many years, *Mustard's Last Stand* has sold franks near Northwestern University's Dyche Stadium, and Chicago offers *Frankly Yours, Uncle Frank's, Franks-A-Lot*, and *Tasty Pup*. For the more discerning frankophile, there is Champaign's *First National Frank*, a theme restaurant complete with teller and night deposit window. Two Chicago nut dealers cannot resist calling themselves *We Are Nuts* and *Nuts to You*. Of course, not all these names are here to stay. The short-lived *Just for the Halibut*, one of a series of restaurants in the same location, reopened as a Greek deli called, oddly enough, *Ess 'n Fress*.

In contrast to Chicago, San Antonio is more limited in its inventory of pun stores, sporting the sidewalk cafe called *The Kangaroo Court* and a nightclub known as *Sunova Beach;* and San Francisco, the city of food, offers the aficionado little more than *Coneheads Ice Cream Parlor,* two barbecue restaurants, *Hog Heaven* and *Holy Smoke,* a chocolatier called *Sweet Revenge,* and the *Higher Grounds Coffee House,* surely the gathering place for local philosophers. Los Angeles seems also behind the times; its few pun foodaterias include *The Big Chill* (frozen yogurt), *The Bread Winner, I Love Juicy* (vegetarian), and *Dem Bones Bar-B-Q.* And not to be outdone, Joyce's Dublin offers *Gulliver's Travel* (travel) and *Molly's Blooms* (flowers).

Although Boston had a *Tower of Pizza* chain for some time (it's no longer in the book), except for *The Farmer and the Del* (deli), there is no current evidence that other hub restaurants are joining the bandwagon. Boston caterers, however, have picked up on the trend, with *Catering to Your Every Whim, Currier and Chives, Food for Thought, The Movable Feast, Peasant Stock,* and *Thyme Square.* The 1987 Chicago Yellow Pages advertises the caterers *An Affair to Remember, Be My Guest, Blazing Salads, The Butler Did It, Having a Ball, It's Your Party,* and *Two's Company.* To this, San Francisco adds the bakeries *For Heavens Cake, Tart to Tart,* and *True Confections,* not to mention *Quiche and Carry.* The Manhattan Yellow Pages offers a few punning fooderies, for example *Eat & Run; 40 Below* (on 40th Street, though perhaps not in the basement of the building); *Taste Buds* (a deli); *The Sweet Life, Sweet Temptations,* and *Weigh to Go* (candy shops); and another frank stand called *Hot Diggity.*

Shopping mall fast fooderies include *1 Potato 2* and *All American Hero.* Not to be outdone, the recently remodeled basement cafeteria in the University of Illinois' Illini Union in Urbana, which is financially self-supporting and must therefore compete with nearby commercial establishments for the local lunch trade, has been renamed *Down Under,* and serves its fare at such trendy counters as *New Deli, Grilligan's Island, Greensland, The Cold Coast,* and *The Orient Expresso.*

These business establishments, with names like overripe Camembert, have grown up with the Yuppies, whose fondness for such lexical twists must be an acquired taste. Even more cutthroat than restaurants for their upwardly mobile custom are the unisex hair salons, which go in for such monickers as *Beauty Mark, Beauty Spot, The Big Tease, Blood Sweat and Shears, The Clip Joint, Cost Cutters, Cut and Dryed, Cut-It-Out, From Hair to Eternity, Hair Today Gone Tomorrow, The Hair Berdashery Hair Salon, Haircutecture, Hairitage, Hair It Is, Hairizons, Hair Majesty, Hair Port, Head Hunters, The Headliners, Head Quarters, Heads or Nails, Hi-Roller Hair Castle, Mane Attraction, Mane Street, New*

Wave, Sharper Image Hair Design, Shear Excitement (also *Shear Artistry, Class, Elegance, Madness, Magic,* and *Pleasure*), *Shear Love* (a clip joint for pets), *Shylocks Hair Co., Tress Pass Hairworks, The Upper Cut, US Hair Force, United Hairlines,* and *Wave Lengths.* Bourbonnais, Illinois, boasts *The Best Little Hair House,* and my own favorite is the beauty shop chain, *Curl Up and Dye.*

Clothing stores, particularly those catering to women, have come out of *The Closet* to sport such punning attire as *The Clothesline, Bottoms Up, Clothes Quarters, Cotton Ginny, County Seat, Fashionation, The Fashion Bug, Hit or Miss, Kiddie Slickers, The Lady's Room, Sacks Appeal, Simply Tops, Smarty Pants,* and *Ups 'n Downs.* Three stores deal exclusively with socks: *This Little Piggy, Sock It to Me,* and *Twinkle Toes.* Women's leather goods can be purchased at either *The Purse Snatcher* or *The Bag Lady.* A haberdasher in Croton-on-Hudson, New York, is called *The Brick Shirt House,* a bold stroke considering that many New Yorkers do not pronounce their *r*'s after vowels. While larger men are content to shop the literally named Big and Tall stores, store owners woo full-figured women with establishments like *Added Dimensions* and *3 Dimensions,* along with *The Ample Blossom, The Better Half* (half and larger sizes), *The Fashion Bug Plus, Ladies at Large,* and *The Forgotten Woman.* Other merchants specialize in certain sizes as well: *The Great American Short Story* (petites), and *The Long & Short of It* (talls and petites). We find Chicago maternity shops called *A Pea in the Pod, Recreations, Expectations,* and *Mothers Work.* One New York discount clothier does business as *The Emotional Outlet* (are the jeans preshrunk?). There are chains of upscale shopping-mall sneaker shops called *The Athlete's Foot* and *The Foot Locker,* a Manhattan orthopedic bootery called *For Feet Sake,* and a Chicago swimwear emporium known as *Liquid Assets.*

Resale, thrift, and second-hand shops often go in for punning in a big way. We find *Play It Again, Presents of Mine, Repeat Performance, Replay, Return Engagement, Second Act, Second Childhood, Second Coming, Second Cousin, Second Helping, Second Time Around, Second Hand Rose,* and *Twice Blest.* Also merciless when it comes to naming, antique and used furniture stores sport titles like *Ages Ago, As Time Goes By, Back Pages, Den of Antiquity, Echoes of the Past, Good Old Days, Missing Pieces, Now and Then, Past Tenses, Past Tymes, Preferred Stock, Regenerations, Room Service,* and *Time Will Tell.* There is even a San Antonio resale store—throwing out both grammar and good taste—called *Too Good to Be Threw.*

Pets are cute, and pet stores now feel compelled to reinforce this idea with cute names: we find *Age of Aquarium, At Your Command* (dog obedience training), *The Barking Lot, The Cat Hilt Inn* (a feline motel),

Dog Day Afternoon, Dog In Suds, Dog's Best Friend (also *Man's Best Friend*), *Doggone It, For Pet's Sake, Groomingdale's, Let's Pet* (I actually know someone who gets her dog groomed there), *Love on a Leash, Paws for Applause, Petcetera, The Pet Stop, Waggin' Wheels,* and *Happy Tails.* Other types of businesses go in for names in this style as well. There are *The Towne Pump* and *The Short Stop* (gas), *Woodie Alan's* (custom-made furniture), a chair retailer known as *Preferred Seating,* as well as *Private Lives,* purveyors of bedroom furnishings, *Off the Wall* (concealed beds), and *Room and Board* (children's furniture). We also find *Splinter Group* (a woodworking shop), and a collection of picture framers called *Frame of Mind, The Framer's Market* (from farmer's market), *The Great Frame Up,* and *The Picture Show. Stats It* is a Chicago photocopy shop, and *Picture This* and *Picture Us* are one-hour photo finishers.

In addition, we find *The Skatium* (a municipal ice rink), *The Court House* (racquetball), *Saving Face* (skin care), *Maid to Order* and *Merry Maids* (housecleaning), *Good Vibes* and *Sound Experience* (stereos), *Easy Weigh* (weight reduction), *The Tape Worm* (not weight reduction, but video rentals), *The Lock Up* and *The Spare Room* (storage facilities), *Flatts and Sharpe Music Company, The Lazer's Edge* (printing), *The Last Wound Up* (mechanical toys), *Magical Mystery Tours* (travel), *Vanishing Act* (electrolysis), *Home Sweet Home* (siding and gutters), and *For Eyes* (eyeglasses). There are two window cleaners, *Clearly Yours* and *One Fell Swoop* (the latter preferring payment in advance, no doubt), and two instrument haulers, *Top Flight Piano Movers* and *Death Wish Piano Movers.* There are *First Impressions* (a résumé service), *Bumper to Bumper* (auto parts), *The Breaking Point* and *Honest Engine* (auto repair), and *Soak Yourself* (hot tubs and saunas). Also, *The Washing Well* (laundromat), *Dead Rite Pest Control,* and both *Accountemps* (part-time and temporary accountants) and *Temporarily Yours* (office temporaries taking off on *forever yours*). One Illinois bait shop calls itself *The Happy Hooker,* and not to be outdone, a suburban septic tank cleaning service does business as *The Wizard of Ooze.* Also redolent but less objectionable are a bouquet of florists: *The Garden of Earthly Delights, Primrose Lane,* and *Grass Roots Garden Shop,* the last a literal rendering of a phrase we normally take figuratively. Health and fitness programs often have playful names: besides *The Body Shop* there are *Fitnastics, Gymboree, Jam-nastics, Jazzercise, Sportastiks,* and *Tan-ercise.* We find a singing telegram service called *Hey Wires,* as well as two specifically adult wire services, *Teddy Bare* and *Grin n' Bare It.* Also, *Bearly Making It* (crafts and hobbies), *Balloonatics* (balloon messages for all occasions), *Left Handed Compliments* (gadgets for the sinister), and *Art Attack Studios* (photographers). Skokie boasts *Centsible Drugs,* Boston has a store for gifted children called *Smart Stuff,* and Chicago has both *Ladies First* (a group gynecological practice) and *Women and Children First,* specializing in feminist books and records.

Many small businesses use the formula *Mr.* _____ in their name, for example, *Mr. Auto Body, Mr. Build* (remodeling and renovation), *Mr. Discount* (furniture), *Mr. Gutter, Mr. Hairweave, Mr. Insulation, Mr. Plumber, Mr. Steak,* and *Mr. Window & Things.* To this New York adds the androgynous *Mr. Chambermaid.* And following *Mister Printer* in the trendy Manhattan Consumer Yellow Pages there is the feminist *Ms. Print* (*sic*), which puns on *Ms.* and *manuscript* but most strongly hints at misprint, something other printers, like Boston's *Fine Print,* take care not to advertise.

Signs and the Times

Cutespeak also makes itself felt in how we name our boats and automobiles. There is a long tradition of punning yacht and power boat names such as *QTπ* or *Sloop du Jour.* With the introduction of vanity license plates in more and more states, car owners have gone in for cuteplates in a big way. One litigious attorney in our town has SUEM on his automobile. A doctor affects VIRUS, and a Latin teacher, JOVIS, while a New York music teacher has MONOT 1 (monotone). One student's car, no doubt a gift from a doting parent, boasts MAZL TOV, while a dilapidated, hand-painted flower-child Volkswagen microbus from Rhode Island displays APATHY. A low-slung Lotus sports car calls itself MUTANT. A pair of academics new to the area evidence loyalty to their old alma mater by investing a small fortune in vanity plates: theirs is the van labeled PENNST 8, the station wagon with PENN ST, and the sporty hatchback tagged PENNST GR8. And a dentist asks the inevitable acronymic question, RUNUM (*Are you numb?*). Frank Nuessel, Jr. (1982) records a variety of cuteplates, including HI U QT, 10SNE1 ('Tennis, anyone?'), 2TH DR ('tooth doctor') and NUTS 2 U, as well as several that managed to evade the watchfulness of motor vehicle bureau censors who are paid to keep our streets and highways clean: RRGASM, BOOZER, AC-DC, and IM GAY.

To this outbreak of auto-vanity we can add two other recent motor sign phenomena. There is the professional-sexual bumper sticker, with such variants as *Teachers do it with class, Divers do it deep, Virologists do it with immunity,* and *Archivists make it last longer.* While this is an auto slogan trend that has already peaked, we find it replaced by the increasingly popular miniature yellow, diamond-shaped road sign dangling from automobile rear windows that began by proclaiming, "Baby on Board" or "Child on Board" but has quickly gone on to convey more bizarre and less literal information.

"Baby on Board" alerts other motorists to the likely presence of youngsters (the signs are not removed when children are not on board). However, the sensible driver avoids smashing into any other vehicle, not just those with children in them, so the effectiveness of the signs is unclear. More likely, these signs are boasts, not just admonitions to be careful, like the maternity t-shirts that read BABY, with a large arrow pointing down (there is now a line of *Baby On Board* maternity wear). The boasts have turned into jokes, however, not based on puns but on bizarre versions of the original signs. *Life Magazine* calls this 1986 fad "yellow fever." On the streets and in the stores we now read such vehicular inanities as "Future Baby on Board," "10 1/2 on Board," "Mother-in-law on Board," "Sex Maniac on Board," "Mother-in-law in Trunk," "Ex-Husband's Girl Friend in Trunk," "Illegal Alien in Trunk" (this from California) and, predictably, "Driver in Trunk." I have yet to see "Nothing in Trunk," but there is a car parked near my office boasting "Stupid Sign in Window." All of these variants may ultimately derive from the hastily done-up "Kick Me" target signs taped to the backs of unsuspecting victims on April Fool's Day, though they have a new twist: in these cases the fool dons the sign on purpose.

Pun Intended

A casual finger-walk through the yellow pages of major metropolitan areas, or the parking lot of any good-sized shopping mall in any vanity state, and if you are not land-locked, as I am in central Illinois, a visit to your local marina should provide similar evidence for store, boat, and car names or other signs based on puns of one kind or another. Product names, long subject to the most bizarre twists and turns of cutietude, are falling into line as well with the introduction of a chocolate-flavored instant coffee called *Double Dutch,* a cat treat called *Goodie Two Chews* (targeting the owners of Siamese?), a remedy for chapping called *Lip Service,* a stuffed snake to put at the base of a door called a *draft dodger,* a garbage disposal called *In-sink-erator,* and two new brands of microwave popping corn, *Pop Secret* and *Amazing Glaze.* I'm not sure the last can be made using the *Stir Crazy* corn popper, or with any of the *Above All* line of under-the-cabinet kitchen appliances now being marketed (there is also an under-the-cabinet food processor called *Cutabove*). Other punning brand names include *Fresh Guys* (cleaning cloths), *Pupperoni* (a jerky snack for dogs), *Habeas Crispus* (a regional brand of potato chip), and two children's items, small *Reebok* sport shoes called *Weeboks* and a line of new-wave kids duds called *Micro Wave*. We also find two hair removers, *Better Off* and *Hair Goes*, not to mention a new cookbook entitled *Pita the Great*. I grew up during the early days of television, cutting my teeth on *Vegematic* commercials. Now our national cable channels offer us a blanket and scarf maker called the *Knit Wit*, if we don't-forget-and-call-by-midnight-tonight.

The make-up industry, long a bastion of the cute name, traditionally uses puns in marketing new products. There is a make-up called *Touch Base*, and there have been lipsticks called *E.S.Pink, In the Flesh, In the Pink*, and *Pithy Peach*, as well as a nail polish with nail-strengthening capabilities called *New Lengths*. Other colors worthy of note are *A rose is a rouge; Coming up roses; Berry rich; Berries jubilee; A la mauve; It's your mauve;* and *Melondrama*. Clothing lines also employ puns: *Back to Back, Suitables, Tanks a Lot, Outside Interests,* and *Brace Yourself* (suspenders), to cite just those I encountered while walking past the racks in a local department store. Nearby I found a line of knives marketed under the *Advant-Edge* brand.

Life Savers has a long history of advertising puns: they have been called *hole-some, enjoy-mint, refresh-mint* and during an election, *the people's candy-date*. Even conservatively named businesses are joining the punwagon. Seagate Technology, a leading manufacturer of disc drives for personal computers, is located at 920 *Disc Drive* in Scotts Valley, California. Urbana's *Diet Center* advertises, "Weight no longer!" Charles Alfieri, Manhattan purveyor of men's hairpieces, slickly proclaims, "We go to your head," and the motto of New York's Quality Pest Control announces, "We stop 'em dead." Chappie's Caterers of Chicago winks, "Have an affair with us"; L & A Portable Cleaning Systems smirks, "Talk dirty to us"; and the Monee (Illinois) Tree Nursery loudly proclaims, "Don't leaf home without us." A recent campaign by grocery bag manufacturers to counter the trend toward plastic packaging adopted as its slogan, "Paper bags have sacks appeal," and a suburban Chicago rug dealer proclaims, "Our prices will floor you." One Chicago arborist deals in "Tree care and all its branches." There is even a refuse collector who insists on reinventing the wheel: on the side of his truck is the old chestnut of the garbologist, "Our business is picking up."

I should make it clear that I am not opposed to wordplay in any of its manifestations, particularly those discussed above. After all, I'm the one furiously compiling the list of examples, which grows with every day—and then of course, there's the title of this book (book titles themselves are another fruitful area for pun collecting). There is really nothing like a good pun, and I resist the inevitable comment that these names are nothing like good puns, because some, like Gotham city's *Drive Me Crazy Auto School,* are very choice indeed. However, the better part of such public displays of humor may ultimately require discretion, if not restraint of trade. A good witticism is enjoyable the first time around, and sometimes the second or third time as well. But frequent repetition sours the best of jokes, and since names are meant to be repeated endlessly, the staying power of funny names is seriously limited.

Worse yet, such names are embarrassing. Imagine telling a friend you bought your new whitewalls from that Shakespearean merchant in Paramus, *Pericles, Prince of Tires,* or that you've switched from Jarndyce and Jarndyce to that discount no frills law firm, *Suit Yourself.* Employees at these businesses have the additional burden of answering the phone all day long with tags like, *"Inanity Fare,* can we help you?" What about the pet store employee who must constantly suggest to callers, "Let's Pet"? Or do they just have one of the dogs breathe into the phone every time it rings?

Unfortunately, the problems that accompany punning names do not always prevent parents from burdening their children with monickers the likes of *Pearl Button, Penny Price, Merry Christmas, Buncha Love,* or *Ima Hogg* (all of these are *real names*). Such naming practices for people are downright cruel, but business owners, who look only at the bottom line, don't seem to get the message. And what, by the way, does *The Bottom Line* deal in? Bookkeeping? Weight Reduction? Proctology?

Our only hope for relief from cruel and unusual corporate punishment may lie in the fact that with enough repetition, a word or expression may lose its transparency. Many a metaphor has died this way. It was not until I was well into revising this chapter that I realized I buy stereo equipment from *Good Vibes,* open my garage door with a *Touch-N-Go* automatic opener, and write occasionally for a journal on editing called *Righting Words.* In addition, the names I've discussed are fashionable, which means that one day the fashion will change, the bumper sticker fade, the license plate crumple. There can be no guarantee, though, that fashion will change for the better, for business names are exhibitionist by nature, and who is to say that *Caesar's Garlic Wars* (Italian food) or *The Cookie Cutter* (hair) are any worse than Cambridge, Massachusetts' *Ernie's Liquor and Lunch* or San Francisco's *Le French Bakery?* Of course there are other forces at work in business names besides the pun. One San Francisco barberteria, bucking the trend in bizarre names like *Le Elegante Beauty Salon* or *Klipotek,* modestly calls itself *Nice Cuts,* and I don't know whether it is humility or simply truth-in-advertising that dictates the name of the Indian vegetarian restaurant in Chicago called *Pretty Fast Food.* In the meantime, cutespeak is on the rise, and there is little to do but monitor our increasing desire to play with our words in public.

IV Language Politics

19 Language Is the Enemy

The main purpose behind business names is to draw customers, and any language use designed to influence people—whether it is advertising, or propaganda, or literature—may be said to be political. Just as we perceive language to express political ethos, we feel that the bias language expresses toward or against particular groups of people is also political. All of us use language as a tool, and sometimes as a weapon, either to distinguish or to discriminate against others on the basis of color, religion, national origin, sex, or some other personal attribute. Sometimes we do this intentionally; at other times we are unwitting perpetuators of a bias that has become built into the language.

The actor Ossie Davis once wrote an essay, "The English Language Is My Enemy" (1967), lamenting the strongly negative connotations of the word *black* and its synonyms in English. While *black* and *white* are not always clearly negative and positive, respectively, Davis's sense of prejudice is not difficult to confirm. Using a thesaurus, one discovers under *blackness* such pessimistic terms as *obscurity, lividness,* and *denigration* (literally, 'making black'). As a verb *black* can mean 'darken, blot, blotch, smudge, begrime, and becloud.' It has connotations of threatening, frowning, forbidding, and foreboding. It suggests baneful, dismal, or sinister doings, as well as uncleanness, immorality, sinfulness and damnation. Reputations, characters, and hearts are blackened.

Whiteness on the other hand generally serves as a positive term. It represents both moral and material purity, cleanness, chastity, and innocence. The expression *a white man* refers to an honorable one (as "That's very white of you" indicates an honorable act), but *a black man* is evil, or a Negro (via Spanish and Portuguese, from the Latin word for black), or both. Black is the color of crime. As an adjective it appears in a variety of phrases referring to imaginary animals as 'fearsome, terrible, or evil.' The comparisons go on and on. Black magic is bad medicine; white magic serves good ends. Blackmail is an unspeakable crime; a white collar is a sign of respectable employment. *A white son* is a favorite, but we deplore a black sheep. And in the horse operas, the baddies wore the black hats, while the heroes dressed in white.

There are a few negative associations for white, but not many. The *white feather* is a sign of surrender, though the *white flag* is the ensign of peace. *White slavery* is far from positive. A *white lie* is truly a lie, but it is not unforgivable, and a *white night* is a sleepless one. To *turn white* means to become extremely fearful or angry, and one sense of *whitewash* is to cover with a thin coat of respectability. *The white death* or *white scourge* once referred to tuberculosis. A *white-livered* person, now more commonly *lily-livered*, is a coward. And white in Chinese culture is the color of death.

Black may be beautiful, but English must sometimes strain to make it so, for the positive senses of *black* are few and far between. To be *in the black* (in contrast to red, not white) means 'to show a profit.' To *black shoes* is to clean them. *Black soil* is fertile, while *white soil* is not. *Black gold* is oil, a most valuable commodity. *Black tie, black belt,* and *black watch* are positive as well. A *black book* may be an official one, just as a *white paper* is an official report (though a *little black book* is something else again). And of course *black* may be neutral. *Blackletter is a style of type.* A *blacksmith* works in iron, or black metal, while a *whitesmith* works in tin, or white metal. Of course there are the more or less neutral black and white plants, animals, and other substances: *blackberry, blackthorn, blackwood, blackbird* (often viewed negatively), *black snake, blacktail, black bread, black lead, whitebait, whitebeam, white ale, white broth, white bread,* and so forth. But *black* is the primary color of gloom, malignancy, disgrace, disease, and death. We speak of *blackguards, blacklists, black markets,* even *black comedy.* No wonder Davis suspects the language is his enemy.

Have We Offended Everyone?

English clearly discriminates against *black* in its vocabulary, placing *white* in a superior position. That *black* is negative in connotation in some African languages, and *white* positive, offers little additional comfort. But English singles out other groups besides blacks for some pretty unequal treatment. Our language discriminates against its speakers not only on the basis of race, but also because of their ethnic origin, religion, age, sex, sexual orientation, physical ability, and even handedness.

Perhaps handedness is the most innocuous of the slants of English, since we don't take it seriously any more. But only a generation or two ago parents and teachers were intransigent in their efforts to convert southpaws to right-handedness (the corresponding *northpaw*, a right-hander, is a rarely encountered slang analogy, though *southpaw* clearly remains the marked term), and even today left-handedness attracts surprised comment. Why was the favored hand an important educational issue? For one thing, the left side of the body was presumed to be weaker, hence to see with the left eye, or work with the left hand, implies inefficiency or incompetence. The right hand is the hand of greeting, while the left may even be thought of as unclean. In Middle English *a left* is a mean, worthless person. A *left-handed marriage* is a morganatic one, in which the offspring cannot inherit. A *child of the left hand* may refer to a child of such a marriage, or to an illegitimate child. In contrast, the name *Benjamin* comes from the Hebrew, 'son of one's right hand.' A *left-handed compliment* is an insult; *out in left field* is metaphorically alone and in the middle of nowhere. And a *left-handed monkey wrench* is a nonexistent tool that is the bane of novice mechanics.

On the other hand, *right* is associated with strength, efficiency, correctness, and reliability. Its contrast with *wrong* adds force to its contrast with *left*. The right side is the principal side of an object, as in *right side up*, and it is the most advantageous side of an affair. The English word *sinister* is the Latin word for 'left,' and *dexterity* comes from its Latin opposite, *dexter*, 'right.' Someone who is ambidextrous, able to use both hands equally well, is really a person with two right, or *dexter*, hands, while a poor dancer apologizes for having two left, though perhaps not quite sinister, feet. In one case, the handedness bias and the sexist bias are combined: in West African Pidgin, the right, or good, hand is called the *manhan*, while the left, or bad, hand is the *wumanhan*.

Discrimination on the basis of handedness is essentially trivial. The most common and the most dangerous language biases concern people's place or country of origin, their sex, and their race or religion. Every set of people has another group they habitually degrade or make fun of. Americans tell a variety of ethnic jokes, for example, though they seem to pick heavily on the Poles. In Poland, however, the Poles tell Russian jokes, while in France, the Belgians are the butt of humor. The Belgians in turn pick on one another, Flemish against Walloon. In the United States, the Texans make fun of Oklahomans, and many Americans pick on Arkansawyers, in addition to singling out residents of particular towns for their sport: *Oshkosh, Walla Walla, Peoria, Brooklyn,* and *Secaucus* are just some of the better known "joke towns" of our culture. Many of us have heard the fiddle tune, "The Arkansas Traveler." According to the *Dictionary of American Regional English* (*DARE*), an *Arkansas traveler* may also refer to a local railway, and

Arkansaw travels (like *Montezuma's revenge* and *Delhi belly*) means diarrhea. A *Chicago* (or *Kentucky*) *pill* is a bullet; a *Connecticut mile* is the distance (usually less than a statute mile) you can go in a minute; and a *California prayer book* is a deck of cards.

In addition to the obvious insulting ethnic epithets which do not need extensive rehearsal here, there are other slang or idiomatic expressions geared to cause offense in varying degrees. Some of these are humorous, others simply blunt, and most involve the low opinion one set has for another. The alleged propensity of particular groups to arrive late for any function gives rise to the expressions *Alaska time, colored people's time, farmer's time,* and *Jewish time* (some of these terms are used by group members as well as outsiders). Our idioms reflect our opinion of other people's hygiene as well as their punctuality. The French call fleas *espagnoles* (the word means 'Spanish'). Likewise, lice are *espagnols,* while in some parts of America they are *Arkansas lizards.* An *Arkansas fire extinguisher* is a chamber pot, and while a *California* (or *Florida*) *room* is a sunny room with many windows, a *California house* is an outhouse.

Many nations freely use their language to characterize the sexuality of "foreigners." The English think of the French as lascivious, and speak of *French kisses, French postcards,* and the *French* (or sometimes *Spanish*) disease. In turn, the French, Italians, and Spanish blame sexually transmitted illness on one another, or on the English, whose reputation for unbridled lust made quite an impression on eighteenth-century Scots and continentals. One English synonym for *condom* is *French letter,* though the French return the compliment by asserting the English origin of this venereal device, which they call the *redingote anglaise,* the 'English overcoat.' Oregonians have been known to sport migration-control bumper stickers warning, "Don't *Californicate* Oregon."

Other national, local, or personal epithets emphasize inferior quality, often through exaggeration or ironic understatement. An *Irish diamond* is actually rock crystal, while in speaking of gems in general, a *female stone* is one of pale or otherwise poor color. *Alabama wool* is cotton. A *Boston screwdriver* is a hammer, a reference to the shoddy construction practice of hammering screws to speed up a job, and an *Arizona paint job* is no paint at all. *Arkansas wedding cake* is corn bread, and *Arkansas asphalt* is not blacktop but a corduroy log road. In baseball a *Texas leaguer* (also known as a *Jap liner, Sheeny Mike,* and *stinker*) is a "cheap" base hit, a ball knocked safely between the infield and the outfield. Speaking of sports and insult, a *Chinese home run* is an easy or cheap one, hit along a short left or right field foul line, and the *Bronx cheer*, or *raspberry*, is not a cheer at all but a rude insult.

Miserliness is another attribute celebrated in our vocabulary: a *Scotch sixpence* may be a mere threepence, but a *Boston dollar* is only a penny. A *Dutch treat*, also called a *Philadelphia treat*, is no treat at all (*to go arkansaw* is the same as *to go Dutch*), while a *Boston quarter* is a five or ten cent tip (more than a *Boston dollar*, but still not enough). *To arkansaw* is 'to cheat, or to kill in an unsportsmanlike manner.' And a *Chinese deal* is one that does not materialize.

The most insulting terms purport to characterize national behavior. A *Chinese fire drill* is a chaotic procedure found in American college dormitories, or in cars stopped waiting for traffic lights to change, in which people run around in mock confusion, flapping their arms and making as much noise as they can. Other terms referring to the Chinese may refer not so much to supposed national character as to geography. Thus a *Chinese three-point landing*, 'a plane crash,' may not allude so much to supposed oriental aeronautic skill as to the fact that Americans think the shortest way to China is straight down (compare also *Chinese handball*, an American urban game in which the ball is hit to bounce off the ground before rebounding off the wall).

According to Hendrickson (1972), the Dutch are the most ill-treated of national groups in terms of English, a fact which Moore (1961) attributes to the intense naval and commercial rivalry between Holland and England. We have already mentioned *Dutch treat*. *Dutch courage* is alcohol-induced foolhardiness, a *Dutch headache* is a hangover, a *Dutch widow* is a prostitute, and a *Dutch defense* is a surrender. A *Dutch nightingale* is really a frog (in the same vein, an *Arizona nightingale* is a mule or donkey, a *Missouri bear*, a hog, and an *Alaska turkey*, a salmon). In contrast, the Italians get off relatively easily (an *Italian football* is a bomb).

Foods are often the subject of this kind of ethnic allusion to inferiority. We eat *Scotch rabbit* or *Welsh rabbit* (now frequently euphemized to *Welsh rarebit*), a dish of melted cheese and toast, but no meat, whose name was not originally intended as an ethnic compliment. Other dishes that are jocularly insulting are *Scotch chocolate*, a drink of sulphur and milk, and *Scotch coffee*, which consists of toasted biscuits boiled in water. *Scotch woodcock* is actually anchovies on toast, *Boston woodcock* is pork and beans, and *Bombay duck* is curried fish. *Arkansas* (or *Georgia*) *chicken* is salt pork, *Texas butter* is gravy made from flour, water, and meat grease, and *Chicago* (or *Cincinnati*) *oysters* are pigs' testicles, although they sometimes refer to pigs' feet as well.

20 Race and Religion

The insulting vocabulary discussed in the previous chapter may be embarrassing, but it is also part and parcel of our language. What directs our choice of words is our attitude toward those we address, and our desire to communicate inoffensively (at least in most cases). Nonetheless, we cannot rid English of insult, nor would we be wise to do so. It is human nature to blow off steam, and we cannot be expected to go around being sickly sweet to everyone we speak or write to. However, we are often motivated in selecting our idiom by the desire to establish goodwill in our audience, and when an associate or correspondent, a friend or stranger, establishes a verbal preference, we are well advised to follow through. Whether it's "Call me Harry" or "That's *Ms.* White," or an unvoiced understanding that black men are not boys, and women are not girls, we do what we can, often unconsciously, to address people in ways they prefer.

The establishment of such preferences may be problematic, because language and fashion change from time to time and place to place, and it is commonly true that tempers run high when it comes to observing—or failing to observe—the language amenities. In what seems to us now an inappropriately titled essay, "Designations for Colored Folk" (1944), H. L. Mencken notes that the standard word to describe people of black African ancestry is *Negro*, used by blacks and whites alike, and his account is spurred in part by the editorial battle that occurred between 1913 and 1930 over whether or not the term should be capitalized in print. Proponents of capitalization argued that it was discriminatory to place a lower case *negro* alongside a capitalized *German, Italian, Jew,* or *Anglo-Saxon,* while the few blacks who opposed the change maintained that it would only reinforce the discriminatory status quo by placing undue emphasis on skin color.

Mencken (1944, 1638–65) reports that in 1937, Dr. Kelly Miller, writing in *Opportunity, the Journal of Negro Life,* traces the history of terms referring to blacks, from the early *Negro,* to *black* itself, which developed negative connotations and was replaced in turn by *African, darky* (a term initially neutral, according to Miller), and *freedman* (popular for about five years after the Civil War). T. Thomas Fortune,

179

editor of the *New York Age,* rejected *Negro* "because of the historical degradation and humiliation attached to it." He coined *Afro-American* around 1880. This seems restricted to rather formal usage, and the analogous but short-lived *Africo-American* proved too cumbersome ever to become popular. In 1936 Robert L. Abbot, editor of the *Chicago Defender,* replaced *Negro* in his journal with the term *Racemen,* though it never achieved much currency. *Sepia* had some brief popularity: in 1944 there was a *Sepia* Miss America contest held in Boston.

Miller concludes that only two terms have any claim to standard status, *Negro* and *colored,* though he rejects the latter as inappropriately vague (all people have color), and euphemistic to boot. Instead Miller prefers *Negro,* a word he finds stronger and more grammatically flexible. Unlike *colored, Negro* can be inflected for number, and apparently unaware of the opprobrium commonly associated at the time with such feminines as *Jewess* and *Quakeress,* Miller finds it a distinct advantage that *Negro* can express gender as well: "Princess, poetess and Jewess have their just grammatical analogue in Negress." Its only drawback, as far as he is concerned, is the closeness of *Negro* to the justly reviled and insulting *nigger.*

As I said above, fashions change, and as a result of the civil rights movement of the 1960s, the standard terms were overthrown once again. Although many of its supporters were radicals in their day, *Negro* became associated with the old order, with the imagined as well as the real Uncle Tom-ism of the past. The standard word, at least for the time being, is *black* again, though there is a new controversy over whether the word should be capitalized—since white is not—either as a noun, or as an adjective in such phrases as *black English.* Recently, too, there has been some support for *African American,* on the grounds that it parallels the other hyphenated-American terms and is therefore most neutral.

Jews and Jesuits

Other American minority groups have changing terminology as well. In a letter to the *Chronicle of Higher Education* objecting to the word *oriental,* Jonathan Chock Chong Chu (March 8, 1989, B4), reports that "some Asians object to the very use of the term. It is all too reminiscent of a time, not so long ago, when 'wog'—worthy Oriental gentleman— rolled easily off the tongues of whites certain of the scientific fact of their racial superiority." Although numerous etymologies for *wog* have been proposed, including another acronym, Westernized Oriental Gentleman, the highly derogatory term, found most often in British usage, is generally explained as a clipping of *golliwog*, a black-faced doll popular at the turn of the century in England, and its primary reference has been to Arabs, Indians, and Pakistanis, though it has clearly generalized to include the Chinese. In any case, *Oriental* and *Asiatic* are now giving way to *Asian*, *Asian-American*, or most recently, *Asian Pacific* in ethnic classification, and *API*, for Asian or Pacific Islander, the alphabet soup terminology of federal affirmative action forms. There is some variation too in the established reference for Americans of Spanish or Latin American ancestry. Competing terms include *Chicano*, *Hispano*, *Hispanic*, *La Raza*, *Latino*, and *Spanish-surnamed* (again, this last is the language of official forms). Writing of Hispanics in the American Southwest, Jane and Chester Christian (1966, pp. 309–10n.) find that *Mexican* "is so often used disparagingly that many who proudly refer to themselves as *mexicanos* in Spanish are insulted if an Anglo calls them *Mexican.*" The Christians classify as polite names that do not refer specifically to Mexican, or which even deny Mexican heritage: *Spanish-speaking*, *Latin-American*, or *Spanish-American*. In addition to the neutral *Anglo* for non-Hispanics, the Christians note that Hispanics use the negative terms *gabacho*, which carries negative sexual connotations, as well as *gringo* and *yanqui*. They refer disparagingly to Hispanics as *pochos*, literally 'bleached, pale,' a term which, like *oreo* for American blacks—which refers to the cookie and means black on the outside, white on the inside—carries the negative connotations of assimilation to Anglo norms.

Many groups—not all of them minorities—have distinct preferences about the words that name them. Women seem divided over the appropriateness of *woman* and *lady* (see the next chapter). Men seem to have some slight preference for *lady*, perhaps because they perceive it as more polite, although usage critics and feminists insist that *lady* is a euphemism and a term denoting secondary status. Jews, at least in America, prefer *Jewish person* or the simple adjective *Jewish*. As Dwight Bolinger notes in *Aspects of Language* (1968), "The word *Jew* has been used unfavorably by so many of the world's big and little defamers that it is sometimes avoided even at the expense of grammar." At one time *Hebrew* was considered the polite term (hence YMHA, Young Men's Hebrew Association, and UAHC, Union of American Hebrew Congregations), though it is no longer current. *The Standard Dictionary* (1890) recommends *Hebrew* for the race and language, *Israelite* for one who practices the religion (for example, the newspaper *The Carolina Israelite*).

Not only do we seek to influence how people address us, we also make an effort to discourage terms of opprobrium, particularly in any formal context. In the 1930s and 1940s, many communities around the country banned any printed matter, whether written by black or white, that used the word *nigger,* even if its negative or dialect status was clearly indicated by italics or quotation marks. Affected were such literary standards as *Huckleberry Finn* (which is still frequently banned for this reason), the works of the prominent black writers W. E. B. Du Bois, Frederick Douglass, Booker T. Washington, Paul Lawrence Dunbar, Countee Cullen, and Langston Hughes, as well as two leading black journals, *The Crisis,* and *Opportunity,* where Kelly Miller's article on *Negro* and its synonyms appeared.

In the 1870s, complaints about two words, *jew* and *jesuitical,* caused a stir in the American press. It has been, at various times, common journalistic practice to identify the race, ethnicity, gender, or marital status of a newsworthy person even if such identification is irrelevant to the story in question (*Blonde Mother of 4 Wins Nobel Prize*). Richard Grant White (1870) discusses a case in which the *New York Times* labeled certain criminals as Jews. A reader objected, asking the question, "Would you speak of the arrest of two Episcopalians, a Puseyite, three Presbyterians, and a Baptist?" White, who felt the label *Jew* was racial rather than religious (and therefore of legitimate interest to the readers of the newspaper!), was disturbed because the *Times* apologized for its error.

White was not the only writer on correct English to be insensitive to the implications of words. Both George Philip Krapp, in his *Comprehensive Guide to Good English* (1927), and Maurice H. Weseen, in *Crowell's Dictionary of English Grammar and Handbook of American Usage* (1928), label *jew down,* meaning 'to cheat, to bargain down the price of something,' as colloquial, and both explain in the front matter to their usage guides that colloquial speech is good, careful, acceptable, informal English.

The use of *jew* as a verb meaning 'to cheat' is cited as early as 1849 by the *OED,* and the *Dictionary of Americanisms* records the word even earlier in this country, in citations dated 1824 and 1825. It did not appear in the dictionaries of Noah Webster or Joseph Emerson Worcester, the two major nineteenth-century American lexicographers, until mid-century, however, and then it was labeled either colloquial or opprobrious. In 1872 Mr. A. S. Solomons wrote to G. & C. Merriam, publishers of Webster's dictionaries, to protest the definition. Merriam agreed to drop it in the next edition, and it is still omitted from their series of *Collegiate* desk dictionaries, although it soon reappeared in the larger, unabridged books.

A usage note on *jew down* in *The Century Dictionary* (1889–97) calls the phrase well established in colloquial speech, having little or no overt reference to the Jews themselves, but adds, "regarded by Jews as offensive and opprobrious." *Webster's New International Dictionary* (1925) warns of the antisemitic character of *jew* as a verb, though it does admit a neutral sense as well: "Used opprobriously in allusion to practices imputed to the Jews by those who dislike them, or now sometimes colloquially without conscious reference to the Jews." Funk and Wagnalls' *Standard Dictionary* derives it from stereotype: "Referring to the proverbial keenness of Jewish traders," but adds a second sense that is somewhat more negative: "To practice sharp methods in trade, such as are vulgarly ascribed to Jews." *Webster's Third*, which was roundly and mistakenly criticized for not providing usage guidance to its readers, comments after its definition of *jew down*, "usually taken to be offensive."

Despite the legitimate insistence of dictionaries on publishing the bad meanings of words alongside the good ones, complaints of discrimination can still be heard. In 1973 Marcus Shloimovitz, a Manchester textile merchant, lost a four-year court battle to have the *Oxford English Dictionary* drop what he considered to be the "derogatory, defamatory and wholly deplorable definitions" of the word *Jew*. Shloimovitz argued that the dictionary editors "should have the decency to make it clear that the definitions are obsolete, archaic and past usage." Being careful not to set a precedent, the judge dismissed the suit on a technicality, ruling that no *personal* damage had been done to the complainant.

In defining *Jew*, the *OED* does note that the word frequently carries, in its early use, an opprobrious sense. But the dictionary does not mark those negative definitions based on stereotype as in any way obsolete, since in fact they are not. Thus *Jew* can serve as an insulting term for any "grasping or extortionate money-lender or usurer, or a trader who drives hard bargains or deals craftily." Still another complaint has recently surfaced, this time against *cabal*, which derives from *Kabbalah*, the Jewish mystical tradition of Biblical interpretation. Since the seventeenth century, *cabal* has had a primarily negative meaning in English, 'a secret or private intrigue of sinister character,' according to the *OED*. *Cabal* as a verb has always been negative in its reference. According to one of William Safire's correspondents, *cabal* is as bad as *jew down* in perpetuating "offensive religious stereotyping" (Safire 1986).

Dictionaries may inadvertently offend other religious and ethnic groups as well. Todd and Hancock (1986) point out that the phrase *street arab*, 'wandering or homeless child,' which appears in the nineteenth century, is anti-Muslim (once *Moslem*, or even *Mohamme-*

dan), though *arab* as a slang term for 'any wild looking or excitable person; peddler,' was often applied to Central Europeans, particularly Jews and Turks, rather than Arabs. A survey of our religious vocabulary shows that it is Jews and Catholics who are most discriminated against in terms of language. Another of William Safire's many correspondents wrote to him complaining about the offensive use of the verb *pontificate*, and speculating that those who object to *jew* and other ethnic slurs rarely take offense when this word appears (Safire 1986). Both the neutral sense of *pontificate*, 'to officiate as a pope or bishop,' and the negative, 'to speak in a pompous or dogmatic manner,' originate in England in the early nineteenth century. It is clear that the pejorative use of these words arises out of some anti-Catholic bias, but it is also clear that despite the negative use of the term in the nineteenth century, many dictionaries have steered the straight and narrow on this one. While the negative sense of *dogmatic*, another word which carries a degree of religious bias, is recorded as early as Samuel Johnson's dictionary of 1755, Johnson, Noah Webster, Joseph Emerson Worcester, the *Century Dictionary*, and Funk and Wagnalls' *Standard Dictionary* either ignore the verb *pontificate* altogether, or record only its positive, literal sense, 'to act like a pontiff or bishop; to say mass.' Contemporary dictionaries including *Webster's Third* (1961), *The American Heritage Dictionary* (1982), and *The Random House College Dictionary* (1980), do record the negative sense, however, and it is clear that in common usage it is this pejorative, figurative sense of *pontificate* rather than the literal meaning which predominates.

Along with *pontificate* and *dogmatic* (whose neutral and negative senses both arose in the seventeenth century), there is *propaganda*. This word enters English in the early eighteenth century as the Congregation of the College of the Propaganda (founded in 1622), a group of Cardinals concerned with the propagation of the faith. *Propaganda*, which means 'propagating,' is transferred to any group or movement to advocate a doctrine or practice in the mid-nineteenth century, and is used as a term of reproach, the sense it retains today. Propaganda is a style of persuasion that we officially discourage in American society, and college freshmen are frequently treated to a unit on the detection and analysis of propaganda in their writing or speech communication courses.

Another word with even clearer anti-Catholic associations is *jesuitical*. Although they acknowledged the nineteenth-century complaint against *jew* as a verb, Merriam's dictionary editors refused to honor another contemporary complaint against *jesuitical*, one of whose senses was defined as 'crafty, sly, deceitful, or prevaricating.' While most dictionary makers agree that *jew down* is at best offensive slang, and at worst outright, raving antisemitism, *jesuitical* seems to the lexicographers more a part of the genteel English literary tradition (itself xenophobic as well as anti-Catholic and antisemitic at times). Worcester's dictionary of 1860 does note after its definition of Jesuit, "their opponents have also ascribed to them those [qualities] of craft and deceit, and have accordingly given odious meanings to the word," and Webster's dictionary of 1864 says of *jesuitical*, "now marked as opprobrious," though subsequent editions do not repeat this warning. To this day the word has not been labeled as defamatory in the Merriam-Webster publications, although *Webster's New World Dictionary* (1982) marks *Jesuit*, 'crafty schemer, cunning dissembler, casuist,' as a "hostile and offensive term, as used by anti-Jesuits," while the *American Heritage Dictionary* (1975) disguises the negative sense of *Jesuit* by simply defining it as "one given to subtle casuistry." Only by checking under *casuist* do we discover the comment, "often used disparagingly."

How Many Usage Critics Does It Take to Change a Light Bulb?

It is unfortunate that the negative senses of words referring to certain groups of people remain current, but that is the fault of the users of language, and not the language itself or its chroniclers. It is not the function of a dictionary of record like Webster's unabridged or the *Oxford*, neither of which presumes to steer its readers along the paths of etiquette and correctness, to ignore usage simply because it is negative. However dictionaries that *do* serve as usage guides owe it to their readers to mark such usage as objectionable and reprehensible when the word in question actually does call to mind the group to whom it originally referred (it is not clear, for example, that *cabal* and *dogma* are as clearly evocative of Jews and Catholics as the other words we have discussed).

On the subject of national insult, John Moore (1961) points out that *slave* derives from *Slav*, and finds in the etymology a reflection of the history of the people. Objecting to a similar usage, John Scheuer wrote to *The New York Times* (June 23, 1980, p. 22) to protest that the word *welsh*, 'to avoid payment, break one's word,' which occurred in a *Times* headline, was offensive to Welsh people. This time the *Times* did not apologize. And William Safire (1986) was called to task for using the verb *gypped*, 'swindled, cheated,' which is a clipped form of *gypsy* (and that in turn comes from *Egyptian*, as gypsies were once thought to come from Egypt). Safire, asserting that the etymology was neither certain nor clear to the average user, defended his word choice. A few years ago a Spanish-surnamed correspondent wrote to the Champaign *News Gazette* objecting to the label *Hispanic* (July 8, 1984, p. A5) because "Spanish-speaking people are as varied as any linguistic group and cannot be grouped simply as a 'non-white' minority." She concluded her letter with a protest against ethnic labels which classify people "as if they were bottles of imported wine." And Robert Claiborne, in his recent usage guide (1986), goes even farther, labeling *race* itself as either a useless term, or one which has too often been used for discrimination, and recommends that all writers avoid it.

Gay and *lesbian* seem to have become the informal terms of choice for male and female homosexuals, respectively, over the objection of some usage critics that this will eventually prevent *gay* from being used in any but its sexual senses. Attempts to avoid highly charged terms are particularly common in the treatment of disease, where euphemism has lately become the order of the day. Thus *leprosy* since the 1930s is more commonly *Hansen's disease*, after the Norwegian physician who isolated the bacillus that causes the disease. Dictionaries continue to use the terms *mongoloid* and *mongolism*, attributed ultimately to the British physician John Down, who in 1866 sought to classify "the feeble-minded by arranging them around various ethnic standards. . . . A very large number of congenital idiots are typical Mongols" (*OED Supplement*, s. v. *mongoloid*). However, because *mongolism* has both objectionable racial connotations and is hurtful to parents, since the 1960s those involved with mental retardation have switched to the more neutral *Down* (or *Down's*) *syndrome*, which is not even listed in some of our most up-to-date desk dictionaries.

We saw in chapter eight that it can be insulting to call someone a grammarian. Clearly one person's neutral word may be negative and offensive to another, and it is sometimes difficult to predict how one's words may be misinterpreted. Recently, for example, two university housing administrators complained in a letter that a major academic newspaper regularly used what they perceived as the extremely derogatory word *dormitory* instead of their preference, *residence hall*, which may be progressive in their eyes but smacks of euphemism nonetheless. Another recent article reports that the term *barbarians* has become objectionable in literal reference to the Germanic tribes that harassed and eventually overcame the Romans, and recommends *frontiersmen* as the new, unbiased standard. Objections have even been lodged against the use of the verb *to stand* because it excludes those who are confined to beds or wheelchairs. The walking world may feel that it can safely ignore such objections from radical or minority fringe elements, since almost any group can claim that some aspect of language is discriminating. But it is sobering to note that the disabled often refer to so-called normal human beings as *tabs,* an acronym that stands for 'temporarily able-bodied.' What better use is there of language than to remind us of our mortality?

21 Sexist Language

In dealing with the more serious types of lexical prejudice, we must remember that language means whatever we agree that it means. Linguistic bias thus tends to reflect cultural bias. In turn, language may be used to perpetuate discrimination, though it also serves as one of the most important tools for removing bias. If *black* and *left* suggest negative characteristics in English, words associated with women fare even worse, and the movement to reverse sexist linguistic bias has aroused considerable interest and emotion—both pro and con—in the past decade or two (for a complete discussion of grammar and gender, see Baron 1986a).

As early as 1950 Wilfred Funk demonstrated that many words referring to women began as positive or neutral in tone but acquired negative—in some cases extremely derogatory—significance over the years. *Courtesan* once meant a female member of court. *Tart* was initially a term of endearment no worse than *cookie, honey,* or *sweetie.* Both words now mean prostitute. *Wench,* which also means prostitute but is used more commonly today only in a jocular sense for 'woman, servant,' originally referred to a child of either sex. *Harlot* at first referred to male entertainers, troubadors, and vagabonds. It came to be used as a more polite term for *whore,* and like many euphemisms, it eventually acquired the derogatory meaning of the word it replaced. The word *whore* itself probably derives from an Indo-European root meaning nothing worse than 'dear,' and the story of its derogation to a purely negative term continues to elude us.

In cases where apparently equal pairs of masculine and feminine terms exist, the feminine often acquires a trivial or pejorative sense in contrast to the masculine. Compare *governor* and *governess, major* and *majorette,* and of course *master* and *mistress.* Occupational terms label either sex—for example *lady lawyer, woman doctor, househusband, male nurse*—but the feminine term always carries with it a sense of inferiority.

Even the names of women bear marks of subordination. Many familiar names or nicknames in English end in diminutives (*Betty, Bobby, Molly, Sally, Tommy*). While males, particularly in the northern United States, often drop the diminutive suffix when they reach adulthood, (*Tommy* becomes *Tom,* and *Billy, Bill*), women's names tend to keep the suffix associated with childhood. A few women's names are feminized versions of men's names (*Antoinette, Charlotte, Georgia, Harriet, Pauline*), a reflection of the secondary status of women in our society. And it has been argued that when a masculine name such as *Carol, Lynn,* or *Shirley* is adopted for women as well—perhaps because men's names are perceived to be more prestigious—parents soon stop using it to name their sons.

It is clear that many women feel they must become linguistically invisible before they can become successful. When the Brontë sisters began to publish their work in the mid-nineteenth century, they chose sex-neutral pen names to disguise the fact that they were women. As Charlotte Brontë ruefully explained, "We had a vague impression that authoresses are liable to be looked on with prejudice." Although usage critics and feminists alike have proclaimed the death of the demeaning words *authoress* and *poetess* for well over a century, women writers are still greeted by male critics in today's supposed literary enlightenment as women first and writers second, and our dictionaries do not consider these sex-marked terms as obsolete.

Invisible Woman

In the novel *Invisible Man,* Ralph Ellison described a feeling among blacks that they form an invisible element in American society. The civil rights movement has done much to reverse this situation. For the feminist cause, the question of linguistic visibility has also become a major issue.

Women are in a double bind when it comes to English. Words marked as feminine make women visible, but do so in order to demean them. In contrast, the common use of the generic masculine renders women linguistically invisible, a situation that subtly controls everyone's perception of what women can and cannot do. Whether we are dealing with *man* as a general term for human beings, male or female, or with the masculine pronoun *he* standing for people of unspecified sex, as in *Everyone loves his mother,* or *A lawyer bills his clients even if they lose,* the exclusion of any specific reference to women has the psychological effect of limiting the reference of such language—and of standard English in general—more or less exclusively to men.

There is no easy way out of such a no-win situation. Some feminists argue that sex-specific terms are necessary to show the world what women have accomplished. The nineteenth-century, self-described *editress* of the popular journal, Godey's *Lady's Book,* Sarah Josepha Hale, favored this solution, and advocated such words as *Americaness, paintress, professoress, scholaress,* and *sculptress.* Henry Fowler, in his *Dictionary of Modern English Usage* (1926), also called for new feminines, including *doctress, editress, inspectress,* and *tailoress.* In addition, Fowler hoped that a number of words would be supplied with a feminine, including *artist, aurist* (ear doctor), *clerk, cook, motorist, palmist, pupil, teacher,* and *typist.* Contemporary feminists may go to greater extremes to bring women into the public eye, writing of *hags* and *crones* and *womyn* instead of *women,* and politicizing *history* into *herstory* to make the point that the doings of women have been ignored by male historians.

The Case of *chairperson*

Chairperson, coined some fifteen years ago as a replacement for the apparently sex-specific *chairman,* and instituted by administrative fiat in schools, businesses, and social organizations throughout the country, has drawn a significant amount of opposition from both sexes. *Chairman,* its opponents claim, is neutral enough, and besides, how dare we tinker with anything as sacred as the English language?

Since the seventeenth century, *chairman* has been the most common title for the head of a committee, but the oldest word to describe this office is the sex-neutral *chair* itself, a metaphoric term that today's language commentators generally find too wooden. *Chairwoman,* of more recent vintage, has always been stigmatized as nonsense, although nowadays, with so much negative attention being paid to *chairperson, chairwoman* has become less objectionable.

There is a fine analogy in *salesperson,* the common-gender alternative to the earlier *salesman, saleswoman, saleslady,* and *salesgirl. Salesperson* appears without fanfare in the early 1900s and is generally greeted as a useful and necessary word, since the position of salesclerk could be filled by someone of either sex, and *salesman* seems always to have been interpreted as a masculine. Some writers initially complained that *salesperson* was business jargon, but the word quickly passed into the standard language, where it remains today as a beacon of unobjectionable and unobtrusive sex-neutrality.

Contributing to the success of *salesperson* is the fact that the word was not associated with the politics of feminism. Because *chairperson* is so intimately tied to today's women's movement, and because the title is more often imposed than chosen freely, the opponents of feminism have joined with the opponents of language manipulation to resist this word and the many others in *-person* that have been coined lately. (The most recent examples I have come across are *waitperson* and *busperson*, sex-neutral alternatives to *waiter/waitress* and *busboy* in the want ads of our local newspaper; still rare in those job columns is the truly impersonal noun *wait*.)

Sometimes our efforts at gender neutrality backfire: many of the *-person* compounds, for example *alderperson, anchorperson, chairperson*, and *spokesperson*, are used most often in reference to women. This defeats the intention of the suffix, turning it into a feminine after all. As journalist and usage critic Roy Copperud has observed, "When we hear chairperson, we know that a woman holds the chair" (1980). Whether *-person* compounds survive depends on many factors, and I would hesitate to predict their fate. *Salesperson* itself may be threatened by the bad press given its newfangled analogs, though it seems livelier than *seller* as a job description.

The Case of *Ms.*

Direct address poses another problem in terms of sex reference. Traditionally, our English honorifics, or titles, are basically limited to *Mr., Miss,* and *Mrs.* The feminine titles generally distinguish marital status, while *Mr.* remains neutral in that sense. Early in this century a few attempts were made to remedy the situation. Several word coiners offered new forms to round out the title paradigm by distinguishing single from married men, and a number of commentators, including the humorist Ambrose Bierce, who argued that titles went against the American egalitarian grain, preferred dispensing with them altogether.

In addition, feminists in the early part of this century, reacting against the loss of psychological and economic identity imposed by marriage, as well as the imbalance in our title system, proposed that *Miss* become the universal feminine title, just as *Mr.* had become the universal masculine one. It is more than likely that this universal *Miss*, abbreviated *M's* or *Ms.*, is the direct ancestor of today's *Ms.* And *Ms.* itself is older than we commonly think. The business community, long in need of a suitable title to use in addressing women whose marital status was unknown, experimented with *Ms.* in the 1930s and again in the 1950s, though the form did not receive a great deal of prominence until the early 1970s, when it was picked up again by the women's movement.

As is the case with *chairperson, Ms.* has been a controversial coinage from the start. Opponents deride it as the lazy, southern, black, or rural pronunciation of *Mrs.,* or the abbreviation for *manuscript* or *Mississippi.* Although the business community now embraces the term enthusiastically, the more conservative literary usage critics have never liked it much, and even feminist usage handbooks warn readers against *Ms.*

Like compounds in *-person, Ms.* has been compromised to some extent. Many single women—particularly younger ones—use it as a trendy substitute for *Miss,* intending to adopt *Mrs.* when they marry. It is not surprising, however, that such inconsistency should affect the title paradigm. *Miss* and *Mrs.* were originally age-graded variants of *Mistress,* with *Miss* being reserved for girls and young women as *Master* was for boys. The feminine titles did not begin to sort themselves out according to marital status until the eighteenth century, and as recently as the early twentieth century *Miss* and *Mrs.* remained interchangeable in nonstandard and dialect speech in England and America. Furthermore, married women have always been free to use *Miss* as a professional title, and many divorced or widowed women retain *Mrs.*

Ms. will remain unpopular with some people, to be sure, and its exact meaning may vary slightly from speaker to speaker, but no one can deny that *Ms.* has made a place for itself in modern English. It need not oust the conventional titles—indeed there is little chance that this will happen in the near future—but it has proven itself both in its own right, and as a polite term to be used until an unknown addressee's preference for some other title has been established.

Women's fight for linguistic equality has been treated both as less serious and as more of a threat to the language than the claim of blacks. But despite the tendency to trivialize the women's movement, and the objections to such terms as *chairperson* and *Ms.,* English usage has shifted in the direction of fairness. For example, *girl* is no longer appropriate in reference to an adult female in formal, standard English, though it persists in the spoken language of men and women alike, where it is used both with and without negative connotations. But one problem, the generic masculine pronoun, continues to give us trouble. As we see in the next chapter, the solution, a new, gender-neutral pronoun for the third person singular, continues to elude us.

22 The Missing Word

We have enough trouble, as we wrestle with English, finding just the right word from a passel of near synonyms to fit a given circumstance. But every now and then we are brought up short by a situation for which no word exists at all, a black hole in our vocabulary. For example, English is a language relatively poor in honorifics, those prefatory titles like *Dr., Ms., sister,* or *boss,* words which indicate something about a person's social status or specify their relationship to the speaker or writer. Some of us who are married meet a black hole when we are forced to address our in-laws directly. Not everyone is comfortable calling a father-in-law or mother-in-law *Mom* or *Dad;* nor do first names always do the trick. As a result, there are people in our society who cannot name their in-laws at all, who call them only *you* and do not speak directly to them unless they can make eye-contact first.

Frequently we need a new word to describe a new wrinkle or refinement or invention. In some cases, finding such a word may prove a problem. For some time now I have had to use a letter opener, a key, or even a screwdriver to pry open the pop tops of the pop top soda cans that come out of our office vending machine—the job is just too hard for fingers alone. A friend of mine saw a device designed for just such a purpose on sale at a store in New York, but he could not remember what the gizmo was called. Obviously the term *can opener* will not do. In fact, the traditional *can opener* is all but useless for opening these supposedly easy-to-open cans. Should these gadgets become widespread, some appropriate name will have to be devised for them (something like *can popper,* for example, or *KanPopper,* the inevitable deformation of the name that makes it registerable as a trademark). But perhaps instead of worrying about nomenclature, the soda manufacturers will solve the problem by making pop top cans that open without hazard to life, limb, and particularly, digit.

In many other instances requiring new words, a term comes readily to hand and is quickly adopted to fill the need. Recently I came across a newspaper ad for a store selling comic books and *graphic novels.* Now when I was a kid I had one of the largest comic book collections in the neighborhood, one which certainly would fetch a handsome price from collectors had it not disappeared from my closet when I went away to college. I have also read a lot of novels in my time, and I am familiar with many of the types that exist: there is the romantic novel and the gothic, the dime novel and the detective, not to mention the Victorian, the historical, the postmodern, and two kinds whose names exist only in foreign languages, the *roman à clef* and the *Bildungsroman.* I know enough about recent publishing trends to have learned that a *novelization* is the rendering in prose of what was originally a movie or television show (to be fair, *picturization* was an early motion picture industry term to indicate a movie made from a book). But I had never before heard of a *graphic novel,* which clearly refers to the adult comic book version of a story.

My ignorance of this new term clearly labels me as a stuffy English teacher, unacquainted with the fashions of popular literature, for I found that my less-isolated colleagues quickly identified the word. One had encountered this form of popular literature in parts of Europe, Latin America, and the Middle East, and told me the Spanish word for it was *novella,* and the Turkish was *fotoroman.* But *graphic novel* is not the only English term for the phenomenon. My secretary told me that a number of *Star Trek* episodes had been released as what she and her friends called *photo novels,* and for all I know there are other ways to refer to these picture books as well, so the exact English designation for the phenomenon may still be up for grabs.

There are indeed a number of cases where many new words are proposed to fill a particular gap, yet no one word ever makes it to the top of the heap. One example of a missing word has drawn much attention in recent years. There is in English no name for the unmarried person with whom one shares both domestic and romantic relationships. *Boyfriend* and *girlfriend* are too adolescent in their reference to suit most adults, and *lover* is too blatant, while *gentleman-* and *lady-friend* smack too much of euphemism. The Census Bureau's acronym *POSSLQ,* 'person of opposite sex sharing living quarters,' is too humorous and sidesteps the matter of sexuality; *liver,* for 'live-in lover,' turns the problem into an indelicate joke; and the pretentious *significant other* doesn't mean anything at all.

Our feeble attempts to meet our expressive needs by creating new words or modifying existing ones suggest that language change of any kind is a difficult process, like pushing a heavy boulder up a hill. First you must invent a word. Then you have to market it. A new word, or neologism, must spread from individual to individual and group to group, going through uncounted stages of acceptance in speech and writing before we can confidently include it in our dictionaries. Some new words seem so apt they quickly pass muster and enter the standard language (*cold war, nylon, Xerox, sexism, humongous*). Others fizzle, fail and quickly pass from memory (*linguistician, matriheritage, desexigration*).

A Needed Word

Despite our failure to coin a better word than *significant other,* the search for the needed word continues. The quest for an epicene, or gender-neutral, pronoun has gone on even longer, and to even less avail. Feminists, grammarians, and usage critics are often at odds about English, but they frequently agree that there is a key word missing from our language: although all of our other personal pronouns are gender-neutral, we have no pronoun for the common-gender third person singular, only the gender-specific forms of *he, she,* and *it.* During the last century and a half, more than eighty remedies have been suggested to fill the gap, yet English has steadfastly refused to adopt a word to replace the generic masculine *he* in a sentence like *Everyone loves his mother* (see Baron 1986a for a complete discussion and a list of these pronouns).

The first common-gender pronouns were coined not out of a feminist spirit seeking to redress sexism in language, but from the purist's urge to restore linguistic efficiency and grammatical correctness to the English language. After all, it was argued by the new word makers, the pronoun agreement rule requires concord between a pronoun and its referent in *gender* as well as number. It is only more recently that the androgynous pronoun has come to be viewed as a way of preventing the masculine from encompassing and obscuring the feminine, a means of righting social as well as grammatical wrongs. In any case, opposition to this new pronoun is strong, and the likelihood that one will succeed is slim.

The need for such a pronoun arises because our English pronoun agreement rule breaks down when it comes to sentences like:

(1) Everyone loves (*possessive pronoun*) mother.

Of the several possibilities to fill in the blank, only (2) is technically correct, yet most experts reject it as awkward or wordy:

(2) Everyone loves his or her mother.
(3) Everyone loves their mother.
(4) Everyone loves his mother.
(5) Everyone loves her mother.

Sentence (3) is probably the most common response in speech, and has been used for hundreds of years in writing by respectable authors.

The so-called 'singular *they*' maintains gender agreement because *their* is common gender. It does, however, violate number agreement, for *everyone* and the other indefinite pronouns are singular in form, even though plural in connotation. Consequently it is frowned on by purists and grammarians and remains highly stigmatized to this day.

Only sentence (4), the generic masculine, is considered standard, though it shows agreement in number, but not in gender. However, the generic masculine is not without its problems.

The Generic Masculine

Just as a plural pronoun may not refer to a singular, a feminine pronoun is not supposed to stand for a masculine, as it does in sentence (5). We either read (5) as aberrant, denying the generic feminine, or we interpret *her* as pointing not to *everyone* but to one particular female individual's mother, as in "Everyone loves Joan's mother."

Historically, English-speaking men have objected to being included in feminine terms, although they expect women to accept the all-embracing masculine without complaint. For example, in the 1960s male teachers vigorously objected to the common reference in educational writing to "The teacher . . . she" (in the same texts, students and administrators were invariably *he*). A scant decade later female teachers chafed at being included in, or made invisible by, the new, so-called generic "teacher . . . he." Without a common-gender pronoun, there seems to be no way out of this dilemma.

The notion of the generic masculine in English goes back to a Latin grammatical doctrine in which the genders are ranked in an order that reflects the hierarchy of the sexes in European society: the masculine is worthier than the feminine, which in turn outranks the neuter. In Latin, adjectives must agree with their nouns in gender, number, and case. Latin grammars apply gender worthiness to situations in which an adjective must agree with a pair of nouns whose genders differ. If one of the nouns is masculine, the adjective takes the masculine form. If neither is masculine, but one is feminine, then the adjective is feminine. The adjective is neuter only if both nouns are neuter.

Fortunately for us, English adjectives do not conform to their nouns. Gender concord only occurs in the personal pronoun system, and there it concerns only the third person singular pronouns, all the others being gender neutral. And while the generic masculine *he* satisfies many of our teachers and editors, the purest of the purists continually remind us that the form violates both the letter and the spirit of the pronoun agreement rule, which explicitly requires concord in gender as well as number. Their solution? A new and needed word.

The search for a new common-gender pronoun antedates our present-day concern with language and sex by some years. Denis Diderot included the common-gender, or epicene, pronouns *lo* (singular) and *zo* (plural) in *Langue Nouvelle*, an artificial language whose outlines he sketched in the *Encyclopedia* (1751), and William S. Cardell, an American grammarian and writer of stories for boys, argued in 1827 that common-gender pronouns were common, indeed desirable features of natural language as well. (Finnish is one language where the third person singular pronoun does not distinguish gender.) And as early as 1869 the conservative language critic Richard Meade Bache comments that "a personal pronoun which should be noncommittal on the question of sex would be a great convenience." It is not surprising then that just about the middle of the nineteenth century enterprising neologists began offering paradigms of new pronouns to fill the void.

The Epicene Pronoun

The earliest epicene pronouns I have been able to trace appeared around 1850. They were *ne, nis* and *nim*, blends of a neuter-sounding *n* prefixed to the masculine pronouns *he, his, him*. A serious though unsuccessful effort was made to push this paradigm, and another blend created at about the same time, combining *his* and *her* to form *hiser,* was actually adopted by a couple of newspapers for a while. A third early pronoun, *en,* appeared briefly in 1868, and in 1884 a flurry of epicene coinage resulted in no fewer than five separate pronoun paradigms.

The best known of the new neutral words was *thon,* the brainchild of Charles Crozat Converse, an American lawyer and prolific hymn writer, who invented the pronoun in 1884 after years of experimentation. Converse argued that since time was money, communication should be rapid as well as grammatically correct. According to its creator, *thon* blends *that* and *one* into a word which resembles existing pronouns, and whose final element smacks of the sexless indefinite. It is more concise than the exact but awkward *he or she* and more correct than either the generic masculine *he,* or what Converse called the "common, yet hideous solecism" of singular *they.*

Thon made it into Funk and Wagnalls' *Standard Dictionary* (1898), and was still listed there in 1964. It also found its way into *Webster's*

Second New International Dictionary, though it is missing from the first and third, and letters supporting its use appeared in the *New York Times* as recently as 1955. Reacting to Converse's proposal, in 1884 Francis H. Williams rejected *thon* because it could be too easily confused with *thou*. (Williams' fears were apparently justified; in a discussion of the word in Otto Jespersen's *Modern English Grammar* [1949], it is misprinted as *thou*.) Instead of *thon*, Williams favored the paradigm *hi, hes, hem*. Edgar Alfred Stevens thought up *le, lis, lim* (based on the French masculine definite article). Charles P. Sherman, unaware of the earlier creation ca. 1850, offered *hiser* and *himer*. And Emma Carleton, who found it shameful "that our language should so long have suffered for a simple pronoun, and no man [sic] have risen to supply the missing word," gave us *ip, ips*, whose resemblance to *it* and Latin *ipse*, she felt, would aid in its adoption.

Since 1884 epicene pronouns have appeared with some regularity. Most word coiners were ignorant of previous efforts to create sex-neutral pronouns, and a number of forms were coined anew every few years. The most commonly reinvented paradigm blends *he* and *she, his* and *her*, and *him* and *her* into variations of *heesh* (also *he'er, hesh*), *hiser* (*hizzer, his'er*) and *himer* (*himmer*). In a couple of cases, *she* precedes: *shem, hem, hes* (1974), *she, herm* (1976), and *sheme, shis, shim* (1977). *She* also combines with *they* to form *shem* (1973, 1982), as well as *shey, sheir* (1979, 1982).

Also popular were paradigms aiming at gender-neutrality, but reflecting the masculine declension *he, his, him*: in addition to *le, lis, lim* we find *se, sis, sim* (1938), *ve, vis, ver*, the last form being based on the feminine *her* (1970), *ze, zis, zim* (1972), and *e, ris, rim* (1977). Most recently, a Chicago marketing firm has offered its clients the paradigm *ala, alum, alas* (1989).

Some reformers preferred recycling an existing word like *it* or *one*; others favored borrowing over coining. In addition to *le* we find French *en* (1868) and *on* (1889), pseudo-Chinese *hse* (1945), *ze*, from German *sie* (1972), Latin *ae* (1978), and Old Norse *hann* (1984). A few forms based on *it* and *e* appear: *et* (1979), *em* (1977), and *E* (1977, 1982). And every once in a while, a lone voice is raised in defense of singular *they*.

The Word That Failed

To date no new pronoun has proved successful, but the paradigms keep coming. It's not that our pronoun system in English isn't highly developed already. We have more than enough of these little words to go around. Indeed, sometimes as we hesitate over *It is I* and *It's me*, or charge blindly into *between you and I* and *Whom did you say was calling?* it seems as if we have too many.

And it's not that pronouns never change. The pronoun system is conservative, it is true. New pronouns don't frequently gain acceptance, and old ones fade away ever so slowly. But the ranks of our pronouns do change: they have undergone both trimming and replenishing over the ages. During the Old English period we had forms for the first and second person dual, to refer to two people, in addition to the singular and plural we are familiar with today.

Our pronoun system may permit the loss of endangered species like the dual or it may come valiantly to their defense. We once maintained a separate second person singular *thou*, which doubled as the intimate or familiar form. It has long since been replaced by the plural *you*. At one point in Middle English all the third person pronouns, singular and plural, masculine, feminine, and neuter, became so much alike in sound and spelling there was some danger of their coalescing into a single form. Such undifferentiated pronouns (*a, un*) persist in British regional speech, but the standard language, introducing *she* and borrowing *they, their,* and *them* from Norse, has veered back toward differentiation in the pronoun paradigm.

In one instance we invented a pronoun by analogy to regularize the system. This is the newest pronoun in our word hoard, *its*, so frequently confused by students and "naive spellers" with the contracted *it's*. It originally had no distinct possessive, and such sentences as "The bird gave it food to it young" were perfectly unobjectionable. *Its*, with the possessive *s* on the analogy of *his, hers,* and *theirs*, appears in the seventeenth century, though too late for inclusion in the King James translation of the Bible.

The difference between the epicene pronoun and our successful new pronouns, *she, they,* and *its*, is that the latter arose as natural variants rather than through the intervention of an individual reformer. In addition, the arguments of the neologists in support of their creations have not been very persuasive. The new pronouns are heralded as better because they are like, or in some cases unlike, the pronouns that we already use. The epicene pronouns are not natural, nor is their meaning necessarily self-evident. So many different, competing forms have been invented that the disinterested observer suspects the coiners of confusion, if not outright malevolence.

Ultimately the new pronouns are advertised as convenient. Some of their supporters go so far as to claim they are essential. A. A. Milne, creator of Winnie the Pooh, felt we would already have such sex-neutral words had English been invented by a businessman [*sic*] or a Member of Parliament. Even the brothers Fowler, in *The King's English* (1906), lament the absence of an epicene pronoun as a real deficiency in our language, although they recognize the difficulties in securing the adoption of a new pronoun: "We shall probably persist in refusing women their due here as stubbornly as Englishmen continue to offend the Scots by saying England instead of Britain."

The Solution

What is to be done? A well-meaning psychologist at UCLA, an ardent supporter of the common-gender pronoun, has called for an elaborate experiment, an exercise in lexicographic market research. By examining new words that have entered English over the years, he will determine the ideal characteristics of neologisms, invent pronouns displaying these ideals, test them against the traditional pronoun paradigm, then mandate the common-gender form with the highest test score.

This sort of rationalized, pseudo-scientific language planning is doomed before it starts. The ideal characteristics that attract us to new words are more elusive than those which motivate us to buy a new product or to vote for a particular candidate in an election. Even if we could determine an ideal pronoun and successfully field test it, we have no way of imposing the new word on speakers and writers in America, not to mention the rest of the English-speaking world.

There is no Academy that rules on matters of the language, nor have legislative efforts been effective in directing nontechnical usage. We have no national system of education whose curriculum will dictate adoption of a new term, nor will our writers and editors agree to be bound by the pronominal opinions of any single manual of style. In short, the missing word must sink or swim on its own, and in view of the repeated failure of the epicene pronoun to win a place in our vocabulary, no such pronoun is likely to stay afloat for very long.

The failure of the epicene pronoun does not mean the triumph of the generic masculine. There are sound reasons for considering alternatives to *everyone . . . he*. For one thing, research has shown that the generic masculine is not a truly neutral form. It conjures up visions of males in the minds of men and women, boys and girls, thereby excluding women from the frame of reference. In addition, more and more women and men are insulted by the exclusive nature of the generic masculine, and if language becomes tagged as insulting we are less likely to use it, particularly in formal writing and speech. We find *girl* used less and less in formal English to refer to an adult female, and *boy* is strictly taboo in the same formal context to refer to an adult black male.

We may lack an epicene pronoun, but there are alternatives for those who prefer explicitly to include both sexes in our discourse. These alternatives are not innovations. They are readily available to users of English, and many of us already use them more or less unconsciously. Singular *they*, despite its stigma as "ungrammatical," has never been rare in English. In some cases, when reference extends across a clause boundary, it is mandatory. We cannot say, "Everyone liked the main course well enough, but he did not care for the dessert."

Another option is the coordinate *he or she*, which need not be awkward if it is used sparingly. (The typographic blends *s/he* and *he/she* are not popular because the first has no distinct pronunciation and the second evokes the slang terms for effeminate male or masculine female.) Finally we may recast a sentence in the plural to eliminate the stumbling block: "Everyone loves his mother" thus becomes "People love their mothers."

In an age of sensitivity to questions of language and sex, the problems inherent in the generic *he* are no longer easy to ignore. Of course we should not rule out the possibility, remote as it may be, that our pronoun system will change to accommodate the gender-neutral third person singular. In the meantime, however, most of us will probably make do by combining the alternatives to the generic masculine: rewriting, coordination, and an occasional singular *they* just to keep the purists on their toes.

23 Language and Liberty

Revising language to eradicate discrimination is a challenge that has appealed to many Americans. To some extent we can trace this connection between language, politics, and social reform to new attitudes that accompanied Europeans to North America. The New World originally presented an attractive if ambiguous prospect to the European mind, a chance to extend the sway of Western culture as well as a vision of Eden where civilization might be designed anew. Here government, industry, and the arts would flourish at a level of rationality that had not been possible since the Fall. Here even the cities would reflect not the chaotic historicity of their old world counterparts but the deliberate order of the universe, ranging their inhabitants along streets and avenues set out to follow the compass points, and neatly numerated, alphabetized, and grouped into arrangements of trees, counties, states, and presidents (readers interested in a full discussion should see Baron 1982b).

Language in the New World offered a similar prospect for extension and perfectibility, and while some reformers of the English language occupied themselves with efforts to keep the colonial tongue from straying too far from its origins, others did not hesitate to suggest that the time was right and the iron hot, that English in the New World could be forged anew in the image of democracy, or rationality, or in the more extreme cases, in the image of both.

Seventeenth-century speculation about the relationship between words and things, between language, the world, and the mind, touched on the connection between language and the polity, and this in turn influenced the way Americans regarded their special linguistic position. John Locke, in his *Essay Concerning Humane Understanding* (1690), employs the political imagery of liberty, democracy, and dictatorship to portray the arbitrary relationship between the word and that thing or idea which it refers to. Locke defends our basic human liberty to coin new words, arguing as well for our right to make language mean what we will. In turn, he objects to that despotism which forces us to accept other people's meanings:

Every Man has so inviolable a Liberty, to make Words stand for
what Ideas he pleases, that no one hath the Power to make others
have the same Ideas in their Minds, that he has, when they use
the same Words, that he does. (225)

The German linguistic philosopher Johann Michaelis wrote his
*Dissertation on the Influence of Opinions on Language and of Language
on Opinions* (1759), an essay which won the prize of the Berlin
Philological Society and which encouraged Noah Webster to write an
essay with the same name. Michaelis, extending the metaphor of
language as democracy, protests against the use of borrowed words in
technical vocabulary because they reinforce the class distinction between the learned and the common people, excluding the masses from
participation in the process of scientific discovery. Echoing Locke's
imagery, Michaelis's objection to the jargon of botanists reads like a
declaration of political rather than linguistic independence:

Words cannot be deprived of their received meaning, but by the
consent of the people, and the gradual introduction of a contrary
custom; whereas an author treats the technical language he makes
use of, with all the arbitrariness of despotism. (88)

Citing Horace as his authority, Michaelis argues that language is
democratic because use or custom is decided by the majority. This
"democratic form of languages" is in turn a means of preventing
confusion and ensuring successful communication that no individual,
whether emperor or language expert, can change. Michaelis reminds
us that even the Emperor Augustus acknowledged his inability to
legislate the adoption of new Latin words. And ironically, Michaelis,
like many language commentators from Noah Webster to John Simon,
regards the opinion of the linguist as suspect too:

Scholars are not so infallible that every thing is to be referred to
them. Were they allowed a decisory power, the errors of language,
I am sure, instead of diminishing, would be continually increasing.
(88)

Although he privileges the role of the educated in directing the
linguistic tastes of the common people—a condition that he finds
inherent in all democratic systems—Michaelis reserves for classic
authors, "the fair sex," and, above all, the people, "who are indeed
the supreme legislators," the inalienable right to create language:

This is a right invested in every one who is master of the language
he speaks: he may form new words, and form new phrases,
provided they coincide with the genius of the language, and be
not over multiplied. (89)

Language reform is to be accomplished in the same way other reforms are instituted in a democracy, through the rule of law, or, failing that, through public ridicule. Furthermore, reform is not to be accomplished "by any act of private authority; that would be a flagrant infringement on the rights of language, which are democratical." Michaelis is pessimistic of the success of artificial, scientific or philosophical languages, such as the one proposed by John Wilkins (1668), because they are the product of an individual and are therefore not only more liable to error, but are opposed in their nature to the democratic spirit of linguistic evolution.

Unfortunately the people as a whole, like the individual, are also prone to error. Discussing folk etymology, the transformation of difficult or foreign words into more familiar ones, for example the formation of *woodchuck* from the Cree Indian *wuchak*, Michaelis warns that, just as language may influence the formation of correct opinion, it may also serve to perpetuate popular error:

> Credit no proposition purely because the etymology implies it, or seems to imply it. Etymology is the voice of the people; which the philosopher always suspects, yet always attends to it. (73)

Democratic American English

The democratic but potentially paradoxical notion that the people rule in matters of language, and that the people can also be wrong, presented few problems to a patriotic language reformer like Noah Webster, who offered his spelling books, grammars, and dictionaries as guaranteed models of correctness to be adopted in America by popular acclamation, thereafter to function with the force of law, much in the manner of the federal constitution. Webster's idea of Federal English was a language uniformly spelled according to his occasionally aberrant notions of orthography. It was to be made free from the regional variations in pronunciation and usage that plagued English in the mother country by means of the establishment of national standards which, in many cases, happened to correspond to the peculiarities of Webster's own New England dialect.

But Webster's arguments for the establishment of an independent American language, while designed in part to promote his series of textbooks, also echoed the political sentiments of the times. In *Dissertations on the English Language* (1789) Webster argues,

> We have ... the fairest opportunity of establishing a national language and of giving it uniformity and perspicuity, in North

America, that ever presented itself to mankind. Now is the time
to begin the plan. The minds of the Americans are roused by the
events of a revolution . . . the danger of losing the benefits of
independence, has disposed every man to embrace any scheme
that shall tend, in its future operation, to reconcile the people of
America to each other. . . . NOW is the time, and this the country,
in which we may expect success, in attempting changes favorable
to language, science and government. . . . Let us then seize the
present moment, and establish a national language, as well as a
national government. (36)

John Adams (1780) felt that in a democracy, where birth and class
were irrelevant, linguistic excellence would serve to distinguish merit.
Pointing to Athens and Rome as proof of the connections between
liberty, prosperity, glory, and language, Adams urged Congress to
establish an academy to oversee the American language, and he
predicted that "eloquence will become the instrument for recommending men to their fellow-citizens, and the principal means of
advancement through the various ranks and offices" in American
society.

The supposed relationship between linguistic and social organization
is also apparent in the nineteenth-century stereotype of American
English as efficient though generally undistinguished. James Fenimore
Cooper is only one of many commentators who notes that the
development of a bourgeois society is a great linguistic leveler. In *The
American Democrat* (1838) Cooper writes, with a tinge of regret,

While it is true that the great body of the American people use
their language more correctly than the mass of any other considerable nation, it is equally true that a smaller proportion than
common attain to elegance in this accomplishment, especially in
speech. (118)

Whitman's American Primer

Adams and Cooper hoped to use democracy to raise the common
denominator of American speech. For Walt Whitman, better English
meant a truly democratic extension of the language to include elements
that are usually regarded as outside the range of acceptability: slang,
regionalisms (particularly place names), neologisms, technical vocabulary, borrowings from other languages, and vulgar speech. Of his
American Primer, written in the 1850s but not published until 1904,
Whitman says, "The new world, the new times, the new peoples, the
new vista, need a tongue according—yes, what is more, will have
such a tongue—will not be satisfied until it is evolved." This new

tongue will reflect American independence and individuality, as well as the newness of the American situation. Whitman rejects the words of the past one thousand years, all of which must be superseded: "These States are rapidly supplying themselves with new words, called for by new occasions, new facts, new politics, new combinations.— Far plentier additions will be needed, and, of course, will be supplied."

Whitman's linguistic embrace includes the nonstandard along with the standard. Going Webster one better, Whitman's approach to lexicography is purely descriptive. He foresees a *Real Dictionary* which "will give all words that exist in use, the bad words as well as any," and he describes in revolutionary terms a grammar that is equally revolutionary: "The Real Grammar will be that which declares itself a nucleus of the spirit of the laws, with liberty to all to carry out the spirit of the laws, even by violating them, if necessary.—The English Language is grandly lawless like the race who use it—or, rather, breaks out of the little laws to enter truly the higher ones."

Whitman finds the English character reflected in our language, which is "full enough of faults, but averse to all folderol, equable, instinctively just, latent with pride and melancholy, ready with brawned arms, with free speech, with the knife-blade for tyrants and the reached hand for slaves." This sense of linguistic self-determination is compounded by the distinctively American linguistic appetite for "unhemmed latitude, coarseness, directness, live epithets, expletives, words of opprobrium, resistance."

But Whitman's populist view of the American language is only part of the picture, for he is also a reformer keen on taming our linguistic independence. While Whitman celebrates the American language with his own brawned tongue, he also manages to find fault with some aspects of our speech.

Like any descriptivist, sooner or later Whitman reveals his own language prejudices. While Webster openly modeled Federal English on the dialect of New England, Whitman finds Yankee pronunciation particularly flat, nasal, and offensive to his ears. Specifically he finds that in the speech of the northeast, "all sorts of physical, moral, and mental deformities are inevitably returned in the voice."

Whitman even reins in his expansive sexuality when it comes to language, calling for a new word that is neither coarse nor euphemistic to describe "the act male and female." And he resists the American obsession with correct orthography: "Morbidness for nice spelling, and tenacity for or against some one letter or so, means dandyism and impotence in literature." But Whitman's linguistic embrace is exclusive as well as inclusive. He strongly objects to the influence of Catholicism in American place names, urging that Baltimore, St. Louis, St. Paul, and New Orleans be renamed, and that "aboriginal," or Native American names replace the saints' names so common in California: "What do such names know of democracy,—the hunt for the gold leads and the nugget or of the religion that is scorn and negation?" Whitman considers the development of native place names essential if America is to become an independent nation and a world leader: "A nation which has not its own names, but begs them of other nations, has no identity, marches not in front but behind."

This America-for-the-Americans attitude is counterbalanced to some extent in an article in *Life Illustrated* (1856) expressing Whitman's desire to introduce some 110 words, most of them French but some from the Italian, for which he sees a need in English. And Whitman's devotion to the speechways of the common people is tempered by his assumption that the new words will trickle down from the literary language to the language of the folk, for the words on his list "have been more or less used in affected writing, but not more than one or two, if any, have yet been admitted to the homes of the common people."

Whitman recommends the adoption of many French words that have since become thoroughly Englished, for example, *aplomb, brochure, bourgeois, cabaret, facade, genre, morgue, penchant, résumé,* and *suite.* Other words on his list are familiar, although still identified as French more than English, for example *allons, bon jour, bon soir, bon mot, en route, faubourg, insouciance, jeu d'esprit, roué,* and *trottoir.* Whitman's suggestion of *portfuille* [sic] is made in violation of his own stricture that a borrowed word must fill a gap in the language, for *portfolio* appears in English as early as 1722.

Three words that Whitman marks as especially desirable have proved remarkably unsuccessful, two of them, *abrégé,* 'abridgement,' and *auditoire,* "place of the audience in a public building," no doubt because the language already contained cognates for them, and the third, *attrister,* 'to sadden,' perhaps because it did not lend itself to nativization according to English verb patterns: even Whitman's democratic language would have trouble embracing *attristed* and *attristing.* Other French words that Whitman recommends have also failed to make their way to the heart of our language, among them *accoucheur,* 'man-midwife,' *bienséance,* 'propriety,' *embonpoint,* 'fat,' *feuilliton,* 'little leaf,' and *voltigeur,* 'vaulter, soldier in the light cavalry' (this last word is occasionally used in nineteenth-century English, particularly as a French military term).

The Failure of Democracy

Walt Whitman attacked Yankee pronunciation, but in a series of articles appearing in *Harper's Bazaar* in 1906 and 1907, Henry James, like Webster before him, defended it. In turn, James challenged the accent of a broader segment of the American population, American women, attributing their inadequate pronunciation to the democratic fabric of our society. According to James, American women, unlike their European counterparts, speak not as ladies but as they like. He claims, in the political diction we have come to associate with descriptions of American English, that "we might accept this labial and lingual and vocal independence as a high sign of the glorious courage of our women if it contained but a spark of the guiding reason that separates audacity from madness."

According to James, the decline of American English has come about because our political and social democracy has caused us to confuse independence with anarchy. James feels that an American, if asked about linguistic standards, would reply, "Well, we don't here, you know—in the matter of speech or any thing else—acknowledge authority!" Furthermore, Americans go out of their way to defend their right to be wrong. According to James, "our women's slovenly speech"—like the other great American linguistic abuse that he singles out, advertising—is "guarded and protected, almost cherished."

A century earlier, Adams saw in democracy the opportunity for citizens to distinguish themselves through linguistic achievement, but James feels that the reverse has actually occurred, that in our perverted sense of social equality we have felt it our duty to sink instead to the lowest possible linguistic level. Although European men and women "stand or fall by their degree of mastery of the habit of employing their vocal organs after the fashion of good society," James finds in America "an innumerable sisterhood, from State to State and city to city, all bristling with the same proclamation of indifference, all engaged in reminding us how much the better sisters may, occasion favoring, speak even as the worse."

In his paternalistic fervor, James praises the rigidly patriarchal, Puritan speech of his native New England, which offered, in his view, an excellent basis for individual intelligence and virtue, "the expressional effect of the few capable of taking care of themselves, and of keeping themselves in hand—capable even of keeping their wives, their daughters, their sisters." And he associates the degeneration of women's speech with their increasing social liberation: "Anything that would sufficiently stand for the word, and that might thereby be uttered with the minimum of articulation, would sufficiently do, wouldn't it?—since the emancipation of the American woman would thereby be attested."

James combines his antifeminism with his notion that the New World has not lived up to its promise. According to James, women's pronunciation is an affront to our national honor. So, apparently, is women's emancipation. But James, who sees himself as keeper of the sacred flame, offers to rescue the masses from their self-imposed linguistic decay, enlightening us in the process, and improving our national speech. An autocrat responsible to no electorate, James characterizes language as democracy and then proceeds to restructure its government. Although his syntax is complex, James's message to American women is plain: since they cannot rule themselves, he will rule for them.

For James, as for many twentieth-century critics of the English language, the bloom is off the rose. The noble experiment of the New Eden is a cultural failure: American democracy has not produced a language worthy of Greece, or Rome, or even royalist England. Certainly, as we have seen, English singles out many of its users for unfair treatment on the basis of race, ethnicity, religion, and sex. Furthermore, while James and most language commentators seek to defend the English language from the barbarians within, we will see in chapter 24 that there has also been a strong isolationist sentiment concerned with protecting American English from foreign competiton.

24 The English Language and the Constitution

No matter what we think of the relationship between the English language and the speakers of English, Americans agree that English is the national language of the United States. Many, however, are surprised to discover that we have no law that makes English the official language of the country. Occasionally there have been attempts to pass such a law.

In November of 1986 the voters of California passed a referendum, known as Proposition 63, making English the official language of the state. Some three-quarters of the electorate voted to make it so, which perhaps is only to be expected, for most people in the United States either speak English or feel a need to learn it, and many view such a language law as a simple reflex issue, like voting in favor of apple pie. For others, both those who support the English first, or English only, movement, and those who oppose the establishment of English, the official language question has become a matter of deep concern.

California was not the first state to designate an official language. Illinois, Indiana, Kentucky, Nebraska, and Virginia already had such laws on their books. The question of an official language is now before us at the national level, as well, in the form of the English Language Amendment to the U. S. constitution (the ELA), first proposed in 1981 by then-Senator S. I. Hayakawa, of California, well known for his writings on semantics. The amendment would establish once and for all the primacy of English, defending it against the imagined onslaught of competing languages, and requiring the learning of English by immigrants.

On the surface, these seem laudable aims. After all, the ELA makes legal what happens anyway. There have always been non-English speakers in the United States, and those groups who have come to this country as permanent residents have always adopted English, a process which often takes three generations to complete. But the ELA is creating just the kind of furor we might expect from a constitutional amendment. Overshadowing and to some extent preventing any dispassionate consideration of the ELA on its own merits, the amendment, turning on such controversial social issues as bilingual education and immigration policy, language loyalty and patriotism, provokes heated and sometimes irrational debate among legislators, civic leaders, newspaper columnists, educators, and the public at large. To point to one blatant example, audience and panelists almost came to blows when the television talk-show host Phil Donahue broadcast a program on the official language question from Miami in 1985. While no action has been taken in Congress on the ELA, official language laws were recently passed in Arkansas and defeated in Texas, Oklahoma, and Louisiana. In 1986 the issue was discussed in thirty-seven state legislatures. It is clear that for now, at least, the ELA is not just going to go away.

The Official Language Question

For a little more than two hundred years, the United States of America has gotten by without an official language. The founders of the United States chose not to designate English as the national language either in the Constitution or in subsequent federal law. Throughout our history, American English speakers, while always vitally concerned with correctness and standardization, have shied away from any form of official language tinkering, rejecting the notion of language academies or state-approved grammars, dictionaries, and spellers, and now both the National Council of Teachers of English and the Modern Language Association have gone on record opposing English-only legislation.

But this reluctance to privilege or mold English does not mean that on the occasions when official American policy tolerates or promotes minority languages, it does so out of any sympathy for cultural pluralism. It was always clear to our leaders that national and linguistic unity went hand in hand, and the United States was never envisioned as permanently multilingual. Practically speaking, we have had to recognize, sometimes officially, sometimes unofficially, the presence of large numbers of non-English speakers on American soil, granting them certain linguistic and cultural rights while at the same time integrating them into the mainstream of American society. The presence of non-English-speaking populations has often promoted official tolerance in the interests of producing an informed citizenry, maintaining efficient communication, and assuring public safety. Nonetheless, English has always been the de facto standard in the United States as a whole, and public policy has dealt with bilingualism as a temporary, transitional facet of assimilation, just as English-firsters would have wanted it, and just as those nonanglophones who come to the United States intending to stay view the situation as well.

English or American?

Throughout our history, we have cycled between policies of bilingual tolerance and an intolerant, English-only approach on the part of local, state, and federal governments. Anti-British sentiment after the Revolutionary War led to suggestions that the newly emerging nation speak a language different from English. Some reformers advocated Hebrew, felt by many eighteenth-century language experts to be the original, Edenic language. Other anti-English patriots suggested Greek, the language of what was seen as the world's first and most prestigious democracy, or French, considered by many, and particularly by the French, to be the language of pure rationality. The impracticality of converting Americans to any new language was always clear, however, and one revolutionary wag advised that we retain English for ourselves and instead force the British to learn Greek.

More popular than giving up English altogether was the insistence by Noah Webster, among others, that we rename our speech *American* rather than *English*. In 1789 Webster was so pro-American that he urged his compatriots to reject British linguistic standards simply because of their association with colonial oppression, even when those standards were demonstrably correct. In the same vein, John Adams predicted that our republican form of government would produce linguistic as well as social perfection, while the British monarchy and British English would continue to decay.

At the start of his language career, Webster envisioned creating a uniform American standard language, free of dialect variation or foreign (particularly French) impurities, and rational in its spelling and grammar. To this end he wrote a series of Federal textbooks, a speller, a grammar, and a reader, using American spellings, place names, and authors instead of British, and published at home rather than overseas. Webster campaigned to have his series adopted in all the states and endorsed by Congress and the universities.

Although he does not allude to the situation in Europe, Webster may have been influenced by French attempts at linguistic centralization as much as by his anti-British fervor. The French Academy had been authorized to produce official language texts, a dictionary, a grammar, and a guide to usage. It attacked this mission with renewed vigor after the French Revolution, partly out of a new national spirit, but also as a means of distancing itself from the *ancien régime,* and it did produce a new edition of its dictionary in the year VII, with an appropriately revolutionary preface. The Academy's grammar did not appear until the 1930s, and none of the academic texts ever achieved the universality intended for them.

Webster also failed in his grandiose scheme to establish a uniform set of approved textbooks. Competition from other texts, both British and American, was simply too stiff, and the states did not pursue the kind of national, educational and linguistic uniformity Webster supported. Nonetheless, he was instrumental in passing the first American copyright laws and in encouraging the purchase of American rather than British books.

Of course not all Americans were so hostile to the mother country. Joseph Emerson Worcester, Noah Webster's arch rival in lexicography, believed that the only practical English standard was that of London and the royal court, and many nineteenth-century language commentators on both sides of the Atlantic rejected the notion of a separate, Federal English, emphasizing instead the common heritage of the two tongues.

Even Webster's radical position on British English eventually softened. He named his great lexicon of 1828 *An American Dictionary of the English Language,* and during a trip to England to promote his publications, Webster, a master of marketing technique, claimed that the few differences between the two varieties of English were trivial and superficial. Despite Webster's change of heart, sentiment for an *American* rather than an *English* language surfaces sporadically in the nineteenth and twentieth centuries. There were *American Grammars* and *Columbian Grammars, American Spellers* (including Webster's own blue-backed speller, originally titled *An American Spelling Book*), even, as we have seen, an *American Primer* written by Walt Whitman. H. L. Mencken's popular study of our speech, *The American Language,* first published in 1919, went through four editions and two supplements, as well as an updated abridgement, and is still in print today.

Language and the Law

Although language has often been a controversial issue in American history, legislative attempts to manipulate language have not generally succeeded. Perhaps the most pervasive English language reform movement involved spelling simplification. Webster was a proponent of this, as were many well-known literary and political figures of the English-speaking world, including Benjamin Franklin, Samuel Clemens, George Bernard Shaw, Isaac K. Funk (of the Funk and Wagnalls' *Standard Dictionary*), Andrew Carnegie, and Theodore Roosevelt. During the later nineteenth century there were a number of failed attempts to get the U. S. Congress to make simplified English spelling the law of the land, and Roosevelt's Executive Order of 1906 enforcing simplified spelling proved ineffectual.

Other language legislation pertains to the official name of our unofficial language. In 1923, Montana Representative Washington Jay McCormick introduced a bill in the U. S. Congress to make *American* the nation's official tongue, and to amend all congressional acts and government regulations substituting *American* for *English* in references to language. McCormick's anglophobia is reminiscent of Webster's. Not only does he advocate dropping all references to the English language, he urges us to do away with any usage that suggests British influence. McCormick hoped to "supplement the political emancipation of '76 by the mental emancipation of '23," and he advised our writers to "drop their top-coats, spats, and swagger-sticks, and assume occasionally their buckskin, moccasins, and tomahawks."

McCormick's bill died in committee, but *American* was clearly in the air in 1923, and similar bills appeared in a number of state legislatures that year. All but one failed: State Senator Frank Ryan of Illinois did manage to push through a law making American, and not English, the official language of the State of Illinois. In its initial form, Ryan's bill was virulently anti-British. Its *whereases* attack those American Tories "who have never become reconciled to our republican institutions and have ever clung to the tradition of King and Empire." According to Ryan, such Anglophiles foster racism and defeat the attempts of American patriots "to weld the racial units into a solid American nation."

The bill as finally worded was toned down considerably, though its original sentiment was clearly unaltered. The Brit-bashing clauses were replaced by a paean to America as the world's welcoming haven. A final paragraph justified changing the name of our language because immigrants to the United States considered our institutions and language to be American. Despite its passage, the Illinois law produced no sweeping changes in usage in the state, where English rather than American continued to be taught in the public schools, albeit illegally, and it was quietly repealed in 1969, when English once again became the official state language.

The Politics of Bilingualism

Just as 1923 was the year of "American," it was also the year that saw a U. S. Supreme Court decision, *Meyer v. Nebraska*, supporting foreign language instruction in American schools, a decision reacting against the English-only sentiment that was then sweeping the country. During and after World War I there was much negative feeling toward German, Polish, and the Scandinavian languages. Local ordinances were passed forbidding the use of German, and one governor's proclamation went so far as to ban all foreign languages in public or on the telephone, a more public instrument then than it is now. Even earlier, in the nineteenth century, some states passed laws requiring that instruction in private as well as public schools be restricted to English, and after World War I sentiment against foreign languages was so negative that some areas banned all foreign language instruction, and a number of states had to pass special legislation to permit languages in school curricula (Kloss 1977).

Tempering the English-only fervor, however, was the fact that American politicians have always sensed the advantages of communicating in the various languages of their constituents. From the outset, important documents like the Articles of Confederation, and a good number of our laws, have been translated into minority languages by federal, state, and territorial governments. The early proceedings of the Continental Congress were published in German, for example, and in French as well, possibly with a view toward attracting the Québecois as future fellow-citizens.

In contrast, many Americans then, as now, reacted to non-Anglo-phones with fear and intolerance. Benjamin Franklin commented on the German settlement in Pennsylvania with some anxiety: "Why should Pennsylvania, founded by the English, become a colony of aliens, who will shortly be so numerous as to Germanize us instead of our Anglifying them, and will never adopt our language or customs any more than they can acquire our complexion?" In 1795, a proposal in Congress to print all federal laws in German as well as English lost by only one vote. Known as "the German Vote" or "the Muhlenberg Vote," after the speaker of the house who reportedly stepped down to cast the deciding negative, this event has been transmuted by pro-English folk tradition into a myth that German came close to replacing English as our national language. This myth was alluded to as a fact demonstrating the tenuous position of English in the new nation by a correspondent in a recent Ann Landers column, though the date was changed to the more patriotically crucial year of 1776.

In perspective, English speakers have been selective in their attitudes toward other languages. At various times they have generally proved more tolerant of the language rights of older, established groups, while decrying the supposed unwillingness of newer immigrants to learn

English and assimilate into American society. French was protected by the Louisiana Constitution of 1845, and Spanish was an official language of New Mexico before 1900. Many states either tolerated or actively supported non-English grade schools for speakers of French, German or Spanish. German regiments, using German as the language of command, served in the Civil War. During World War I, the treasury department advertised bonds in every language spoken in the country, and Franklin Roosevelt used the non-English press to publicize his New Deal policies.

Despite such bilingual tolerance, whenever English speakers feel threatened by increased numbers of non-Anglophones, they take action to promote English or to curb competing languages. For example, one unwritten criterion for statehood has always been the presence in a territory of a clear majority of English speakers, a factor which delayed statehood for Michigan (initially settled by the French), New Mexico (forced because of its Spanish and Native American populations to wait for statehood until 1912 though it was annexed in 1848), and most recently, Hawaii (annexed in 1898, it achieved statehood in 1959), and still prevents it for Puerto Rico. While New Mexico was never officially a bilingual state, several provisions of the constitution of 1912 protect Spanish speakers while attempting to move them toward fluency in English. Louisiana is the only territory that was granted statehood (in 1812) while its Anglo-Saxon population was outnumbered, though one historian suggests that in 1807 Jefferson entertained the idea of settling 30,000 English speakers in the territory to create an instant English-speaking majority (Kloss 1977).

The same erroneous claims made today against America's Spanish and Oriental populations, that they maintain alien cultural and linguistic ways in defiance of their obligations as residents or citizens, were lodged against the southern and central European immigrants of generations past, and language restrictions such as tests of literacy and English pronunciation were imposed to limit the access of certain ethnic and religious groups to voting and employment. The New York City public schools were particularly affected by such pronunciation screening, and for a generation or two only those who could master a stilted, hypercorrect form of speech were licensed to teach there. As recently as the 1950s, students preparing for careers in education at a major midwestern university were advised not to seek employment in New York because their midwestern accents would immediately disqualify them. In addition, students with any sort of perceptible accent, whether foreign or domestic, were diagnosed as having speech defects and were sent in droves to speech pathologists for remediation.

Just as the schools sought to admit only proper speakers to the teaching ranks, the linguistically elite staff so chosen did what they could to modify the language habits of their pupils. A number of specific varieties of English as it is used both by native speakers and by immigrants have come under censure through the agency of the public schools. During the immigration boom of the late nineteenth and early twentieth centuries, the schools presented a more or less uniform English-only stance; mainstreaming and not bilingual education was the order of the day. The schools were supported in their refusal to recognize any language but English by psychologists who, drawing evidence from flagrantly biased testing instruments, viewed bilingualism as a liability, and concluded either that non-English speakers were genetically inferior in intelligence or that bilinguals suffered impaired intellectual development because of internal language competition (Hakuta 1986). The only curricular hints at the presence in the classroom of non-native English speakers were a small number of transitional English classes for immigrant children, and published lists of errors in pronunciation, diction and grammar likely to be made by members of the various immigrant groups.

In addition, northern urban schools sought to eradicate traces of undesirable southern speech that might appear in students who had migrated from the south. In many cases, these students were black as well as southern, and the practical effect of this policy was to stigmatize the language of American blacks. Speakers of Black English were often accused of speaking English either poorly or not at all. Again, in the 1950s, leading American educational psychologists claimed that black children failed in schools because they had no language whatsoever. The Ann Arbor, or King decision of 1979 is frequently cited by those not familiar with the case as promoting Black English rather than standard English as the language of school instruction. Nothing could be farther from the truth: although the federal court decision affirmed the status of Black English as a legitimate variety of English, it ordered the Ann Arbor School Board to provide its teachers with the best existing linguistic knowledge so that they could more effectively educate their students "to read in the standard English of the school, the commercial world, the arts, sciences and professions" (Bailey 1983).

A Law with Teeth

What makes California's Proposition 63 different from earlier official language acts like that of Illinois is the fact that the California law has teeth. It amends the state constitution to prevent the legislature from passing laws diminishing or ignoring English, but more important, it allows any individual or business within the state to sue if the law is violated. At the time of this writing, U. S. English, the group that led the fight for the passage of Proposition 63, is contemplating suits against Los Angeles and San Francisco for alleged violations of the language law.

While the supporters of U. S. English and the new California statute deny that their efforts are aimed at the state's highly visible Hispanic and Asian communities, the group's fund-raising questionnaire, the "National Opinion Survey on Language Usage in the United States," targets the languages of these groups. The survey asks *What is the language in which you ordinarily think, speak, and write?* and, although the 1980 U. S. Census lists Spanish, followed by Italian, German, French, and Polish as the most frequently spoken non-English "home" languages, the survey proposes as responses, besides English, only Spanish, Chinese, Korean, Vietnamese, and *other.* U. S. English was formerly chaired by a physician whose concern that too many of the world's non-European tired, poor, huddled masses are making it to these shores led him to found the Federation for American Immigration Reform, known by the ironic acronym of FAIR.

By linking immigration with the question of a national language, the current English-first debate does not differ much from earlier attempts to deal with the fact that the United States is and has always been a multilingual country whose basic language is English. Furthermore, while many believe that the ELA is aimed primarily at Spanish speakers, recent studies show that Spanish speakers rapidly adopt English, and that Spanish can be maintained as a minority language only as long as Spanish immigration continues (Marshall 1986). Spanish is then no different from any of our other minority languages. However, researchers are now finding that the large numbers of Hispanics who have become monolingual English speakers are not benefiting from their linguistic competence in terms of increased salaries and job opportunities: apparently the discrimination against them is deeper than language alone.

The ELA's backers press the de facto status of English as our official language and stress the problems of miscommunication and noncommunication in a polyglot society. Pointing to the social strife in multilingual countries like India, Belgium, and Canada, they warn that without legislation protecting English, similar social disruption will occur at home. In contrast, opponents, who also accept a de facto official English, argue that the ELA defends English against an imaginary foe. They see the amendment as attacking the new waves of non-Anglophone, non-Anglo immigrants coming to our shores. According to its detractors, the ELA subverts the traditional American tolerance of native-language maintenance needed for an orderly transition to English, making the sometimes slow process of entering the mainstream slower still, if not impossible. They note that unrest and violence have only occurred abroad when language rights previously enjoyed by an area's citizens are suddenly revoked in order to promote an official language, and darkly hint that the ELA will do more harm than good to the fabric of American society.

Compounding the problem, the rational appeal of one nation speaking one language also attracts to the ELA the support of well-meaning citizens—perhaps a majority of Americans, English and non-English speakers alike—who find the idea of linguistic and ethnic prejudice otherwise abhorrent. It is clear that these well-meaning citizens, including a majority of the state's school teachers, and not the radical fringe, are responsible for the massive support given Proposition 63.

One obstacle to the ELA's success is the uncertainty over its effect. On one hand, it might simply prove symbolic. In the case of Arkansas and Illinois, Official English laws have not restricted minority language rights or interfered with the assimilation process. On the other hand, it is not clear that either the House or Senate version of the ELA has been framed to anticipate undesirable interpretations. The House and Senate versions of the proposed English Language Amendment, or ELA, are quite different. The Senate version, which simply establishes English, need not affect the status of other languages. It should not put bilingual education programs in jeopardy, nor should it require that ballots, street signs, and emergency services in multilingual areas be limited to English. However, the House version specifically prohibits the use of any language other than English except as a means of establishing English proficiency. This could restrict the use of multilingual tests, forms and ballots, as well as translators for legal and emergency services. The ELA might change language use in America profoundly: one legal analyst concludes that an extreme interpretation of the ELA might not only outlaw foreign language requirements in college curricula, it could prevent the voluntary teaching of any foreign language except for the limited purpose of helping a non-English speaker to learn English (Marshall 1986). Ironically, adopting the ELA may not only fail to facilitate the adoption of English, it may in fact deter the learning of English by isolating non-English speakers further from the American mainstream.

On balance, the benefits of an English-only amendment are not entirely clear. That the framers of the Constitution, who dealt with the same problems of multilingualism that face us today, chose not to adopt an English-first stance is instructive: their attitude should lead us to question the necessity of an amendment whose purpose seems not linguistic but culturally and politically isolationist in its thrust.

25 Private Words

I make many mistakes.
—Raymond Chandler *The Big Sleep*

Most of the language speculation that we have dealt with in this book, whether it is about teaching English, standard English, changing English, or English and only English, concerns the use of language for public discourse. But even public discourse can seem oppressively private to the uninitiated. I learned how exclusive public language can really be when I accepted an exchange lectureship a few years ago at a French university. Earlier in these pages I boasted of my reading knowledge of French. But my ability to speak what is often called the language of romance or rationality, depending upon your prejudice, is nil, and no amount of classroom training prepared me for the problems I encountered understanding the French of native speakers. During my first month of immersion in French I struggled with kilos and francs and liters and degrees centigrade. I made many mistakes. The sentences of spoken French ran by me in the air so fast I couldn't identify the individual words. The feeling of dizziness this engendered gave way to one of suffocation, accompanied by a high degree of language anxiety. All this culminated in a frantic dream where I found myself intoning fluent French without being able to understand a single word I said.

After a few weeks, of course, I became more comfortable with French, but it remained for me a private language, one that belonged to someone else. My sole consolation was that my French students, who were English majors destined to teach English to other French students, knew far less English than I did French. Of course neither French nor English is a private language—they just seemed that way to the *foreigners* or *étrangers* trying to learn them. But the experience led me to become interested in the study of true private languages.

On the other end of the spectrum from public languages like English and French is the notion of the private language, a language developed for use by a small group, or in extreme cases, by a single person, and designed to exclude outsiders. Criminal argot forms one such private language; technical jargon forms another. Unlike public language, whose purpose is to break down the bars to communication, a private language is either intentionally or functionally opaque—the reality it represents is secret, and expressions are masked or coded so that only initiates, whether members of the same profession, clan, or social group, can fathom their significance.

Thieves cant, or criminal argot, has been a popular topic of study for several centuries. Some words from this argot have been picked up as slang by the standard language over the years. Many of us know what a *con* is, for example, or a *mark*, or a *scam*. The movie *The Sting* further enlightened the American people to the terminology of the confidence racket. The linguist David Maurer (1964), a specialist in the language of American professional criminals, notes that sometimes the passing of a thieves' term into wider use involves a change in meaning. According to Maurer, male thieves refer to themselves as *guns*, while a female thief is a *gun moll*. The word *gun* in this case derives not from the firearm, as is popularly assumed, but from the Yiddish *gonif*, 'thief.' *Moll* functions simply as a gender marker. Picking up the folk etymology rather than the true one, and combining it with a view of women which sees them playing a role subservient to men, Hollywood deprofessionalized the term *gun moll* in the era of the gangster picture from the original 'woman gangster' into a synonym for 'gunman's girlfriend.'

Maurer published a detailed analysis of the special words used by pickpockets, or *whiz mobs*. *Mobs* work in teams, with a strict division of labor and an elaborate terminology. The *tool* (also the *hook, wire, cannon, mechanic* or *claw*) selects the *mark*, or victim, and makes the actual *score, hook, dip,* or *sting*. The *stalls* are accomplices who *work* the crowd, taking their cue from the *tool*, moving in to make the *frame* which puts the mark in position for the score. Once framed, the tool *fans* and *locates* the victim, or *chump*, determining the presence of something worth taking and pinpointing the position of the wallet or purse before actually hooking it. The entire process, under ideal conditions, should take less than twenty seconds from sighting the mark to taking the wallet. Some tools, called *prat diggers*, specialize in hip pocket wallets (*prat* is the slang term for buttocks, as in *pratfall*); others prefer *britch kicks*, 'side pants pockets,' or the more difficult *insiders* or *coat pits*.

Criminal usage is an exception to the rule that most private languages do not receive much attention from linguists and language commentators. Private languages are difficult to study partly because they are transient phenomena occurring on the fringes of communication, and partly because investigators have difficulty gaining admission to groups

using these secret forms of speech, or *cryptolects*. The *travelers* of
Europe, Great Britain, and the United States, as well as other anglo-
phone areas of the world, a group which includes but is not limited
to *Gypsies*, use the various traveler cants, or Romany dialects, as a
private "language of the roads" to mark both ethnic identity and to
exclude outsiders from a communication. The linguist Ian Hancock
(1986), of Romany descent, has specialized in these previously neglected cryptolects. For example, Hancock presents a version of the
Lord's Prayer in what is known as The Cant, which begins, "Our
gathra, who cradgies in the manyak-norch, we turry kerrath about
your moniker." Modern Cant contains a good mix of English vocabulary
along with such basic non-English words as *gaje*, the term for 'non-
Gypsy,' and according to Hancock, a number of Cant words—called
"peddlars French" by one sixteenth century commentator though their
exact origins remain unknown—have made their way into Modern
English, including *booze, gear, queer,* and *rum*.

In California, a more localized private language called *Boontling*
arose in the 1890s around the town of Boonville in the Anderson
Valley. As the linguist Charles Adams (1971) describes it, Boonville
was at that time fairly isolated from the rest of the state, and local
residents evolved the Boontling jargon to serve a variety of functions.
To some extent men used it as the secret language of sheepshearing
crews and baseball teams, from which women were excluded, though
in practice women quickly learned it. In addition, adults used the
jargon to keep discussions secret from children, though children
managed to figure out the code as well. Boontling was most effective
in separating natives of the valley from outsiders, who could not easily
fathom the code of deformed pronunciations, abbreviations and clipping, and personal associations of the "you had to be there" kind that
form the basis of Boontling.

For example, Adams lists in his glossary of the jargon such terms
as *dirty neck*, 'a person in the intermediate stages of degeneration,' in
contrast to a *deejer*, or someone who is *deejy*, both deriving from
degenerate with the addition of an appropriate suffix. *To rubberneck*
means in Boontling 'to listen in on a party line.' And a *shattaquaw*,
from *Chautauqua*, is a talkfest. To *netty* means 'to dress fancy,' and
derives from the name of a woman who overdressed. A speaker of
Boontling (from *Boonville lingo*), or Boont, is called a *harper*, and *nonch
harpin'* is the use of the extensive taboo aspects of Boont. On the other
hand, *to hark Boont* means to speak the lingo incorrectly.

Many Boontling terms are nicknames. *Dime* was the name of the
owner of the local dime store, and *Dupont* referred to a local man
who once tried, unsuccessfully, to make his own blasting powder.

Teebow was a woman—the Boontling term for woman is *tea drinker*—who could bow a mean fiddle. Because this same woman became deaf in her later years, the adjective *teabowed* came to mean 'hearing impaired.'

As times changed and Boonville became more connected to the world, Boontling declined. However the same processes that generated this California cryptolect continually operate on a smaller scale to produce private language within families and other close-knit groups. Children are particularly playful with language, and many of their coinages become institutionalized within a family's lingo. Nicknames are the most public representatives of what starts out as private language. At the age of three, a friend's daughter began to call herself Gumby because the name she was given, Alexandra, was, as she explained it, "too gooey and too sticky." She named her younger brother Owl Boy, which has no connection whatsoever to his real name, Remy, which is seldom heard in their household.

Soon after she began to talk, my younger daughter, Rachel, began coining and adding suffixes to names, much in the manner of the Hindi honorific *-ji* and the Japanese *-san: daddy* in Rachel's lingo became *dido*, which was in turn transmuted into *dido-wok, dido-way* and *dido-go-way. Mommy* quickly became *mommy-wok, mommy-go-way, momby* and *momba.* Her favorite stuffed dog is both the traditionally formal *puppy* and the inventively familiar *puppy-woni, woni-woni,* and *puppers.* Rachel called her sister Cordelia, *Dida,* sometimes *Dida-wok.* When she got a little older that became *Deria;* now she is *Sisties.* For Rachel, lights were *do,* while *bui* in Rachelspeak meant 'look.' Rachel's first sentence, *Bui, a do,* 'Look, a light,' contained but one normal word, the indefinite article, which led us to wonder if she would ever speak a more public variety of English.

Some children's invented words echo real-world sounds, while others are phonetic deformations of common words made accidentally or on purpose (mispronunciations, according to stricter parents than I). Rachel called strawberries *gerbies,* and another child we know referred to grapes as *beeps.* A friend's son said *ickies* for *cookies,* and while his parents may not have cared for this temporary idiosyncrasy, my own family gleefully adopted it for a time. Another friend's children named the cardboard tube inside a roll of paper the *doot da doot* in imitation of the trumpet-like sound they make with the paper instruments. Rachel's noun *growmot* for *grown up,* as well as her *retend* for *pretend* and *renember* for *remember,* have now passed into the family lexicon, as has *Yu Nork,* her spoonerized pronunciation of the city where one of her grandmothers lives.

Other child-created words do not have such clear etymologies. For reasons known only to her, Rachel called a sponge a *feh*. We don't know where Rachel—who is now almost five—came up with two of her mealtime favorites, *doum* (rhymes with *room*), which is mashed potatoes, and *munyo*, or seltzer water. She is a finicky eater, and we got her to try oatmeal by calling it *doum cereal*. We also attempted to calm her fear of looking out an airplane window by telling her we were flying over *doum*, not clouds.

One Last Word

Parents also coin private language, whether family nicknames or child-oriented euphemisms for bodily parts and functions. But because euphemisms quickly acquire the stigma of the taboo they are meant to soften, and because private language is often intensely personal as well, much private language can be embarrassing when it is published abroad. Consequently it is difficult to get people to discuss their own private language, particularly such things as the pet names they use in intimate situations, with any degree of openness. Moreover, because it generally impedes communication (though it may often function as a private form of shorthand for the in-group), much private language, like private jokes, does not interest those who are on the outside, except for certain linguists and folklorists.

In contrast to the hidden, private forms of speech, there has been, from time to time, an interest in the artificial creation of new public languages designed to facilitate communication even better than the languages already in existence, and to eliminate the need for private forms of discourse. In the seventeenth century, linguists imagined— and some tried to devise—a language whose vocabulary and grammar was directly related to reality. In this "philosophical" language, each word corresponded unambiguously to one and only one thing or idea in the natural world. With such a language, one could see a direct correlation between amount of knowledge and vocabulary size. If human knowledge is infinite, the word hoard of the philosophical language would be infinite as well, but unlike our natural languages it would be infinitely measurable and manageable. Language would be an ideal medium of instruction since each word would be a clear reflection of its meaning, rather than a source of confusion or a potential hindrance to understanding. Imagine how easy it might be, using an auxiliary philosophical language, not just to teach, but also to assess learning with a great degree of accuracy as well, or to calculate, as some states are now trying to do, exactly what a school or college education adds to a person's knowledge. Unfortunately, none of the attempts at a philosophical language have had any success, and such a language does not now exist.

Equally tantalizing, and equally impossible, why not imagine a language in which all possible meanings are compressed into one single word? Perhaps the opponents of verbosity would look kindly on such a tongue. In any case, there is a story which anthropologists tell about an anthropological linguist (we must be careful not to say *grammarian*) somewhere off in the bush who accidentally discovered this unheard of language phenomenon: a group of native, or primitive, or under-developed, or preindustrial (or whatever the currently popular phrase) people, living in the valley beyond the mountains, whose language— never before described—consisted of one and only one word. To begin his field work, the linguist selected an appropriate informant and began to elicit linguistic information using gestures. He pointed at a cow and his informant responded with a word something like *svii*. Pointing to a tree brought the same response from the informant, *svii*. So did pointing at the sky, the sun, the moon, water, earth, stones, people, and everything else. The linguist dutifully taped the session, transcribing the recording later in his tent using phonetic symbols.

This was really something. No language could possibly exist with only one word. Yet whatever the linguist pointed to, out came *svii*. This discovery would shatter all previous linguistic speculation and turn the anthropological community on its head. Here was the sort of find that made one's reputation, and brought in grants and honors from universities around the world. In his mind, the linguist began to plan the article announcing his discovery.

Returning once again to Western civilization, our linguist met a colleague on her way out to study another of the local cultures. Unable to contain himself, he blurted out his news, a group of natives whose language consisted entirely of the single, monosyllabic word *svii*. The colleague looked puzzled, then thought for a bit, and finally asked, "Is that the group of hunters and gatherers living in the valley beyond the mountains?" Yes, it was. "Then I've just seen something about them," she explained. "Hoskins studied them only a year ago and sent me a draft of her monograph on their language." The linguist looked apprehensive, but it was his colleague's next comment that proved most deflating: "I was just reading that monograph." And she pulled it from her baggage and began thumbing through it rapidly. Finally she found what she was looking for. "There, you see," she said, pointing to the page. "*Svii* is their word for 'finger.' "

As *kangaroo* may have been for Capt. Cook, it was all one big mistake. Of course, fictional language mysteries are easier to solve than real ones. In Raymond Chandler's novel, *The Big Sleep,* General Sternwood's competent butler Norris tells private investigator Marlowe, "I make many mistakes." We all make many mistakes when we deal with English. But the story of the anthropological linguist shows that, like everything else in the modern universe, language can be maddeningly relative. Words are not always what they appear to be. Sometimes we imagine the discourse is about distant abstractions, when it is really nothing more than fingers.

As I have tried to demonstrate, all our words, the common as well as the rare, are important, and each one has a history, sometimes real, sometimes imagined, often both. The word *grammar* may be on the outs, for now—or declining, if you will excuse the pun—and the study of grammar may inspire fear, but whatever our linguistic bias, language challenges our deductive and inductive powers, egging us on to new and greater discoveries, while at the same time tripping us up with new and greater mistakes. It is both fitting and ironic to end our look at English fact and fancy with a tentative statement of another language law, which we may call the Paradox of Constant Humility. We considered in chapter nine the development of a First Law, which asserts that efforts to control our language use are likely to go awry. It is now time to articulate our Second Law of English grammar:

> The humbling thing about language is that we cannot expect to find out what is right unless we gracefully accept the fact that we may go wrong along the way, if not at the end as well.

Bibliography

A. E. 1884. "Need of a Telephone Vocabulary." *Lippincott's Magazine* 33:418–19.

Adams, Charles C. 1971. *Boontling: An American Lingo.* Austin: University of Texas Press.

Adams, John. [1780] 1852. "To the President of Congress." In *Works,* edited by Charles Francis Adams, 8: 249–51. Boston: Little, Brown.

Aiken, Janet. 1930. *English Past and Present.* N.Y.: Roland Press.

Algeo, John. 1977. "Grammatical Usage: Modern Shibboleths." In *James B. McMillan: Essays in Linguistics by His Friends and Colleagues,* edited by James C. Raymond and I. Willis Russell, 53–71. University: University of Alabama Press.

Ayres, Alfred. 1882. *The Verbalist.* N.Y.: D. Appleton.

————. 1901. *Some Ill-used Words.* N.Y.: D. Appleton and Co.

Bache, Richard Meade. 1869. *Vulgarisms and Other Errors of Speech.* 2nd ed.

Bailey, Richard W. 1983. "Education and the Law: The *King* Case in Ann Arbor." In *Black English: Educational Equity and the Law,* edited by John Chambers, Jr., 1–28. Ann Arbor: Karoma.

Bain, Alexander. 1887. *English Composition and Rhetoric.* N.Y.: D. Appleton.

Baker, Josephine Turck. Editorial Comment. *Correct English* 6 (1904): 169.

————. 1907. *Correct English: How to Use It.* Baltimore: Sadler-Rowe.

Baker, Robert. 1770. *Reflections on the English Language.* London.

Baker, Sheridan. 1981. *The Practical Stylist.* 5th ed. N.Y.: Harper and Row.

————. 1984. *The Complete Stylist.* 3rd ed. N.Y.: Harper and Row.

Barber, Charles. 1976. *Early Modern English.* London: André Deutsch.

Barnes, William. 1878. *Outline of English Speech-Craft.* London.

————. 1880. *Outline of Rede-craft (Logic) with English Wording.* London.

Barnhart, Clarence L., Sol Steinmetz, and Robert K. Barnhart, eds. *The Barnhart Dictionary of New English Since 1963.* 1973. N.Y.: Barnhart/Harper and Row.

Baron, Dennis. 1981. "The Epicene Pronoun: The Word That Failed." *American Speech* 56: 83–97.

————. 1982a. *Going Native: The Regeneration of Saxon English. Publication of the American Dialect Society,* no. 69. University: University of Alabama Press.

————. 1982b. *Grammar and Good Taste: Reforming the American Language.* New Haven: Yale University Press.

————. 1986a. *Grammar and Gender.* New Haven: Yale University Press.

————. 1986b. "An Endangered Language." *English Today,* April: 21–24.

————. 1987a. "No way to treat a lady—or a gent." *Righting Words* 1 (January/February): 24–28.

————. 1987b. "Federal English." *Brandeis Review* 6 (Spring): 18–21.

————. 1987c. "Public Cutespeak." *Verbatim* 13 (Spring): 18–19.

————. 1987d. "The Uses of Usage." *English Journal* 76 (December): 59–60.

————. 1987e. "A Literal Paradox." *Righting Words* (forthcoming).

————. 1988a. "Our Presto-changeo Language." *Righting Words* 2 (January/February), 15–17; 20–21.

————. 1988b. "The Ugly Grammarian." *English Today* 16 (October): 9–12.

————. 1989. "Going Out of Style?" *English Today* 17 (January): 6–11.

————. (In press). "Watching Our Grammar." *Essays for English Teachers,* edited by Gail Hawisher and Anna Soter. Albany: SUNY Press.

Barzun, Jacques. [1975] 1985. *Simple and Direct: A Rhetoric for Writers.* N.Y.: Harper and Row.

Bernstein, Theodore. 1965. *The Careful Writer.* N.Y.: Atheneum.

————. 1977. *Dos, Don'ts and Maybes of English Usage.* N.Y.: Times Books.

Blair, Hugh. [1783] 1860. *Lectures on Rhetoric and Belles Lettres.* Philadelphia.

Blount, Thomas. 1656. *Glossographia.* London.

Bollinger, Dwight. 1968. *Aspects of Language.* N.Y.: Harcourt, Brace and World.

Breslin, Jimmy. 1982. *Forsaking All Others.* N.Y.: Simon and Schuster.

Brewer, E. Cobham. 1898. *Dictionary of Phrase and Fable.* Philidelphia: Henry Altemas.

Brewer, W. A. 1987. "The Folkmorph-*busters*." *American Speech* 61: 371–76.

Brooks, Cleanth, and Robert Penn Warren. 1970. *Modern Rhetoric.* 3rd ed. N.Y.: Harcourt, Brace and World.

Brown, Harry M. 1980. *Business Report Writing.* N.Y.: D. Van Nostrand.

Butters, Ron. 1987. " 'Hubba-hubba': Its rise and fall." *American Speech* 61: 363–65.

Camden, William. [1605] 1637. *Remaines Concerning Britaine.*

Cameron, Deborah. 1985. *Feminism and Linguistic Theory.* London: Macmillan.

Campbell, George. [1776] 1823. *The Philosophy of Rhetoric.* London.

Cardell, William S. 1827. *Philosophic Grammar of the English Language.* Philadelphia.

Christian, Jane Macnab, and Chester C. Christian, Jr. 1966. "Spanish Language and Culture in the Southwest." In *Language Loyalty in the United States,* edited by Joshua Fishman, 280–317. The Hague: Mouton.

Claiborne, Robert. 1986. *Saying What You Mean: A Commonsense Guide to American Usage.* New York: W. W. Norton.

Colby, Frank. 1944. *Practical Handbook of Better English.* N.Y.: Grosset and Dunlap.

Converse, Charles Crozat. 1884. "A New Pronoun." *The Critic* (2 August): 55.

Cook, Claire Kehrwald. 1985. *The MLA's Line by Line: How to Edit Your Own Writing.* Boston: Houghton Mifflin.

Cook, Luella B., and Lucy H. Chapman. 1936. *Using English: Third Year.* N.Y.: Harcourt, Brace and Co.

Cooper, James Fenimore. 1838. *The American Democrat.* Cooperstown, N.Y.

Copperud, Roy. 1980. *American Usage and Style: The Consensus.* N.Y.: Van Nostrand Reinhold.

Crews, Frederick, and Sandra Schor. 1985. *The Borzoi Handbook for Writers.* N.Y.: Alfred A. Knopf.

Curme, George O. 1935. *Parts of Speech and Accidence.* Boston: D.C. Heath.

Davis, Ossie. 1967. "The English Language Is My Enemy." *Negro History Bulletin* 30 (April): 18.

Delaware Technical and Community College. 1982. *Writing Skills for Technical Students.* Englewood Cliffs, N.J.: Prentice-Hall.

Dessoulavy, Charles Louis. 1917. *Word-book of the English Tongue.* London: George Routledge and Sons.

Diderot, Denis. 1751. *Langue Nouvelle. Encyclopédie, ou Dictionnaire Raisonné.* 9: 268–71. Neufchatel.

Durand, Margéurite. 1936. *Le genre grammatical en français parlé à Paris et dans la région parisienne.* Paris: Bibliothèque du français moderne.

Earle, John. 1890. *English Prose.* London: Smith and Elder.

Evans, Bergen. 1961. *Comfortable Words.* N.Y.: Random House.

Evans, Bergen, and Cornelia Evans. 1957. *A Dictionary of Contemporary American Usage.* N.Y.: Random House.

Fairfax, Nathaniel. 1674. *A Treatise of the Bulk and Selvedge of the World.* London.

Fielden, John S., Ronald E. Dalek, and Jean D. Fielden. 1984. *Elements of Business Writing.* Englewood Cliffs, N.J.: Prentice-Hall.

Fishman, Joshua, ed. 1986. "Language Rights and the English Language Amendment." *International Journal of the Sociology of Language* 60.

Flesch, Rudolf. [1949] 1974. *The Art of Readable Writing.* N.Y.: Harper and Row.

Follett, Wilson. 1966. *Modern American Usage.* Edited by Jacques Barzun. N.Y.: Hill and Wang.

Fowler, H. Ramsey. 1983. *The Little, Brown Handbook.* 2nd ed. Boston: Little, Brown.

Fowler, Henry W. 1926. *A Dictionary of Modern English Usage.* Oxford: Clarendon Press.

Fowler, Henry W., and Francis G. Fowler. 1906. *The King's English.* Oxford: Clarendon Press.

Francis, W. Nelson, and Henry Kučera. 1982. *Frequency Analysis of English Usage.* Boston: Houghton Mifflin.

Funk, Charles E. 1950. *Thereby Hangs a Tail.* N.Y.: Harper and Row.

Funk, Wilfred. 1950. *Word Origins and Their Romantic Stories.* N.Y.: Funk and Wagnalls.

Genung, John Franklin. 1900. *The Working Principles of Rhetoric.* Boston: Ginn and Co.

Gould, Edward S. 1867. *Good English; or, Popular Errors in Language*. N.Y.

Greenough, Chester Noyes, and Frank W. Hersey. 1918. *English Composition*. N.Y.: Macmillan.

Hakuta, Kenji. 1986. *The Mirror of Language*. New York: Basic Books.

Hall, Donald. [1976] 1985. *Writing Well*. 5th ed. Boston: Little, Brown.

Halliday, M. A. K. 1970. "Language Structure and Language Function." In *New Horizons in Linguistics*, edited by John Lyons, 140–65. Harmondsworth: Penguin.

Hancock, Ian. 1986. "The Cryptolectal Speech of the American Roads: Traveler Cant and American Angloromani." *American Speech* 61: 206–20.

Hanson, Charles Lane. 1908. *English Composition*. Boston: Ginn and Co.

Harmer, L. C. 1954. *The French Language Today*. London: Hutchinson's University Library.

Hofland, Knut, and Stig Johansson. 1982. *Word Frequencies in British and American English*. Bergen: Norwegian Computing Centre for the Humanities.

James, Henry. 1906–1907. "The Speech of American Women." *Harper's Bazaar* 40 (November): 979–82; 40 (December): 1103–06; 41 (January): 17–21; 41(February): 113–17.

Jespersen, Otto. 1949. *Modern English Grammar*. Place: pub.

Johnson, Roy I., A. Laura McGregor, and Rollo Laverne Lyman. 1939. *English Expression*. Boston: Ginn and Co.

Kane, Thomas L. 1983. *The Oxford Guide to Writing*. N.Y.: Oxford University Press.

Kennedy, Arthur G. 1935. *Current English*. Boston: Ginn.

———. 1942. *English Usage: A Study in Policy and Procedure*. N.Y.: D. Appleton-Century.

Kenner, Hugh. 1982. "The Word Police." *Harper's* (June): 68–71.

Kloss, Heinz. 1977. *The American Bilingual Tradition*. Rowley, Mass.: Newbury House.

Krapp, George Philip. 1927. *A Comprehensive Guide to Good English*. Chicago: Rand McNally.

Kruck, William E. 1981. *Looking for Dr. Condom*. PADS 69. University: University of Alabama Press.

Lanham, Richard A. 1979. *Revising Prose*. N.Y.: Charles Scribner's Sons.

Lannon, John M. 1985. *Technical Writing*. 3rd ed. Boston: Little, Brown.

Lawrence, Margot. 1986. "Tudor English Today." *English Today* 8 (October): 27–29.

Leonard, Sterling A. 1929. *The Doctrine of Correctness in English Usage 1700–1800*. University of Wisconsin Studies in Language and Literature no. 25. Madison.

———. 1932. *Current English Usage*. Chicago: National Council of Teachers of English.

Lever, Ralph. 1573. *The Arte of Reason, Rightly Termed, Witcraft, Teaching a Perfect Way to Argue and Dispute*. London.

Locke, John. [1690] 1694. *Essay Concerning Humane Understanding*. London.

Lounsbury, Thomas. 1908. *The Standard of Usage in English*. N.Y.: Harper and Bros.

Lowth, Robert. 1762. *A Short Introduction to English Grammar.* London.

MacCracken, H. N., and Helen E. Sanderson. 1919. *Manual of Good English.* N.Y.: Macmillan.

Maimon, Elaine P., Gerald L. Belcher, Gail W. Hearn, Barbara F. Nodine, and Finbarr W. O'Connor. 1981. *Writing in the Arts and Sciences*. Boston: Little, Brown.

Marius, Richard, and Harvey S. Wiener, eds. 1985. *The McGraw-Hill College Handbook*. N.Y.: McGraw-Hill.

Marckwardt, Albert. 1940. *Scribner Handbook of English*. N.Y.: Scribner.

Marsh, George Perkins. 1859. *Lectures on the English Language*. N.Y.

Marshall, David F. 1986a. "The Question of an Official Language: Language Rights and the English Language Amendment." In Fishman 1986.

————. 1986b. "An Endangered Language?" *English Today* (April): 21–24.

Maurer, David. 1964. *Whiz Mob: A Correlation of the Technical Argot of Pickpockets with Their Behavior Pattern*. New Haven: College and University Press.

McCrimmon, James M. 1980. *Writing with a Purpose*. 7th ed. Boston: Houghton Mifflin.

McMurtry, Jo. 1985. *English Language, English Literature*. Hamden, CT: Archon Books.

Mencken, H. L. 1937. *The American Language*. 4th ed. N.Y.: Knopf.

————. 1944. "Designations for Colored Folk." *American Speech* 19: 161–74.

Michaelis, Johann David. [1759] 1769. *Dissertation on the Influence of Opinions on Language and of Language on Opinions.*

Mills, Gordon H., and John A. Walter. 1970. *Technical Writing*. 3rd. ed. N.Y.: Holt, Rinehart and Winston.

Moore, John. 1961. *You English Words*. Philadelphia: J. B. Lippincott.

Morris, William, and Mary Morris, eds. 1975. *The Harper Dictionary of Contemporary Usage*. N.Y.: Harper and Row.

Mullins, Carolyn J. 1983. *A Guide to Writing and Publishing in the Social and Behavioral Sciences*. Malabar, Fl.: Robert E. Krieger.

Nagy, William E., and Richard C. Anderson. 1984. "How Many Words Are There in Printed School English?" *Reading Research Quarterly* 19: 304–30.

Nagy, William E., and Patricia A. Herman. 1987. "Breadth and Depth of Vocabulary Knowledge: Implications for Acquisition and Instruction." In *The Nature of Vocabulary Acquisition*, edited by Margaret McKeown and Mary E. Curtis. Hillsdale, N.J.: Laurence Erlbaum Associates.

Newman, Edwin. 1974. *Strictly Speaking*. Indianapolis: Bobbs-Merrill.

Nuessel, Frank H., Jr. 1982. "License Plate Language." *American Speech* 57: 256–59.

Orwell, George. [1946] 1984. "Politics and the English Language." Rpt. in*The Harper and Row Reader,* edited by Wayne C. Booth and Marshall Gregory 133–42. N.Y.: Harper and Row.

Pascoe, Graham. 1988. "To the Barricades."*English Today* 4. (1): 7.

Porter, Frank T. 1875. *Gleanings and Reminiscences*. Dublin.

Puttenham, George. [1589] 1936. *The Arte of English Poetry*. Edited by G. D. Willcock and A. Walker. Cambridge, England: Cambridge University Press.

Quirk, Randolph, Sidney Greenbaum, Geoffrey Leech, and Jan Svartvik. 1976. *A Grammar of Contemporary English*. London: Longman.

————. 1985. *A Comprehensive Grammar of the English Language*. London: Longman.

The Random House Dictionary of the English Language. 2nd ed. New York: Random House.

Raymond, James C. 1980. *Writing (Is an Unnatural Act)*. N.Y.: Harper and Row.

Richards, I. A. 1943. *Basic English and Its Uses*. N.Y.: W. W. Norton.

Robinson, Ian. 1975. *The New Grammarians' Funeral*. Cambridge, England: Cambridge University Press.

Roundy, Nancy. 1985. *Strategies for Technical Communication*. Boston: Little, Brown.

Sampson, Martin W., and Ernest O. Holland. 1907. *Written and Oral Composition*. N.Y.: American Book Co.

Safire, William. 1986. *Take My Word for It*. N.Y.: Times Books.

Scheuer, John. 1980. Letter. *New York Times*, June 23: 22.

Shapiro, Fred R. 1987. "Etymology of the Computer 'Bug': History and Folklore." *American Speech* 62: 376–78.

Shaughnessy, Mina. 1972. *Errors and Expectations*. N.Y.: Oxford University Press.

Shaw, Harry. 1981. *The Harper Handbook of College Composition*. N.Y.: Harper and Row.

Sherman, L. A. 1893. *Analytics of Literature*. Boston: Ginn and Co.

Simon, John. 1980. *Paradigms Lost*. N.Y.: Clarkson Potter.

Simpson, David. 1986. *The Politics of American English, 1776–1850*. N.Y.: Oxford University Press.

Smith, G. Gregory, ed. 1904. *Elizabethan Critical Essays*. London: Oxford University Press. In 2 volumes.

Smith, Logan Pearsall. 1948. *Words and Idioms: Studies in the English Language*. London: Constable.

Sprat, Thomas. 1667. *History of the Royal Society*. London.

Standard Dictionary of the English Language. New York: Funk and Wagnalls.

Swinton, William. 1877. *A School Manual for English Composition*. N.Y.: American Book Co.

Todd, Loreto, and Ian Hancock. 1986. *International English Usage*. London: Croom Helm.

Visser, F. Th. 1973. *An Historical Syntax of the English Language*. Leiden: E.J. Brill.

Vizetelly, Frank. 1907. *Desk-book of Errors in English*. N.Y.: Funk and Wagnalls.

Voss, James F., Terry R. Greene, Timothy A. Post, Barbara C. Penner. 1983. "Problem-Solving Skill in the Social Sciences." *Psychology of Learning and Motivation* 17: 165–213.

Webb, John. 1669. *An Historical Essay Endeavoring a Probability That the Language of the Empire of China Is the Primitive Language:* London.

Webster, Noah. 1784. *A Plain and Comprehensive Grammar.* Hartford.

————. 1789. *Dissertations on the English Language.*

————. 1828. *An American Dictionary of the English Language.* New York.

Webster's Third New International Dictionary. 1971. Springfield, Mass.: G. & C. Merriam.

Weekley, Ernest. [1911] 1961. *The Romance of Words.* N.Y.: Dover Press.

Wentworth, Harold, and Stuart Berg Flexner, eds. 1975. *Dictionary of American Slang.* 2nd ed. N.Y.: Crowell.

Weseen, Maurice H. 1928. *Crowell's Dictionary of English Grammar and Handbook of American Usage.* N.Y.: Crowell.

Whalen, Doris. 1978. *Handbook for Business Writers.* N.Y.: Harcourt Brace Jovanovich.

White, Richard Grant. 1870. *Words and Their Uses.* Boston.

Whitman, Walt. 1856. "America's Mightiest Inheritance." *Life Illustrated* 1 (April 12): 55–56.

————. 1904. *American Primer.* Boston: Small, Maynard and Company.

Wilkins, John. 1688. *An Essay Towards a Real Character, and a Philosophical Language.* London.

Williams, Joseph. 1981. *Style: Ten Lessons in Clarity and Grace.* Glenview, Il.: Scott, Foresman and Co.

————. 1985. Talk given at 1985 meeting of the New Society for Language and Rhetoric. Chicago.

Willis, Waldo H. 1965. *Better Report Writing.* N.Y.: Reinhold.

Wolfram, Walt, and Donna Christian. 1976. *Appalachian Speech.* Washington, D.C.: Center for Applied Linguistics.

Wooley, Edwin C. 1907. *Handbook of Composition.* Boston: D.C. Heath.

Writer's Workbench Software. [Release 2.0.] 1982. Piscataway, N.J.: Bell Laboratories, Inc.

Zinsser, William. 1980. *On Writing Well.* New York: Harper and Row.

Author

Dennis Baron is Professor of English and Linguistics, and Director of Freshman Rhetoric, at the University of Illinois at Urbana-Champaign. He has been a high school English teacher and has directed summer workshops for teachers in writing instruction. He has been a member of NCTE's Commission on the English Language, and his commentaries on the English language have been broadcast by WILL-AM in Urbana. A student of language reform and attitudes toward the English language, his publications include *Grammar and Good˙ Taste: Reforming the American Language* (Yale University Press, 1982), and *Grammar and Gender* (Yale, 1986). He is currently working on *English First: The Official Language Question in America,* a book tracing the attempts since the eighteenth century to make English our official language.